PANZER GUNNER

The Stackpole Military History Series

THE AMERICAN CIVIL WAR

Cavalry Raids of the Civil War
Ghost, Thunderbolt, and
    Wizard
Pickett's Charge
Witness to Gettysburg

WORLD WAR I

Doughboy War

WORLD WAR II

After D-Day
Armor Battles of the Waffen-SS,
    1943–45
Armoured Guardsmen
Army of the West
Australian Commandos
The B-24 in China
Backwater War
The Battle of Sicily
Battle of the Bulge, Vol. 1
Battle of the Bulge, Vol. 2
Beyond the Beachhead
Beyond Stalingrad
The Brandenburger
    Commandos
The Brigade
Bringing the Thunder
The Canadian Army and the
    Normandy Campaign
Coast Watching in
    World War II
Colossal Cracks
A Dangerous Assignment
D-Day Deception
D-Day to Berlin
Destination Normandy
Dive Bomber!
A Drop Too Many
Eagles of the Third Reich
Eastern Front Combat
Exit Rommel
Fist from the Sky
Flying American Combat
    Aircraft of World War II
Forging the Thunderbolt
Fortress France
The German Defeat in the East,
    1944–45

German Order of Battle, Vol. 1
German Order of Battle, Vol. 2
German Order of Battle, Vol. 3
The Germans in Normandy
Germany's Panzer Arm in
    World War II
GI Ingenuity
Goodwood
The Great Ships
Grenadiers
Hitler's Nemesis
Infantry Aces
Iron Arm
Iron Knights
Kampfgruppe Peiper at the
    Battle of the Bulge
The Key to the Bulge
Kursk
Luftwaffe Aces
Luftwaffe Fighter Ace
Massacre at Tobruk
Mechanized Juggernaut or
    Military Anachronism?
Messerschmitts over Sicily
Michael Wittmann, Vol. 1
Michael Wittmann, Vol. 2
Mountain Warriors
The Nazi Rocketeers
No Holding Back
On the Canal
Operation Mercury
Packs On!
Panzer Aces
Panzer Aces II
Panzer Commanders of the
    Western Front
Panzer Gunner
The Panzer Legions
Panzers in Normandy
Panzers in Winter
The Path to Blitzkrieg
Penalty Strike
Red Road from Stalingrad
Red Star under the Baltic
Retreat to the Reich
Rommel's Desert Commanders
Rommel's Desert War
Rommel's Lieutenants
The Savage Sky
The Siegfried Line

A Soldier in the Cockpit
Soviet Blitzkrieg
Stalin's Keys to Victory
Surviving Bataan and Beyond
T-34 in Action
Tank Tactics
Tigers in the Mud
Triumphant Fox
The 12th SS, Vol. 1
The 12th SS, Vol. 2
Twilight of the Gods
The War against Rommel's
    Supply Lines
War in the Aegean
Wolfpack Warriors
Zhukov at the Oder

THE COLD WAR / VIETNAM

Cyclops in the Jungle
Expendable Warriors
Flying American Combat
    Aircraft: The Cold War
Here There Are Tigers
Land with No Sun
Phantom Reflections
Street without Joy
Through the Valley

WARS OF THE MIDDLE EAST

Never-Ending Conflict

GENERAL MILITARY HISTORY

Carriers in Combat
Cavalry from Hoof to Track
Desert Battles
Guerrilla Warfare
Ranger Dawn
Sieges

PANZER GUNNER

A Canadian in the German
7th Panzer Division, 1944–45

Bruno Friesen

STACKPOLE
BOOKS

Text and photographs © 2007 by Bruno Friesen
Maps © 2008 by Helion & Company Limited

Published in paperback in 2009 by
STACKPOLE BOOKS
5067 Ritter Road
Mechanicsburg, PA 17055
www.stackpolebooks.com

PANZER GUNNER, by Bruno Friesen, was originally published in hard cover in 2008 by Helion & Company Limited. Copyright © 2007 by Bruno Friesen. Paperback edition by arrangement with Helion & Company Limited. All rights reserved.

Cover design by Tracy Patterson

Printed in the United States of America

10 9 8 7 6 5 4 3 2 1

Library of Congress Cataloging-in-Publication Data

Friesen, Bruno, 1925–
  Panzer gunner : a Canadian in the German 7th Panzer Division, 1944–45 / Bruno Friesen.
    p. cm.
  Originally published in hard cover: West Midlands, England : Helion & Company, 2008.
  Includes bibliographical references.
  ISBN 978-0-8117-3598-8 (pbk.)
  1. Friesen, Bruno, 1925– 2. Germany. Heer. Panzer-Regiment, 25. 3. Germany. Heer. Panzer-Division, 7. 4. World War, 1939–1945—Regimental histories—Germany. 5. World War, 1939–1945—Tank warfare. 6. World War, 1939–1945—Campaigns—Eastern Front. 7. World War, 1939–1945—Personal narratives, German. 8. Soldiers—Germany—Biography. 9. Soldiers—Canada—Biography. 10. Canadians—Germany—Biography. I. Title.
  D757.5725th .F75 2009
  940.54'1343092—dc22
  [B]
                              2009001479

Contents

Foreword

In 1950, after my 11-year exile in Europe, I had been back in Canada for only a few weeks when Ted Nettleton, the middle-aged personnel manager at the B.F. Goodrich tyre plant on King Street West in Kitchener, Ontario, mentioned to me that a certain old sea captain was known to say, "Don't tell people your troubles; half of them don't care, and the other half are glad of them."

My employment interview at Goodrich must have revealed that I was greatly concerned because a lot of my fellow citizens looked askance at me for having served in the enemy armed forces during part of the Second World War, and that I had years of catching-up on formal schooling ahead of me.

From 1950 to 1993, I, heeding the cautionary advice given to me by Ted Nettleton, rarely disclosed that I had been sent to Germany in 1939, and that I had been forced to live outside of Canada continuously for well over a decade.

In 1994, however, with the fiftieth anniversary of the end of the Second World War in Europe just ahead, I decided to divulge some of my overseas experiences.

I first describe, in this book of mine, what it was, I believe, that got me from Canada to Germany in 1939. I then relate how I fared in Germany before I joined the *Wehrmacht* on November 1, 1942. Thereupon, I present, chronologically, stories of some of my adventures as a German soldier before May 7, 1945. These chapters I regard as the book's core. Thereafter, I write about my post-war jobs in Germany and my long-delayed return to Canada.

The following subsequent milestones in my life fall within the scope of the book: employment at B.F. Goodrich Canada Ltd.; marriage to Helga Meyer in Waterloo, Ontario, in 1951; ten years of Advanced Technical Evening Classes, yielding, for me, A.T.E.C. Certificates I, II, and III, issued by the Ontario Department of Education, and registration as a Certified Engineering Technologist; 5½ years of full-time studies at university, resulting in the degrees of Bachelor of Arts, Master of Arts (English), and Master of Philosophy (English); 19 years of teaching English at an Ontario College of Applied Arts and Technology; retirement at age 65 in 1990; and volunteer work at the Canadian War Museum.

My occasional use of German in the stories is calculated to impart to them greater realism as well as, quite possibly, to afford the reader glimpses into the mentalities of the characters, something purely unilingual stories based on such subject matter would do to a much lesser extent. Of course, the reader may elect to dispense with the italicized German and rely entirely on the parenthesized translations.

Copies of documents of mine which are germane to the book's contents appear on separate pages. The originals, some of which I carried with me at the front lines, have remained in my possession ever since I got them.

Among my originals, all of them uncommon, are the pocket-size, one-page Battle-Line Avowal of the Soldiers of the 7th Panzer Division, a document from late 1944 or early 1945 – so rare that the Divisional history, published in 1986, makes no mention of it.

Although I have not had to rely on archival support for my stories, I have consulted the following book repeatedly: General der Panzertruppe a.D. [Retired] Hasso E. von Manteuffel *Der 7. Panzer-Division im Zweiten Weltkrieg: Einsatz und Kampf der "Gespenster-Division"* (Friedberg, Podzun-Pallas-Verlag, 1986). Using only the translation of its title, henceforth I refer to the above book as *The 7th Panzer Division in World War II*, mostly in documenting my translations of passages from Manteuffel's original. It is not to be confused with Manteuffel's English-language *The 7th Panzer Division: An Illustrated History of Rommel's "Ghost Division" 1938–1945*, also listed in my bibliography.

Acknowledgments

I am pleased to acknowledge gratefully the help of each of the following six persons who influenced, for the better, the writing of my stories.

Major Don Holmes, a good friend of mine and an erudite listener and reader, encouraged me, as far back as 1994, to begin writing my war stories. As each such story, which stems from my 2½ years of German military life, appeared, I could expect Don to recommend that I expand some passages, or that I condense others. His long interest in my writing, which eventually included my pronouncedly autobiographical prolongations, reminded me of the importance of observing all aspects of the iron rule of prewrite, write and rewrite. Don is truly a watchful adviser.

Dr. Gerhard Friesen, who is my brother and a Professor Emeritus of German, read all of my manuscript and offered much constructive criticism, in which he reminded me to include "warts and all" in my descriptions. I should, he said, refrain from using euphemisms in preference to raw, real-life expressions. Thus, he discouraged non-authentic stylistic shifts in my writing.

Kathie Friesen, Gerhard's wife, urged that all English equivalents of the German expressions in my writing be understood immediately by the reader. The fact that Kathie has a graduate degree in German from Johns Hopkins University made her especially well qualified to comment on the translations. Always most conscientious, she repeatedly produced word-processor pages from my sheaves of typed manuscript, and displayed great enthusiasm for our undertaking.

Since 1994, Gerhard and Kathie urged me to add to my writing autobiographical chapters covering the years before and after my service in the Wehrmacht. I followed that advice.

Dan Glenney and Dr. Serge Durflinger, even before each had read and commented on a few of my war stories in 1998, recommended strongly that I make my writing appeal to Canadian readers by emphasizing in it my Canadian birth and background. Since 1998, at the Canadian War Museum in Ottawa—where he is a Director, Serge a Military Historian and I a Volunteer—Dan has championed my authoring a publication with this unique Canadian viewpoint.

Always, Helga, my wife, excelled at providing me with the ambience ideal for the recording, in writing, of what William Wordsworth calls "emotion recollected in tranquility." Because she had heard most of my stories over the years, she expressed the caveat that I, in committing them to paper, employ standard English and standard German to the greatest extent possible—good advice for any narrator of war stories.

Thank you, Don, Gerhard, Kathie, Dan, Serge and Helga, for your invaluable contribution to *Panzer Gunner*.

CHAPTER 1

Shipped Out to Germany

Thousands of times, I have been asked, "What made you go *back* to Germany?" Thousands of times, I have replied, "I didn't go *back*; I was born in Canada and had never been to Germany."

In March, 1939, two months before my fourteenth birthday, I was yanked out of Suddaby Public School on Frederick Street in Kitchener, Ontario, and, together with my brother Oscar, who was 1½ years younger than I, and three other youngsters from Kitchener, was put on a train to New York. There, the five of us boarded the express steamer *Europa* for the voyage to Bremerhaven in Germany.

Making travel preparations in Kitchener for Oscar and I had not amounted to much more than hurriedly and quietly getting together our Canadian passports and our free tickets. That brief spell had elapsed without our being given any reason for our having to leave Canada or, for that matter, for our having to maintain silence regarding our impending departure. Often I have wanted to fathom why, surrounded by secrecy, Oscar and I were shipped out to Germany almost 70 years ago.

My father, a stationary engineer at Forsyth's shirt factory in Kitchener at the time, would read well-circulated copies of various German illustrated periodicals. That I knew. He would, I also knew, drop in after work at Colarco's fruit and vegetable store, near the city hall in Kitchener, and, I suppose, have a chat with *Signor* Colarco about Axis developments.

Yes, my father was pro-German, but I have to look far beyond Colarco's counter to explain, if I can, what it was that made him and my mother decide to send Oscar and me to Germany.

Having arrived in Canada from the Ukraine in 1924, my parents – please consult the relevant maps for the location of the district in the Ukraine from which they hailed – after working for almost a year on a Pennsylvania-Dutch Mennonite farm near Waterloo, Ontario, moved to the Portage la Prairie district of Manitoba. The Canadian Pacific Railway had advanced many Mennonite immigrants the money for their fares to Canada under the condition that they settle on lands adjacent to CPR tracks.

I was born on Section 1–13–9 in Westbourne municipality on May 25, 1925, and was just old enough to start school in Waterloo after my parents had abandoned their land at Westbourne and returned to Ontario. In Manitoba, they had tried in vain to farm 160 acres, part of an agriculturally inferior tract bought by ten families while it lay under snow. Annually, widespread spring flooding prevented the timely seeding of practically all of that expanse.

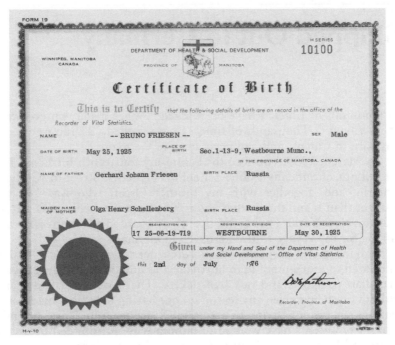

Birth Certificate

Among all Mennonites burdened by it, the CPR loan was referred to as our travel debt, and for them that debt remained, for years, a financial millstone.

The Great Depression of course was the primary cause of so much misery. It robbed my father of any hope that he might emerge debt-free in Canada.

My parents had never been to Germany. Neither had my grand-, great-grand-, or great-great-grandparents. However, because of their first language–German–all of them had maintained strong cultural and economic ties with Germany. The German-speaking population of the Mennonite colonies in the Ukraine had for decades mail-ordered their agricultural machinery, their reading material and, starting in the early 1900s, even their automobiles from Germany. In "Soviet Armour Ambushed at the Lake at Lessen in West Prussia," one of my following stories, I refer in detail to some of my forebears' strong traditional German ties.

Before we moved to Kitchener in 1937, we lived at 132 King Street South in Waterloo. Every Saturday evening, a coterie of Mennonites, including my parents, would congregate at 132. A polyglot bunch they constituted, speaking High German, Low German, Russian, Ukrainian–and some English. High German is the official language in Germany, Austria, and Switzerland. Low German or *Plattdeutsch–platt* is German

Map 1   Mennonite Migration from the Vistula to Southern Russia

for *flat*–is the informal German spoken in flat, or lowland, northern Germany.

Every letter from relatives or friends in the Old Country that did get through to the group in those hard times was neatly written in High German, no matter how low-grade the stationery, as was every letter of response.

On Saturday mornings, the W-K, or Waterloo-Kitchener, United Mennonite Church on George Street in Waterloo conducted its one-room German school in the church basement. I acknowledge that during my early months in Germany I made good use of most of the rather rudimentary German I had learned at W-K; however, it turned out that the unworldliness of the school's one level of text book, strengthened by the school's one instructor, a strait-laced lady from a fine Russian Mennonite family, had left me incapable of enquiring, in refined German, where the next toilet was.

In 1985, about 50 years after I last attended German classes at W-K, the surviving members of the family of a former custodian of the German school's text books presented me with the book I had used on at least one Saturday morning so very long ago. It was mine all right, so to speak, for it bears my full name and what was then our address scribbled boyishly onto the inside of its back cover.

This old book, in itself, attests to the Russian Mennonites' faithfulness to the German language. Its full title is *Deutsches Lesebuch für Volksschulen in Russland (German Reader for Primary Schools in Russia)*. Published in 1919 by Gottlieb Schaab in Prischib, a town adjacent to the north-western corner of the Molotschna, one of the oldest Mennonite colonies in the Ukraine, it is one of a dozen or so identical copies that were used for years at W-K, and would have been brought to Canada from Russia, probably in the early 1920s, by persons to whom the German language meant a great deal.

In my own modest library, there reposes, next to the reader I have just referred to, a book entitled *Poems of Nicolaus Lenau*. It has an embossed spine and covers, and was published in 1877 in Stuttgart in Germany. My annotation on the inside of the front cover reads as follows: "Received as a

Author at 13 years old - At the age of 13 years 10 months, shortly before Oscar and I were sent from Canada to Germany in March of 1939.

Oscar Friesen - Oscar Friesen at 17 years old, who would be later killed
at Houffalize in Belgium in 1944.

gift from Father at the main railway station in Wilhelmshaven before I left for Canada." This book, one of a large trunkful that my father had taken with him from the Ukraine to Canada, and from Canada to Germany, signified his love of literature. I am certain that he cherished this particular book more than many of his others.

Nicolaus Lenau is the pen name of Niembsch Edler von Strehlenau (1802–50). A resident of Hungary, Lenau chose his subject matter largely from outside of Germany. It is not surprising that my father displayed a great affinity for Lenau's work.

Throughout most of his adult life, my father wrote many poems and much prose, all under the pseudonym Fritz Senn. I have a 311-page book, published in Winnipeg in 1987 after his death and entitled *Fritz Senn: Collected Poems and Prose*. Much of his writing reveals his intense nostalgia for his beloved Mennonite world in the Ukraine.

My mother often related that, as a single young man in the Ukraine, our *paterfamilias* had spent much time with his books. He was, she emphasized, the youngest of nine children in a well-to-do family, and he hadn't been expected to work hard. That, she said, had left him with a lot of time for literary studies.

Probably contributing to my father's pro-German stance was the fact that, starting in 1917, he was, for a few years, a member of the Mennonite Self-Defence Organization, a paramilitary cavalry established to protect the affluent Mennonite colonies in the Ukraine from the infamous Machno's bandits. This defence organization was trained briefly by German officers and non-commissioned officers. Many purely pacifistic Mennonites condemned those of their brethren who fought the anarchistic forces.

By early 1939, my father's ideas concerning emigration from Canada to Germany had become solidified, largely because of the influence of the Confederation of Germans [Abroad], a Third Reich-backed, propagandistic organization operating in league with many of the German social clubs in North America.

At the time, the Concordia Club, the Kitchener area's largest German club, had its premises above one of the two movie theatres–either the Capitol or the Lyric–on King Street West in Kitchener. On Saturday evenings, the parents, both nominal Mennonites, of the three boys who accompanied Oscar and me to Germany would parade most, if not all, of their ten kids close to the dance floor at the Concordia Club.

Although my parents never frequented the Concordia, our family did, in the summer of 1938, attend the club's annual picnic on cow dung-dotted Kaufman's Flats, beside the Grand River, just upstream from Kitchener. At that picnic, my father was happy to earn a few dollars extra by washing beer glasses in the vicinity of the bar in the beer tent. The occasional glass of suds which one of the busy, perspiring bartenders handed to him in the heat under the canvas must have constituted his bonus.

Probably the Confederation was instrumental in having the train and steamship tickets for Oscar and I paid for from within Germany. In return, the recruiters involved undoubtedly hoped that they had planted boundless love for the Third Reich in the members of our family.

I believe that Fritz Senn or, if you prefer, Gerhard Johann Friesen, could not see himself as a farmer or factory worker in Canada. Germany beckoned mightily, so he sent, as the initial step in his unpublicized plan to transplant his entire family to that promised land, his first- and his second-born there, albeit at a very inopportune time. My mother simply consented. Oscar and I left Kitchener for New York on March 20, 1939, and sailed from there on March 22.

At any rate, we five seemingly outcast boys discovered, in one of the lounges aboard the *Europa*, a phonograph surmounting a boy-high cabinet of polished, reddish-brown wood, filled with records. Daily throughout the crossing, we had our fun making the thing play for hours at a time. I stress our having so much fun with the phonograph because for us things became absolutely mirthless upon our arrival in Bremerhaven, about one week after we left New York.

My souvenir log of that Atlantic crossing by the Europa shows that she left New York on March 22, 1939, and that she passed Cherbourg, France, and breakwater on March 27, having covered 3,128 nautical miles in 4 days, 22 hours, and 6 minutes. For the Europa to get from Cherbourg to Bremerhaven—the souvenir log also shows that she had to travel another 535 nautical miles to get there—must have prolonged our trip by about two days, making it seven days.

At this point, I had best introduce into my narrative two entire newspaper articles as well as excerpts from another two. Published in the *Kitchener Daily Record* between March 16 and 24, 1939, the four articles are preserved on microfilm at the archives of *The Record* in Kitchener, Ontario. Please see Appendix A for the copies of three of the articles.

The subject microfilm reveals its age; nevertheless, the copies made of it on my behalf by Gerhard and Kathie Friesen reflects the concerns about Nazi activity in Canada around the time of Oscar's departure and mine. Note that the *Kitchener Daily Record* published our names on Friday, March 24, 1939 two days after the *Europa* had sailed from New York.

Jews Boycott K-W Product
Action Said Result of Nazi Activity throughout District

Attorney-General Conant's reported investigation into alleged Nazi activity in the Twin City and district was not in evidence here today and both city and provincial police declined to comment on the announcement.

But while there was no indication that outside police were checking on the reports, several angles came to light. It was learned that Bruno and Oscar Friesen, 821 King Street East, accompanied the four Esau children to Germany.

POLICE KEEP QUIET

Indications that local business might suffer from adverse publicity given the community came to light when *The Record* was informed at least one manufacturer's goods were boycotted by Toronto Jews. The latter claimed they would have nothing to do with merchandise manufactured locally.

"I have nothing to say for publication," Sgt. W. C. Oliver of the provincial police told *The Record*. He refused to confirm or deny a report that outside police may be sent here to probe Nazi activities. Inspector Jordan, in charge of the local detachment, was out of town and could not be reached.

CHAPTER 2

A Stranger in *Deutschland*

After disembarking in Bremerhaven, we were taken to Hohenkirchen, an old village about 20 kilometres northwest of Wilhelmshaven, the naval city on the North Sea coast. The district association of farmers had half a dozen farmers, their large N.S.D.A.P. (Nazi) membership badges in evidence, seated at one end of the long table in the Hohenkirchen council chamber; grouped at the other end of the same table, we boys awaited our fate. How who got whom I do not know. The farmers might as well have thrown the dice to arrive at some kind of distribution.

What I do know is that I was assigned to Gerhard Iben, pronounced Ee-ben, of Carlseck, a hamlet something like four kilometres northwest of Hohenkirchen, and within sight of the North Sea dyke. Promptly the stern-faced lady of the Iben house, bent on finding out how much German I knew not, asked me to read the name of their weekly newspaper. Because the *J* and the *F* in Gothic type look very much alike, I read aloud *Fefersches Wochenblatt*; I should have read *Jeversches Wochenblatt*. At that, the entire family guffawed. Present were the Ibens' two daughters, both of whom attended high school in Jever, pronounced *Yay-fir*, the district capital 16 kilometres west northwest of Wilhelmshaven.

A day or two after my arrival in Carlseck, I was handed an oversize piassava broom and told to remove the thick moss covering an entire wall of one of the brick buildings. As I attacked the moss, a couple of middle-aged sightseers with horse and buggy drove up. Reins in hand, the nosey rustic said to his equally nosey wife, *"Dat is Gerd sien Amerikaner"* (That is Gerd's [Gerhard's] American). In addition to sounding a lot like a reference to my being regarded as the Ibens' chattel, those words showed the locals' ignorance of the existence of Canada.

Every visitor who came to the Ibens specifically to behold the *Amerikaner* had to agree with the master of the house's pronouncement that Germany had saved a young lad of German blood from degenerate life in *Amerika*. What could I say? Had my parents not sent me to *Deutschland?*

Upjever, near Jever, at the time had a military airfield which still exists for the *Bundeswehr*, successor to the *Wehrmacht*. In 1939, planes from Upjever sometimes practised low-level flying over the fields at places like Carlseck, just about scaring the yokels on the ground into deep, water-filled ditches.

When there was once talk at the table of half the tribe having been buzzed by two flying machines stationed at Upjever I mentioned that in Canada we boys had fashioned model aircraft from balsa wood, using twisted rubber bands as motive power for their propellers. 'Impossible!' the Ibens and whoever else was there blurted out. I should, they scolded, stick to the truth and not talk about planes in *Amerika*; instead, I should talk about the planes at Upjever–real, live German military aircraft. In every respect, *Deutschland, Deutschland* above all else governed the thinking of the ignorant, humiliating bastards that the word Carlseck stood for!

Less than half a year later, I was no longer confined to performing tasks like trying to rid a brick wall of stubborn, centimetre-thick moss. During harvest time in 1939, for instance, I carried many sacks full of heavy grain from the threshing machine, up a ladder–not up any stairs– and into the granary, actually the attic above the family's living quarters.

I served as the family's underprivileged junior hired man. Their senior hired man, a good-enough chap by the name of Gerd Brandt, volunteered for the German infantry to get away from Carlseck.

My room was what is called an aftermost, or back, kitchen, a small place adjacent to the upper end of the long cattle stable. I say *upper end* because the stable was built on a slight incline to facilitate partial drainage, towards its lower end, of the excrement gutters situated imme diately behind the rows of cattle.

Crudely fastened, by means of four thumbtacks, to the inside of the grey wooden door of my uncomfortable abode hung a magazine clipping showing the black-and-white copy of a portrait of Adolf and, in the margin below his likeness, his telling signature consisting of a snippet of *Adolf,* followed by a down sloping, tornado-like vortex representing *Hitler.*

My wash water I usually fetched, at least in the frost-free months of the year, a pail full at a time from the frog-infested, moat-like ditch almost surrounding the farm's clustered buildings.

Home, Sweet Home!

Once every week–I was a foreigner living in what was called a border area–I had to walk to the police station in Hohenkirchen, report to the police and walk back to the farm. If I was lucky, I would meet one or two of the Canadians at, or near, the police station. They, too, had to show up there in person.

Upon returning to the farm at Carlseck, I would, without fail, be quizzed about what I had observed along the way. How is so-and-so's oats coming along, and how many head of cattle are grazing on his land?

Gone for good, I knew, was the old neighbourhood gang back in Canada. Gone were the roller skates in summer. Gone was the Albert Street hill in Kitchener–our ski and toboggan hill with the synagogue and the city's water tower at its apex, and Rumpel's Bush at the bottom of its eastern slope. Gone was so much.

Gone, abruptly, was my childhood.

Surprise! A few weeks before the outbreak of Second World War my parents with the rest of their kids–three of them, all Canadian-born–made it to Germany. To Wilhelmshaven, to be exact.

The apartment assigned to them was on the ground floor of a First World War-era walk-up on Kasernenstrasse, a short street with Roonstrasse and its immense *Kriegsmarine* barracks opposite its one end, and the high, barbed-wire-topped brick wall of the submarine base opposite its other. Half a dozen blocks north of Kasernenstrasse towered one of the city's landmarks, the Kaiser Wilhelm Bridge, also called *K-W-Brücke*, with the *K-W* as in *Kitchener-Waterloo*. Still in operation, this old swing bridge connects the city with the commercial beach, the location of, for instance, the sea-water aquarium.

In the walk-up, the toilets–not the bathrooms because there weren't any–for all of the apartments were off the stairway landings, between the floors. Not only that. Next to each toilet door was the coin-operated gas metre for the corresponding apartment. One had to feed one's metre frequently and on time or it would, without warning, shut off the gas.

On the far side of Kasernenstrasse, Emmie Seiler, a spinster, operated a small grocery store. Emmie wanted the new family on the street to have a treat, so she sold my mother some Roquefort. Not knowing that Roquefort contains veins of mould, my father thought that the cheese was spoiled. He exclaimed, "*Die meint wohl, wir essen im Dunkeln!*" (She must think that we eat in the dark!) Their table in Canada and, before that, in the Ukraine had hardly seen the delicacies that were common in Western Europe. We, my parents included, were learning many things daily.

My father was soon introduced by the N.S.D.A.P. (*Nationalsozialistische Deutsche Arbeiter Partei*, or Nazi Party) to his first German place of employment, an electrical business owned by Julius Harms, a master electrician and politically well-connected bigwig whose wife Amanda had, I later learned, been a cocktail hostess in her younger years. Julius's business premises were located on Marktstrasse, in the heart of Wilhelmshaven.

The new employee at Harms's little empire was known as the stores administrator. Rolls, large and small, of various gauges of electrical wire, untold numbers of diverse fasteners, ladders of different lengths, special tools–that sort of treasure my father administered.

When the Old Man–that's a term we boys had often used in Canada–visited me at Carlseck, his jaw dropped. He soon took the train back to Wilhelmshaven and enlisted the help of the city's political boss, *Kreisleiter* (district political leader) Meyer, to secure my release from the Ibens. Meyer, who seemed to be endowed with humanitarian qualities, promised to have the Old Man's two boys join the family in Wilhelmshaven. Oscar was in servitude on a farm at Carolinensiel, down the North Sea coast, just west of Hohenkirchen.

Indenture for Apprentice Electrician

In the tightly organized N.S.D.A.P., every *Kreisleiter*, subordinate to his *Gauleiter* (political leader of a province), was in charge of the following classes of functionaries: *Ortsgruppenleiter* (political leader of a ward in a city, or of a county), *Zellenleiter* (political leader of a part of a city ward or county), and *Blockleiter* (political warden of a block). *Blockleiter* abounded in a large city like Wilhelmshaven.

Even *Kreisleiter* Meyer was unable to take me away from Carlseck without coming up with a very good reason for my switch from the country to the city. The solution: a genuine, old-fashioned apprenticeship for me. Still, it took another six months before I had Julius Harms as my master, or before he had me as one of his three apprentices, learning the trade of electrician. Once again, I had no say in what was happening to me.

Suddenly I had an indenture binding me to three years–from April 26, 1940, to April 25, 1943–of good behaviour, hard work, regular attendance of the trades school–and barely any pay. During the first year, 3.00 *Reichsmark* per week; during the second year, 4.00 *Reichsmark* per week; and during the third year, 5.00 *Reichsmark* per week. Figuratively speaking, one *Reichsmark* equalled one dollar at the time. Payday was each Saturday–after the driveway, the yard and the warehouse at Marktstrasse 39 had been swept clean by noon.

The stipulation that I attend Hitler Youth service as part of my apprenticeship appeared in typing under the printed heading *Besondere Bestimmungen* (special conditions) on the last of the four legal-size pages that constituted my indenture: The apprentice must attend Hitler Youth service regularly.

Contrary to expectations, the one man in the company who had the most authority to pressure us apprentices politically did no such thing; consequently, neither did anyone else.

Our saviour was Carl Poth, whose last name rhymed with *boat*. A master electrician and Julius Harms' right-hand man, Carl had served as a Petty Officer in the Kaiser's navy in World War I, about a quarter of a century before I got to know him.

Carl trusted his people, and they trusted him. He once told me that Hitler Youth service amounted to hocus-pocus. That sort of talk could have put him into a concentration camp. It was hard to believe that his son had a full-time position at the *Hitler-Jugend* headquarters in Wilhelmshaven.

On the job, an apprentice could frequently tear his clothing. The quick fix for any tear, especially a large one, was to stitch it with bare copper wire of a small gauge. Towards the end of the week, one's work outfit would look a bit tattered, just as mine did one day when I met Amanda in the vicinity of the Marktstrasse.

Sizing me up soon after I had been spotted by Amanda, Carl said, "You look pretty shabby." He was right. However, he didn't leave things at that. A few days later, he presented me with a ration coupon for new work pants and jacket. He had rapport with his subordinates, especially with the apprentices.

Old Carl, a serious-looking little guy, liked to keep a cigar going, at least intermittently, when he made his rounds of the job sites.

My father hadn't worked for Julius very long before *Kreisleiter* Meyer found a position for him as cashiers' bookkeeper at the income tax office in Wilhelmshaven. To get to know the fiscal ropes, he had to take an extensive course at the school of finance in Flensburg, up near the German-Danish border.

By that time, my parents had realized what life in an overpopulated country at war was, and would continue to be, like. My father must have voiced his disillusionment because, on one occasion, *Kreisleiter* Meyer rebuked him by saying, "Do get rid of your Canadian attitude!"

Julius's electrical firm had a great many government contracts for work at the naval dockyards in Wilhelmshaven. I spent weeks at a time learning from well-versed journeymen and even young masters of the trade how to install electrical wiring by the mile–by the kilometre, really– in various huge buildings such as the machine construction building No. 3 while moving about on scaffolding as high as a tall ship's rigging. Expressed in one German novel of the sea, an old sailor's advice to a

Lehrbrief	Prüfungszeugnis
Bruno Friesen	Bruno Friesen
geboren am *23. Mai* 19*25*	geboren am *23. Mai* 19*25*
zu *Westborne* Kr. *Westborne*	zu *Westborne* Kr. *Westborne*
hat vom *20.5.1940* bis zum *20.5.1943*	hat am *17. Aug.* 19*43* die Gesellenprüfung
bei *Firma: Harms*	für das *Elektro-Inst.*-Handwerk bestanden.
zu *Wilhelmshaven*	Praktische Leistungen: *Gut*
das *Elektro-Inst.*-Handwerk erlernt.	Theoretische Leistungen: *befriedigend*
Kenntnisse: *Gut*	*Wilhelmshav.*, den *17. August* 1943
Fertigkeiten: *Gut*	Der Gesellenprüfungsausschuß der Innung *des*
Betragen: *Gut*	*Elektro-Inst. Handwerks*
Wilhelmshaven, den *17. August* 1943	

Jorneyman Electrician's Certificate

novice crewman aboard a sailing ship goes as follows: "One hand for the ship; the other hand for yourself." That line applied to anyone engaged in the kind of electrical work we did at hazardous heights.

My getting around in the naval dockyards made me aware of great weaknesses in the country's security.

For instance, one day in 1940, a friendly and enthusiastic teen-age dockyard worker offered to show me aboard Germany's largest battleship, the *Tirpitz*, which lay alongside an outfitting pier. The ship, to which the following dates would apply, was fast taking shape in the presence of the proud dockyard workers: laid down October 20, 1936; launched April 1, 1939; and completed February 25, 1941.

At the shoreward end of the long gangplank leading to an open area on the ship's weather deck, a young *Kriegsmarine* sentry had his post. Dockyard workers, many of them carrying toolboxes, streamed past him on their way to the giant's innards.

To walk onto that ship, I simply mingled with the many workers, who bore neither name tags nor passes. Their work clothes were the standard blue pants and jacket. Just like mine.

Below deck, wherever my guide and I went—and that was a total of only a few hundred metres—the danger of our being found out and apprehended increased tenfold. Nowhere did we linger, for every tradesman, for instance, and his helpers could readily tell that we bareheaded youths were in no position to ply any trade. Besides, trades people habitually made it a point to become acquainted very quickly with persons from

other trades who worked in their proximity, just as my dockyard pal and I
had gotten to know each other on the job. Consequently, like a pair of
young, new-in-town vagrants sizing up a succession of alleys unfamiliar to
them, he and I moved warily through some of the *Tirpitz*'s steely passages
before we headed back towards the gangplank traffic.

Had I been arrested aboard the *Tirpitz*, or in her vicinity, I would,
fortunately, have been dealt with fairly leniently as a 15-year-old young
offender.

Yes, I paid the *Tirpitz* a hurried visit about four years and three
months before, on November 12, 1944, several British Tallboy bombs
caused her to capsize with the loss of some 1,200 lives at Tromsö, near the
northern end of Norway's long Atlantic coast.

Across the Kaiser Wilhelm Bridge in Wilhelmshaven and down to the
right, close to the base of the huge dike between a kind of minor coastal
road and the tideland, the *Kriegsmarine* had built a new cartography
building. The inside of the place wasn't entirely finished; sections of it
needed good-quality electric lighting, and that was where we fellows from
lighting house Harms came in.

The cartography building housed thousands of naval charts that were
entrusted to a team of cartographers, every one of whom was exempt from
military service because of his advanced age. A particularly talkative
chartist, who had lived in England, liked to have his colleagues call him
"Hughie."

The cartography building's hydrographic charts, domestic and
foreign, were all classified as secret, yet we chaps from Harms handled
dozens of them at our leisure–another soft spot in Germany's security.

Trades school meant half a day a week away from work. N.S.D.A.P.
protocol demanded that at the beginning of each such half day in class, one
of the students had to march to the front of the room, turn about, and
holler, while extending his right arm straight forward so that his
outstretched right hand was at the level of his right eye, "We begin our
instruction with a threefold greeting to our *Führer! Sieg Heil!* [Hail to
victory!] *Sieg Heil! Sieg Heil!*" Next, the cheerleader would do his best to
enunciate, loudly, some N.S.D.A.P. maxim. "Work ennobles!" was a
favourite with the apprentices because of its brevity. Another acceptable
utterance, also not hard to recall, was "Rather be the hammer than the
anvil!"

For a while, before I would be "it" up front, I listened around and, from
a young fellow who, with his parents, had come to Wilhelmshaven from the
coal scuttle (the coal-rich part of the Ruhr valley), I got a non-political
saying that I actually used. I simply recited, loudly and clearly, "Whoever
hooks cabbage in the summer has sauerkraut in the winter." I got away with
it. The instructor and the rest of the class may have thought that I hadn't
been in Germany long enough to come out with something befitting the
occasion.

All but one, the members of the Gerhard Friesen Family in the summer of 1941 at
Wilhelmshaven, Germany. I am not included becaused I took the photo.

By 1941, our family resided in Fedderwardergroden, a west-end
suburb of Wilhelmshaven. The place was nicknamed 'rabbit housing'
because its many row houses were reminiscent of long lines of pens for
domestic rabbits.

In Fedderwardergroden, as in the city, insufficient food ration stamps
were symbolic of near-breadless days, and luminous pin-on badges, of
gloomy nights.

Contributing almost daily, and certainly almost nightly, to the miserable living conditions in and around Wilhelmshaven were the Allied air
raids that drove mainly the young and the old into the various kinds of air-
raid shelters for hours at a time.

Unlike the core areas of the larger cities such as Wilhelmshaven, its
suburbs had no 30-metre-high, cylindrical above-ground air raid shelters
with metre-thick concrete walls and slightly conical, thick concrete tops.
The interior of each such shelter consisted of a concrete ramp spiralling
upward, with no steps whatsoever, about a central concrete column. A
couple of metres away from the column stood the rows of wooden
benches, fixed radically to the ramp.

The basement air-raid shelters in the houses in a new suburb like
Fedderwardergroden–the place had been built just before the Second
World War–had, I would say, been designed in anticipation of war and
bombing raids. The extra-thick, laminated-wood doors and window shut-

ters, and the frames for them, as well as the sturdy hardware, were all part of the buildings' original construction. Nothing makeshift.

Whereas Wilhelmshaven's centre, including its naval yards, attracted many big high-explosive bombs and incendiary bombs, Fedderwardergroden would usually be hit with only the small, hexagonal incendiaries, each some 45 centimetres long. Often, they rained down seven to a bundle–six outer bombs strapped to one central bomb.

Half way through 1941, my father, then 47, was, without notice, called up for service in the Army as a Special Duties Officer with the rank of Corporal. Generally, a Special Duties Officer would function as an interpreter-translator. My father had grown up in the Ukraine. He had lived there from his birth in 1894 until 1924; that is, for 30 years. He certainly knew Ukrainian and Russian. About 18 years after he and my mother had emigrated from the Ukraine, my father experienced what was probably one of the highlights of his life. He was, in the Ukraine, able to visit Halbstadt, his birthplace, and other places he knew from his youth. However, he certainly had to pay an exorbitant price for the thrill.

Late in the summer of 1942, about 2½ years after I had begun my apprenticeship, I had to appear at a registration for the military draft, including physical examination and tentative classification. Half a hundred unclothed young men hung around inside a pub, each waiting to take his turn at standing at attention inside the white circle drawn with chalk on the hardwood floor of the bowling alley, part of the premises.

Five metres from the chalk circle, three military officers seated at a long table decided, mainly by just looking at the individual nude before them, what branch of the *Wehrmacht* Adonis should be suitable for. In reality, they looked primarily for replacements for the branches of the *Wehrmacht* that had suffered the greatest losses. The infantry was a sure bet.

I had heard that in the cities, especially, such a *triumvirate* liked to earmark the mechanical and electrical tradesmen for the armoured troops. My qualifications, sparse as they were, counted, and I was told that I would be hearing from a Panzer Personnel Replacement Battalion.

The entire registration process had an archaic, none-too-rigorous, and even comical air about it. As well as suffering other minor indignities, such as being ordered to look alive, every guy being screened in the chalk circle had to about-face on command, bend forward, and expose to the officers his anus by manually spreading his buttocks. At that stage of the *Musterung*, spotting piles was what the officers were concerned with, 'twas said.

I don't recall the German name of that pub in Wilhelmshaven, but I do know that some 2¾ years later it was known as The Starboard Light, operated for members of the British Element of the CCG, the Control Commission for Germany.

In early October of 1942, I had my enlistment order, telling me to appear, on November 1, 1942, at the Panzer Personnel Replacement Battalion 10 in Gross-Glienicke, just west of Berlin, out Potsdam way.

At this point, I have to say that on August 17, 1943, I passed the final examination for my journeyman's certificate as an electrician. I had obtained a short leave of absence and showed up in uniform at the trades school. Because I was serving in the *Wehrmacht*, I was credited with half a year of school and practical experience, meaning the time from November 1, 1942, to April 25, 1943. It was called 'granted half a year'.

CHAPTER 3

The First Six Months
of My Military Service

By the very beginning of November, 1942, the barracks of the Replacement Battalion 10 in Gross-Glienicke were overcrowded to the extent that new recruits had to be put up in the large Panzer garages behind the barracks blocks. Although the unit had no Panzers, the relatively new barracks had been provided with garages.

Each morning, for a couple of weeks, many recruits, picked at random, were ordered to do lots of push-ups in the urine-soaked areas next to the garage doors, where dozens of men had relieved themselves the night before. For the first few days, before the recruits were issued their field-grey uniform they had to do the push-ups while still wearing their civilian clothing.

Each recruit at the Replacement Battalion 10 eventually got his pay book. He also got his oval identification disk of rustproof metal, with three elongated break-away perforations at its longer axis. Each half of the disk showed three items of information: his blood group, his original military unit (*Stammkompanie* or cadre company), and his enrolment number in that unit. My disk, which I still have, reads as follows:

O
Stamm. Kop. Pz. Ers. Abt. 10
862

The 0.5-mm-thick disk's axes measure 7 cm and 5 cm. The noiseless disk hung from around one's neck by means of a sweat-proof, shoelace-like cord looped through two holes close to the outer edge of its upper half; the lower half, to be retrieved in the event of one's demise, had but one hole close to its outer edge.

The Replacement Battalion's garages stood close to one side of the paved parade square, at whose very centre towered a steel flagpole from which the Reich's flag flew. It was on that damned square, daily the scene of much real tragicomedy, which the recruits had to assemble to swear the oath of allegiance.

On the day of the swearing-in ceremony, four 25-ton Panzer IVs, brought in from some other Panzer unit in Berlin, were positioned, one at each corner of the square, with their frontal armour directed towards the flagpole, and with their main guns at maximum elevation, as if mimicking the German greeting, or Nazi salute.

Each of the four guns looked as though it were aimed inadvertently at the flag, directly below which, in the presence of the top brass, stood, on

German Army Identification Tag

parade, a dozen recruits who had been picked to represent their comrades, all of whom stood at attention on the square, well away from the flagpole. Those 12 reps would have to echo, on behalf of their buddies, the stern words of the far-reaching oath.

The proxies at the flagpole obediently repeated in bits, as administered, the words of the oath which, in its entirety ran as follows: "I swear by God this holy oath that I will render to the *Führer* of the German Reich and the German people, Adolf Hitler, the Supreme Commander of the *Wehrmacht*, unconditional obedience, and that I will, as a brave soldier, at all times be prepared to give my life for this oath." For sure, seeing themselves sworn in by proxy constituted a singular experience for most of the men.

The field-grey uniform each of us recruits in Gross-Glienicke was given didn't include an overcoat, probably because generally we stayed warm by moving fast while out in the open. During the breaks, however, we felt the biting cold. In the Berlin area, the minimum outside temperature averages close to 0 degrees Centigrade for most of November and December.

Outside, on many a cold day, each of us occasionally warmed at least his gloveless, numb hands by backhandedly swatting, for a while, the fingers of one hand, then of the other, against the trouser-clad backside of a buddy bent over forwards. Since this peculiar practice, which entailed reciprocity, was performed in response to an N.C.O.'s order, it seemed to be based on German military tradition.

At Gross-Glienicke every day was filled with activities, many of them unscheduled, designed to instil utter obedience in a recruit.

Having lain packed, all night long, in a barracks room originally meant for a third of that number of men, 18 guys, upon hearing the N.C.O. of the Day holler "Get up!" and blow his sports whistle out in the hallway, ran for the washroom. There, at least one N.C.O. lurked, fully expecting to catch men turning on the water taps while still wearing their undershirts.

"You dirty pig, you!" he would holler at any culprit who, without bare upper body, as much as looked at any of the taps. Any sign of moisture at the neck of one's undershirt brought on a tirade. "You soft cock! You sissy! You masturbator! Get out of that shirt!"

After being subjected to such abuse, or after having witnessed it, the recruit did not hurry to a dining room for a hearty breakfast. No, sir, he returned to his still-unventilated room and cut a slice off what was left of his one-third of a take-out loaf of Army bread, bread that was to last him for several days. If he had no more margarine, ersatz honey, or rubbery sausage, he simply resorted to plain bread with thumb and index finger as the spread.

A mess tin lid full of lukewarm *Negerschweiss* (literally 'black man's sweat', but meaning coffee) a man could get at the quartermaster's window, that dimly-lit hole in the wall with a half-height door, down at the end of the hall.

The small rations prompted the saying "The quartermaster has cut his finger," meaning that he, in preparing small portions had cut his finger.

Keeping rations in one's locker was sanctioned, as long as, for instance, no unclean knife blade or crumbs were in evidence there. Theft of rations–or of anything else–if resulting from a locker left unlocked, could lead to the victim being charged with inducing a comrade to commit theft.

The next part of the day's activity began with assembly on the parade square. There, too, some of the N.C.O.s would be bent on catching more 'shit birds', meaning filthy persons, by shining run-down flashlights–the flat, button-on German military jobs with the black-out cover–into the ears of the recruits. They also checked the men's hands, especially the fingernails, for cleanliness.

Allowing the N.C.O.s to gloat over the men's discomfort, at least temporarily, the Sergeant Major took over. His goddamned report book had its place in an unbuttoned gap in the front of his jacket. Get your name into that black-covered book and you'd do extra duty somewhere, somehow that very day. The Sergeant Major wouldn't necessarily imme-diately use the abusive language characteristic of the rest of the unit's N.C.O.s–although he was a master at it.

After several tries at assembling with special attention to Toe the line!–no toes of boots were ever shiny enough or lined up straight enough right away–and "At ease!" as well as a thorough roll call, the men soon marched off. Whoever hadn't eaten well–and who had?–hardly felt like launching into some ditty about girls. Nevertheless, that was the way to go. Hours of "Left wheel! and Right wheel!," and the like, followed by an hour or so of callisthenics loosened the men up for the day.

Every inch of the way, the N.C.O.s looked for trouble. A guy poorly standing at attention was called a excrement voided as a turd roughly the shape of a question mark or a cockeyed fuck-up and was ordered, "Pinch your buttocks together!" and "Take the slack out of your skeleton."

The soldier's midday meal did not come from his small hoard of victuals in his locker; rather, a kitchen bull or cook slapped the man's mess tin about half full of food at food issue at the barracks' kitchen.

Sometimes the noonday meal consisted of a hodgepodge such as bean soup with meat added or pea soup with bacon. Often quoted, the following saying applied to both of these soups: "Every little bean causes a faint sound; every pea, a bang!" The trouble with those soups, which usually amounted to mush because they had been stirred excessively, was that the soldier wasn't certain about their meat content.

With some foods, such as fried potatoes with small sausages the man could easily see what he was getting in the way of meat. The 1941 *Army Service Manual No. 86* entitled *Field Cookbook*, p. 43, contains the following passage pertaining to the serving of meat: "Prior to issuing food, divide the meat into portions. The soldier wants to see his portion of meat. Therefore, if possible, the meat must not be cut small and mixed into the food, or even be present only in the form of fibres in the food."

The same source, p. 107, under the heading "10 Commandments for the Field Cook," emphatically reiterates part of p. 47: "Last, cut meat into portions on meat cutting board, keep portions warm inside food-carrying containers, and serve individually. Reason: the soldier wants to see meat!"

Although they had to observe strict rationing–they never handed out seconds–the cooks, not the quartermaster, dispensed the kind of food that sustained the recruits at Gross-Glienicke.

The *H.Dv. 86*, of which I have a photocopy, also bears the following two imprints on its front cover as well as on its title page: *M.Dv. Nr. 894* and *L.Dv. 86*. The manual was, therefore, valid not only for the *Heer*, but also for the *Kriegsmarine* and the *Luftwaffe*. It was published August 16, 1941, by the High Command of the *Wehrmacht*.

After the short noon break, the soldiers at the Replacement Battalion usually spent the rest of the afternoon outside. Often they marched to the shooting range for shooting instructions and shooting practice.

Owing to their infantry-oriented basic training, which included field-stripping and reassembling the German foot soldier's primary weapons in total darkness, all of the recruits visiting the range understood the machine gun model 1934, the Mauser Carbine 98k, and both 9-mm pistols, namely the *Luger* and the *P38*.

When field-stripping any of these firearms, a man had to put the small parts into his overturned field cap to keep them from getting lost. Since the parts were oily, the lining of the cap, especially, became spotted and required washing with soap and water. The inside of one's cap and the white side of one's collar band buttoned to the inside of the collar of the field-grey uniform jacket were always the first items of clothing to be inspected by the N.C.O.s. Most potato peelers and toilet cleaners in the barracks had been caught with duds with bacon fat on them, duds spotted with body oil and, in the case of the field caps, with firearms oil.

Failing, supposedly, to salute properly here, there, and everywhere caused no end of headaches for the recruit. However, at the shooting range a man could be crapped upon, or snarled at, both forms of dressing-down, for saluting a superior. Throughout the *Wehrmacht*, saluting was forbidden at firing ranges or inside washrooms, especially if the latter included toilets.

Still, the N.C.O.s played hell with the men at the range. "Don't make your right eye squint into the left pocket of your jacket!" and "Quit trembling as though you're fucked out!" were typical admonishments bellowed by the N.C.O.s at the firing line.

Eventually some fortunate fellow using the 7.92-mm Mauser Carbine 98k would shoot an extraordinarily tight group at 100 metres. The marksman was rewarded with a train ticket–and a very brief leave.

For those who trained with the 98k, the following words, which constituted the often-heard opening sentence of the printed training instructions for that rifle, remain unforgettable: the Carbine 98k is a weapon with which to shoot, stab, club and swat.

Sometimes the last part of the afternoon was declared to be a cleaning and mending hour, which the men called an hour for farting and fucking. To make sure that the Privates attended to their boots and clothing instead of playing skat, or some other popular game of cards, a few of the N.C.O.s hung around the barracks rooms until suppertime.

Ah, yes, supper! That word meant taking a peek into one's locker for something along the line of one's frugal breakfast. Generally, supper was about as meagre as this paragraph is short.

Figuratively, the dictum "Being on duty" means being on duty, and boozing means boozing, the opposite of being on duty. It signified the strict dichotomy between attending to business and relaxing, or, for instance, what the soldier did before supper and what he did after supper.

In his room after supper, a man could take off his boots and his jacket for the first time in about 12 hours, allowing him to relax cautiously in what was known as his beer drinker's suit. I say he could relax cautiously because there was, for instance, an important distinction between properly keeping his suspenders over his shoulders, or allowing them to dangle, very improperly, from buttons at the waist of his trousers. Of course, he had no beer in his quarters, just as he had no liquor there.

The biggest hindrance to true post-supper relaxation in a barracks room was the din of voices coming from the many guys. Mainly because of the loquacious types, no one could possibly hear everything that was talked about within those four walls.

Noisy conversation disadvantaged the quarters' senior soldier–among recruits the Private elected to do the job–who was always expected to know the exact number of men present in the room. Furthermore, he was to be aware of the issues–there were many, most involving N.C.O.s–that influenced the men's disposition collectively. If, for instance, a fellow recruit deserted or committed suicide, the senior soldier might be asked to testify.

At the very least, the senior soldier occupying a close-to-the-door place at the long barracks-room table had to be adept at snapping to attention and yelling "Attention!" whenever an N.C.O. or an officer walked in, although whoever saw such a visitor first had to jump up and utter the yell.

With regard to many voices in one room, I recall that about two years after my time in Gross-Glienicke, when, once again, I was quartered in the company of a slew of men, a black-bordered envelope addressed to me arrived by field post. The terse message was that Oscar had been killed in action near Houffalize in Belgium during the German Ardennes offensive. He had been shot in the abdomen by Allied aircraft fire. I doubt that more than two or three of those present in the room were able to take note of those sad tidings. For one thing, most of them were busy excitedly discussing the mail they had just received; for another, life simply went on as far as they were concerned.

Fortunately, none of the recruits' rooms at Gross-Glienicke had a radio, not even a mass-produced, tinny midget radio receiver in a dark-brown Bakelite housing, or an inexpensive radio receiver, the big brother to the midget radio. Josef ("Joey") Goebbels's brand of propaganda wasn't listened to by the Privates in the Panzer barracks, at least not by means of radios.

At 10 p.m. the order "Lights out!" came as a relief. Hearing those words, some joker lying on his sack was sure to holler "Draw your knives!" as if preparing for some nocturnal criminal activity. However, pretty soon a different kind of disturbance, namely snoring, took over.

Some of my upcoming war stories contain further references to Gross-Glienicke, but for now let me tell you what happened there at the end of our basic training, on Graduation Day, which just about coincided with Christmas in 1942.

In a large hall, bottles of wine had been placed on the tables, one bottle for every two graduates with a huge flag bearing a black swastika on a circular white field approximately two metres in diametre hung down one wall. Close to the lower end of the flag stood the head table, at which the Commanding Officer and his training cadre were seated. The presence of the N.C.O.s at that table just about guaranteed that, even in such a setting, we would be subject to some shocking way of theirs of smartening up recruits.

Sure enough, right after our meal a ghoulish Sergeant recited the many stanzas of an explicit poem about a drowned virgin whose body remained unrecovered–a maiden to whom no man could, unfortunately, ever demonstrate the wisdom of *carpe diem* (seize the day). That poem's two-line refrain sticks in the mind: "And through the sexual tract doth feel / Its winding way a long, long eel."

After two months of basic training, the Privates were sent to various Panzer schools for additional training. Their training completed, the men went to Panzer Regiments in Germany, each of which was the replacement unit for its Panzer Regiment in the field. My Regiment, namely the part of it in Germany as well as the part constituting the core of the 7th Panzer Division abroad, was Panzer Regiment 25.

One can easily see why an eight-week stay at a Personnel Replacement Battalion would not generate a high degree of *esprit de corps*. There, a conscript did not train the company of men from his own province.

Early in 1943, on our trip by train for most of the way from the Replacement Battalion to the Army tank driving school at Lyck in East Prussia, we were in the charge of four young, unseasoned Corporals wearing brand-new rank insignia. I'd have sworn that each of them had, at the very end of 1942, signed up for 12 years with the Panzer Forces, and had, for that reason alone, been promoted. The four hadn't come from Gross-Glienicke.

Supposedly to maintain discipline throughout the trip, which for them was merely an extension of their somewhere-in-Berlin barracks, *the stage on which to play their lofty role in the rigorous atmosphere of mid-war*, the quartet of *Schweinehunde* (literally pig dogs or dogs used in herding pigs, but also meaning the imaginary offspring of wild swine and stray dogs) would, at every stop, no matter how brief, arbitrarily order half a dozen guys out of the train, and onto some spot where, next to the tracks, heavy items–for instance, steel railroad-car brake shoes were piled in layers.

Standing outside in the bleakness, perhaps even at night, the six fellows would be ordered to grasp rusty brake shoes, one with each hand, and perform knee bends in unison while reciting a couplet so simple that it could have originated with any one of the four Corporals: "Eventually, I, too, want to attain the tank battle badge."

Especially at the Panzer driving school, a more difficult version of the knee bends accompanied by a saying was in vogue. It requires six men to hold their arms extended forward at shoulder height–there were no heavy weights used for this one–and to do their knee bends individually according to the 1–5–3–6–2–4 firing order of a six-cylinder engine, at the same time reciting their saying.

Six men bobbing in imitation of a straight-six engine's pistons made for a very rough-running motor. No 12-point buck, meaning a man who had signed up for 12 years of service in the *Wehrmacht*, ever succeeded in

Tank driver's licence, front and back

doing a tune-up, so to speak, on six Privates, regardless of whether he had them pumping away at low speed, at intermediate speed, or at high speed. However, the demi-lifer didn't want perfection at all; he wanted, in each instance, a reason to prolong one of his stock show-'em-who's-the-boss exercises.

For us Privates, Lyck, pronounced *Lick*, was a vast improvement over Gross-Glienicke. The N.C.O.s were of a much better breed than those at G-G, and tank driver training replaced basic training.

Three photos taken at the Tank driving school at Lyck in East Prussia

Situated just outside of Lyck, the driving school's buildings were a few years older than the one-pattern late–1930s Panzer barracks in cities farther inside of Germany. The district about the school–Lyck lay about 650 km east northeast of Berlin–consisted of open country, something a tank driving school required. An undulatory stretch of the Lyck terrain, known as the waves of the Danube, made for hours of long, hard practice at shifting the turret-less Panzer IA's manual transmission with its five forward gears and one reverse gear.

My *Wehrmacht* driver's licence for armoured tracked vehicles was issued on April 30, 1943, not at Lyck, but at Gross-Glienicke, to which the others and I had returned from Lyck. I was then not yet 18. By way of Panzer Regiment 25 some of the new drivers that I knew were sent to the Kursk area for the large-scale Panzer battles that began there about two months later, namely early in July.

The photographs give interesting information about life at Lyck. Additionally, note, for instance, the small Christmas wreath suspended from the ceiling, and the tiled stove or masonry heater, part of which is visible in the photo of exactly thirteen men, including me, in a barracks room. Also note that in another photo four of those thirteen are standing alongside one of the driving school vehicles. Note, too, the Soviet tanker's padded leather helmet, a souvenir from the German Eastern Front, worn by the instructor.

Note that, in the photo of a Panzer IA being driven past close-cropped trees growing next to the road, the driver's vision slit in the vertical wooden windshield is much smaller than the instructor's window.

Finally, as far as the last of my Lyck photos is concerned, note that it shows me in front of the guardhouse.

Not shown in any of the photos is a nearly-new British recovery vehicle, captured in North Africa that stood unused in a corner of one of the Panzer garages. The number of foreign armies' equipments and vehicles that were to be found on Panzer bases in Germany was surprising.

Because I have dwelt on life in the Panzer barracks at Gross-Glienicke and because the reader will therefore appreciate a change of pace, I have chosen to weave numerous descriptions of Panzer drivers' doings into most of the following war stories, or to base entire accounts on them. The longest description of the latter kind, Chapter 14, is entitled "Driving the Jagdpanzer IV: Avoiding Transmission Abuse." A much shorter one in Chapter 11 bears the title "Those Farting Tank Drivers."

Although I write a lot about Panzer driving, I write even more about Panzer gunnery. In all of my ensuing stories about Panzer battles, I am a Panzer gunner, not a Panzer driver.

Panzer driving tactics taught at Panzer driving schools are dealt with where appropriate later in this book.

CHAPTER 4

1943–A Year of Panzer Barracks and Intermittent Absences

For me, most of the year 1943, after I had finished tank driver training, proved to be a kind of revolving-door existence because of my repeatedly having to leave some Panzer barracks, then having to return to them. Twice, at least, an absence of considerable duration from the barracks amounted to my being granted an unsought deferment from service at the German Eastern Front.

The first deferral came about when, at the Panzer Regiment barracks at Erlangen, about 20 km north of Nürnberg, I began to be plagued by carbuncles. One particularly bad cluster of four grew in my lower back, causing massive swelling, or edema, preventing my right kidney from functioning properly, and making my body retain much liquid. The fellows–they saw my swollen face and hands–thought that the barracks food was doing wonders for me. I certainly was gaining weight. However, finger pressure exerted on my flesh left temporary depressions. Before long, I was sent, for about a month, to the urologists at a military hospital at Bad Brückenau, a spa about 100 km northwest of Nürnberg.

Just as the rest of the town of Bad Brückenau enjoyed absolute peace and quiet, so did the hospital. Only two patients to a room, with many other rooms unoccupied. Plenty of good food. The only other place at which I was to get extra food in the way of seconds was close to the German Eastern Front the following year.

Lance Corporal Hermann Pasold, a fellow patient known to us by his nickname, Männe, was a none-too-sick operator who hailed from Erfurt, I believe. Männe worked on the nurses until one of them, a physically big girl, gave him what he most desired–in one of the vacant rooms on our floor.

Because Männe's next urine sample contained a profusion of spermatozoa, the medical staff suspected that he had suddenly become sexually overactive. The word spread, and Männe was discharged before he had the opportunity to provide many more specimens of his urine. We learned after Männe's departure that the big nurse was regularly having sexual intercourse with at least one of the medical officers at the hospital. Männe thought he was, to use the cliché, God's gift to women. I'd wager that he went right on playing Lothario, no matter where.

Come to think of it, Männe believed that one of his many attributes was a fine tenor voice. On a Sunday, in an inn in some village within walking distance of the hospital, he would persistently let loose a few arias, expecting to be rewarded, by the innkeeper, with a bottle of wine. That was Männe: wine, women and song.

The year was far from over when I, my boils in remission, returned from Bad Brückenau to the starkness of the Panzer barracks at Erlangen, from where some of the guys I knew from tank driver's school had just been sent to the front.

Thereafter, Panzer Regiment 25 moved to Schweinfurt, where, for starters, we took part in a huge parade involving the garrison on the occasion of Adolf's birthday, a very rainy April 20. All that activity was rather harmless; however, things were getting worse by the day.

The Schweinfurt Panzer barracks had a miniature training ground next to them. A pure punitive obstacle course. Out there, in one instance, one of the non-coms got his face full of small splinters from the hardwood bullet of a 7.92 x 57 practice round, after which the unfortunate shooter and his pals were made to do hours of fast crawling. The N.C.O.s at the Panzer barracks in Schweinfurt had a particularly bad reputation. Often, they were close to being out of control.

In those severe times, young soldiers who were required to serve in places like the Schweinfurt Panzer barracks soon learned the meaning of endurance. The harsh treatment they experienced manifested itself in many of their sayings, one of which ran as follows: everything passes, even a life sentence. Those words strongly implied an analogy between barracks and penitentiary.

The Panzer soldiers' numerous sayings, and their songs, affected me greatly; they enriched my German.

After Schweinfurt, Bamberg became the home of Panzer Regiment 25 until the end of the war. When I was discharged from a military hospital on April 10, 1945, I received written orders to report in Bamberg.

Another development that helped to keep me from being sent to the German Eastern Front in 1943 was that, after Marshal Pietro Badoglio announced, on September 8, 1943, the Italian armistice with the Allies, German troops rapidly occupied most of Italy. Personnel that could be spared at the Panzer barracks in Bamberg were dispatched to Italy to help bolster the occupation forces temporarily, not as Panzer crews, but as guards of one kind or another.

The 7th Panzer Division, of which Panzer Regiment 25 was a part, had been stationed in France from May, 1940, until February, 1941, before most of us who were being sent from Bamberg to Italy had become members of the *Wehrmacht*, or had completed our Panzer training, so we hadn't experienced the good life in France. We were, largely, young fellows, about 18 years old on the average.

Just what our destination was in Italy we were not told, but Italy, in lieu of France, would, we supposed, mean a fine life for us for a while.

Russia would come soon enough.

Photo of my Father and I (indistinct, but the only one I have showing me in the black
Panzer uniform)

Our troop train, en route through the Alps to Italy, had stopped in
Villach in Austria one morning. Standing at the feet of mountains
towering left and right of the tracks that carried much transalpine traffic,
we had to wait an hour or so.

From the adjacent empty track, two Canadian prisoners of war,
members of a roadbed improvement work party, scrutinized a few of us as
we were leaving our boxcar to get fresh water at the station, a bit farther
down the line.

Suddenly taking his eyes off us, one of the two POWs hurled a ballast
stone at a mongrel pigeon tarrying on a tie. I complimented the pitcher
with "You're damned good at it." He had knocked the bird out. The two
men probably wondered for a long time how come a young guy with a
Canadian accent was travelling among German troops.

By mid-September of 1943 I had been away from Canada for a long
four and a half years of hard knocks; I have often recalled that for me it
was a pleasure to say a few words in English to the Canadian at Villach.

A day or two after Villach, we detrained at Trieste, a major seaport on the
Gulf of Trieste, at the head of the Adriatic. We had been sent there to assist in
guarding the port, which then had a population of about 250,000. That's
what we were told at first.

Without encountering any hostility whatsoever, we moved to the
outdated, unoccupied Bersaglieri barracks located on high ground over-
looking a large part of the city.

All of the hastily vacated quarters were bare. Possibly the tables and chairs had been removed just before our arrival, but I'll wager that no lockers had ever graced the dormitories assigned to the men. Massive clothes hooks jutted from three of the four walls of each such room, reminding me of the many double hooks in the classes' cloak rooms in the three public schools I had attended in Canada. We enjoyed neither beds nor mattresses at that Ritz Bersaglieri; we had simply gone from the crushed German straw on the floors of the boxcars to the Italian straw of roughly the same feel, colour and smell covering parts of the floors of our rooms in the barracks. Furthermore, we had not been left racks of any kind for our rifles.

Basically, each of the many no-flush toilets arranged in rows of six or so in the various parts of the barracks consisted of a funnel-like hole in the concrete floor. Armed with his own hoarded toilet paper or a handful of Italian bedding straw, a visitor to the john had to watch himself–his suspenders, his heels, his wallet–as he, with his backside bared, squatted directly above such a slippery crater of no return, each of his feet carefully placed on a light-coloured, smooth tile shaped like the sole, arch, and heel of an upside-down Italian military boot of small size. Easy to clean, though, that kind of bowl-and-cubicle-free Italian latrine. Hose it down. Period.

Behind the barracks blocks stood the unlocked garages, in which Italian military gear, new and used, lay piled high. Layered haphazardly among clothing, for instance, olive-coloured crates, with *BOMBA MANU* (hand grenades) stencilled on them in white, made that area downright dangerous.

"*Dort lebt man wie der Herrgott in Frankreich*" (There one lives like the Lord God in France), an old, proverbial simile that can be applied to any locality in which a soldier is enjoying a comparatively luxurious life, certainly did not hold for Trieste during our first few days in the barracks there.

Then, towards the end of the first week–we were still busy making the place liveable, and hadn't been away from it at all since our arrival–we began to believe that we, in our part of Italy, would be blessed with that cozy *Herrgott* feeling after all: Chianti, brought into the barracks surreptitiously in mess tins, was being consumed in the rooms. Since none of our talent had the supernatural power to turn straight Italian tap *acqua* into strong Italian *vino*, there had to be a wine supplier in the neighbourhood.

About half a dozen Italian kids, their average age perhaps 14 would accept lire through some tight hole in the high barracks fence, and, half an hour later, would, at the same opening, deliver the bulbous, partly straw-adorned bottles of Chianti. They would also take the empty bottles with them after the *vino* had been poured into mess tins. Sure, those Trieste kids profited, but not one of our men ever got gypped out of his money, or even part of it.

Before long, naturally, some of the guys overindulged; some mess tins became puke pots, many of the sunken toilets became badly spattered, and the cat was out of the bag.

The soldiers' exclamation *"Da war der grosse Hund los!"* (The big dog was unleashed there!) meaning that all hell broke loose characterized the resultant crackdown during which, first of all, every bit of the wine that the soldiers had on hand was poured down some of the gaping toilets. The second, and final, stage of the enforcement took longer; the announcement, once again, of the no-booze-in-the-barracks order was driven home with an hour of stiff, sober drill and marching, the latter mostly in double time.

The big event over, the big dog was again leashed. The premises were deemed to be dry for good. The proverbial cushy life of Riley–so far, the boys had caught but a glimpse of that life–would have to be found elsewhere in the area.

Soon the boys would be able to slake their largely imaginative, intense thirst in some pub well outside of the confines of the barracks. Also, they would soon let the brothels contribute to their good life, although they would find out that no drinks were available there.

The Association of Juvenile Italian Bootleggers had, as far as their wine trade with the barracks was concerned, of course been put out of business by the big dog; however, a few die-hard boozers found other ways of getting *vino* in.

Caught before long, those smugglers each got seven days' detention. The ground-floor detention cells at the Ritz afforded their occupants an excellent view of the parade square; conversely, the passers-by could see the cells and the guys in them. As the culprits stood there on the inside, looking out through the barred windows, they appeared to be far removed from the good life, especially since the rest of the guys had begun to get down into the city, either on duty or on short periods of leave.

Getting Around in the Streets of Trieste

Other than recalling the life in the barracks, I most vividly remember, as far as Trieste is concerned, travel in the streetcars, patrols as well as visits downtown, and guard duty at the old tobacco factory next to the main railroad station.

Often reaching speeds of more than 100 km per hour, the bora, a bitterly cold wind that blows from the mountainous northeast onto the Adriatic region of Italy and Yugoslavia, has been known to knock down people and overturn vehicles. In Trieste, this wind seemed to concentrate its fury at numerous street corners. Bucking the walls of wind in those localities proved to be next to impossible for pedestrians. Far easier, we soon learned, to ride the streetcar whenever we travelled outside the barracks.

Usually, we used the convenient direct line that ran downtown from our abode, and vice versa. Always, some conductor habitually prodded us with "Step in farther! Step in farther! Please! Please!" On most days, a couple of squads of our men armed with rifles rode the streetcar without ever causing the civilian passengers to be alarmed. On the contrary, a good many of our fellow passengers, using their Austrian-flavoured German, conversed freely with us.

Patrol duty in Trieste was almost exclusively a matter of our having to be downtown at night. Unlike stationary guard duty, in which we participated frequently at a POW camp in the city, patrolling a certain area on foot afforded us a fair measure of mobility despite the darkness.

Sometimes groups of three of us from the barracks would be assigned to two-man patrols of the military police for the early part of the night, but tagging along with those typically callous, overbearing fellows inevitably made us feel restricted. We got around much better when we–a Sergeant, perhaps, and two men–were on our own, ready to learn as much as we could about nocturnal Trieste.

Never so late as to be in violation of the nightly curfew, some of the residents of Trieste would, for instance, hold an important social gathering–from out on the street the affair sounded like muffled auditions for an Italian opera–behind solidly shuttered windows. Their door, just as solidly secured, would, however, be opened for us curious fellows, allowing us to witness what could be called a big party in progress.

At each such gathering that we saw, the proceedings would be directed by an elderly master of ceremonies whose sweaty glow betrayed his love of much drink and song and food. Many times, when making our rounds, we came upon the eat-drink-and-be-merry atmosphere of an evening feast in Trieste.

Inevitably, it was a matter of our having to resist accepting the advice offered by the well-known "Where people are singing, sit down at ease, for wicked people know no songs." We weren't dressed for the occasion. The steel helmets and the rifles and, for that matter, the uniform … We didn't fit in. We moved on, into the night.

When downtown in Trieste on leave for a change, many of us felt compelled to spend an hour or two at some commercial bathhouse to catch up on our personal hygiene. After all, sleeping on straw and voiding urine and excrement into a near-medieval type of plop toilet could contribute to sickening B.O. Besides, even after we had occupied the Ritz for several weeks, the plumbing hadn't been made reliable enough for us to count on regular showers.

Anyway, the basic rental bathroom in an Italian bath–the place also had rooms with far more elaborate layouts–had to be seen to be believed. A rectangular, tiled room with a bathtub standing alongside each of two parallel walls. Between the tubs, a waterproof room divider. On the wall at the far end of the room, in the direction in which the bathers, sitting in their tubs, would look, a large mirror, by means of which each bather could see the other–before the mirror became steamy.

For us, the hot water and soap was the main thing, not the kinky interior.

Experiencing the Trieste Brothels

Generally, a group of on-leave adventurers from the barracks, upon entering a brothel in Trieste's downtown in the evening, would, first of all, be seated on a couple of dozen chairs standing along the four mirror-clad walls of a kind of ground-floor arena.

Enticing their customers from that pool, perhaps eight fairly young, good-looking and sexy brothel whores, directed by their brothel mother, or madam, would efficiently pursue their business.

During the early stages of each visit to a brothel, the young men would want to savour the social aspect of it all. Those who had been to that very brothel, and who knew, or thought they knew, certain whores there, would point out some bashful boy whose sex life seemed to require a bit of professional stimulation. Thereupon, one of the whores would sit on Junior's lap, work one hand through his fly, and fondle him hornier than he had probably ever been.

Soon the youth would be ready for his trip upstairs. With his comrades wildly cheering the whore's expertise and his resolve to engage in sexual intercourse like a man, the whore would lead him away from the dizzying, reverberant theatre, to the bottom of the stairs out in the corridor, not far from the front door and the street.

Next, not more than a few steps up the narrow staircase, the whore would calculatingly engage him in yet another bit of Italian whorehouse drama by lifting, and holding high, the back of her short skirt, exposing her bare, well-shaped bottom. Presented almost primordially, life-size and at eye level, that splendid female erogenous zone, with its vulva unveiled, beckoned him on.

Under the powerful spell of the whore's vagina, the young man craved only lots of ultra-deep penetration and an almost never-ending orgasm.

The whore, on the other hand, really had no greater desire than to engage her lustful customer in hurried, shallow coitus. She knew that very soon after he had ceased to pump his youthful semen into her, she would need to continue to abide by the quasi-motion-and-time-studied routine of a brothel whore, a life to which a certain saying applied then, just as it applies now: "*Der nächste Herr, dieselbe Dame.*" (The next gentleman, the same lady.)

For sure, a brothel in Trieste was not the place in which to find true sexual bliss. Yet, such a place constituted the setting in which many a young fellow–usually in the presence, to a certain degree, of some of his peers–experienced what amounted to one of his premarital rites of passage.

Now and then, sexual intercourse in the presence of spectators could–with the permission of the madam, of course–happen in the pit of the brothel. A willing whore and a still more willing soldier, and the performance of primeval, foreplay-free vaginal intercourse while standing, with entry from the rear, would quickly commence.

The whore, bending forward from the waist, would brace herself by placing her hands on the seat of a chair standing in the middle of the room. The soldier, with only his boots off for the sake of some comfort, would hold his whore by the bare hips and ram his erection home. A fraction of a minute later, he, having diddled with abandon, would involuntarily lift his heels high off the floor as he ejaculated.

The boys would love every moment of the show, and the madam would be certain that favourable word would get around Trieste, causing even more soldiers to pile into her brothel.

An imaginative patrol, having looked in on something like an Italian soiree, could very easily move on to a search–ostensibly for guys AWOL (absent without leave)–of the entire premises of a brothel or two that had closed for the night.

Inside the brothel and past the loudly protesting, obstructive madam, the entire patrol would briefly look into the reception room on the ground floor, and then go up the stairs to the second floor, where each whore had her own so-called work room, which she had left for the night.

One single bed. One bedside table, on it a small, shaded lamp. One small sink, a mirror above it.

On the whore's no-longer-resilient mattress, a wrinkled sheet, its middle third, mainly, cumulatively discoloured by spots and streaks resulting from semen left there by a vast succession of men.

In the partly pulled-out drawer of the whore's bedside table, a jumbled multitude of black-and-white portraits, and mementos from many of the men with whom she had lain individually on her unclean sheets.

Centred in the whore's small sink, a large bowl containing a deep-blue chemical concoction, one shot of which, syringed by the whore into the urethra and around the glands of her client's erection, supposedly rendered him safe, for the moment, from infecting her with venereal disease, or from being infected by her.

Looked at far more closely than would have been possible in the distracting presence of its resident whore, such a second-floor room proved to be the kind of place that could well have inspired the visions that led to the soldiers' following saying: "Gonorrhoea, syphilis and chancre–Oh! was he a sick man!"

Having checked out the first and second floors of the brothel, the patrol still had to look closely at the third floor, to which, generally, all of the whores had retired for the night.

Again quickly brushing past the still very much impeditive madam, the three men began to behold a wondrous sight. Some of the whores, their comforters guaranteeing cosiness, lay in their clean, spacious beds, in real bedrooms. In other rooms, also well furnished, the rest of the sorority, in negligee, either chatted relaxed or indulged in a late snack featuring fried onions.

The quality and cleanliness of the third floor confirmed what the *cognoscenti*–those who, on their patrols had seen many a brothel from bottom to top–generally stated that the average Trieste whore kept herself, her wardrobe, and her living quarters a lot cleaner than her professional chamber.

Lord, that final floor did spell sleeping with a woman! It spelled the superb kind of sexual intercourse befitting a voluptuary anthropomorphic deity called the Lord God in France. Never mind the fast, cat-like copulation sold downstairs.

In the end–the madam, sensing that her visitors were about to leave, had become quieter–the basically kind hearted patrol leader may well have recalled a couple of popular lullaby-like lines from Paul Lincke, a Berlin-inspired composer of operettas: "Little girls must go to bed when, at a late hour, the stars shine in the sky."

Leaving the madam to regain her composure, and the whores to recover their strength–maybe the next evening two dozen guys in a vigorous gang or two from the Ritz Bersaglieri would arrive at that brothel–the patrol, bent on doing at least one more erotic brothel inspection that evening, hurried to the nearest brothel, no more than a block down the street.

The World of the Collection Camp

Our main function in Trieste was, it turned out shortly after our arrival there, the performance of guard duty at the prisoner of war collection camp housed in a large, old two-storey building that had, we were told, long been a tobacco factory.

Abutting the Piazza Della Liberta, as did the adjacent main railroad station, the collection camp required far fewer guards outside than inside.

Outside, a guard would have to contend with the bora for two hours at a time–if he was not resourceful. Luckily, the Italian railroad police maintained a number of small, enclosed watch shelters, some of which had windows that happened to afford a good view of large parts of the outside of the camp.

Crammed into what was meant to be a one-man booth, two men–a friendly Italian railroad cop and an adaptable German soldier, his fortunate guest–had to pass their watches standing upright, all the while being careful not to get too close to the cop's red-hot makeshift electric heater, consisting of something like a 50-cm long loop of bare, spiralled resistor wire whose ends the cop had somehow poked into the poles of a wall terminal.

Sometimes, having tried to learn at least bits of a foreign language in the closeness of the shelter for the better part of two hours, the soldier, upon emerging, would honestly be able to say, among other things, "*Io niente parla italiano, ma io parla inglese e tedesco.*" (I do not speak Italian, but I speak English and German).

Attesting immediately to the more stressful world faced by the guards inside the camp, a machine gun, model 1934, with bipod and, to its left, one full ammunition box ruled repressively from atop a small table in what could be called the lobby, inside the main entrance.

Whoever had positioned that MG34–it stood there when we first arrived, and it still stood there when we left for good–had fed only one 50-round belt of ammunition into it, and trained it on the door of the largest room off the lobby–the room holding dozens of anti-Fascist Italian soldiers. We gladly kept he MG34 standing on the table, although we could have quickly changed its aim, had the need to do so arisen, and fired it. Also, we could have reloaded it instantly.

Trying to stay away from the direction in which the muzzle of the MG34 was pointed, a two-man guard kept their eyes on the many Italians' doorway, which, as one entered the lobby through the front door, lay to one's right. A one-man guard stood immediately outside the open door of a smaller room which lay to one's left, across the lobby from the Italians. That small room held but one prisoner, an Italian Colonel – one of Badoglio's men.

About 50, the bespectacled gentleman wore his still-natty army uniform. Judging by the well-fed looks of him, he had long enjoyed the good life. However, he was a tormented individual. You see, many of the bedbugs in the building were getting to him.

The Colonel on one occasion explained to his guard, a Private in field grey, that he had devised a way to prevent the bugs from climbing up to him from the worn wooden floor at night–he had the foot of each leg of his cot standing in a sardine tin with some sardine oil in it. Still, the bugs were making hell of his stay at the collection camp.

A neat person, the Colonel had all of his six shiny sardine-tin bedbug traps placed uniformly. The fact that he had been allowed to keep the sharp-edged tins in his room confirmed that he wasn't considered to be dangerous.

The multifaceted old solider also told the Private that he had figured out that the bedbugs would, in the nightly near-darkness of his room, congregate on the ceiling and then, sensing the heat of his body lying directly below, drop themselves onto him. Airborne bedbugs, in other words.

One day, as we–two armed squads, a total of about two dozen men–travelled from the barracks to the old tobacco factory for guard duty there, a well-dressed, lovely young brunette boarded our streetcar. Instantly, many of the men gave the lady a rousing welcome worthy of a celebrity.

The majority of the fellows aboard had, after close to a month's stay in Trieste, become amateur whoremongers, mostly by consorting with the whores at one of the larger houses in the city; they had, consequently, easily recognized that brunette who, while at work as a whore in that particular establishment, wore a close-fitting, skirtless two-piece outfit in black.

Obviously greatly insulted by the rude reception, the ladylike whore quietly left the streetcar at the next stop, undoubtedly a lot earlier than she would have normally. Under the circumstances, she would not endure the presence of men who failed to consider that a brothel is, so to speak, not a *piazza*, or, perhaps that a *piazza* is not a brothel.

Actually, those brothel regulars, elated at seeing one of their own sweet whores outside the brothel, had forgotten a prescript that had become familiar to every one of them long before he went to Italy: "A gentleman enjoys and does not tell."

Eight cocky Alpini, Italian mountain troops, for some good reason segregated from the large number of Badoglio boys across from the Italian Colonel's quarters on the main floor of the camp, worked hard at keeping up their fighting spirit. Theirs was a room on the second floor of the camp, not far from the loading docks at the back entrance. If ever there was a bunch that looked as though it was very likely to attempt to escape, they were it.

At times, usually while feeling his oats, each of these fellows would ostentatiously don his high-crowned, green-felt Alpini hat, adorned with a long, shimmering tail feather no doubt plucked from a big Italian rooster. Such an imposing hat, typically issued at least slightly oversize to boot, made its wearer appear relatively diminutive, like a would-be grownup.

Not at all diffident, those troupers now and then adeptly aimed their repertoire of half-disguised obscene gestures at their guards.

In yet another of the chilly, bare rooms at the camp, we had charge of 12 New Zealanders, POWs who had been recaptured shortly following their release when Italy switched to the Allies on September 8, 1943.

One of the 12, a curly headed, cheerful fellow of about 25, spoke on behalf of his buddies, asking their questions and hinting at their needs. He said that he had been a newspaperman in New Zealand.

They always divided evenly whatever army bread I was able to bring to them. They were a good bunch.

After the war, I wrote to the mayor of Wellington, a Mr. Appleton, asking for his help in locating mainly the soldiers' curly haired spokesman in New Zealand. The mayor's office did send to me a letter and the photocopy of a short newspaper article—the latter undated and no source stated—expressing my request; however, not one of those 12 who stayed temporarily in the old tobacco factory in Trieste got in touch with me. Who knows where they ended up?

The Trieste Experience Summed Up and Lessons Learned

We left Trieste by boxcar, the way we had come roughly two months earlier. The city had shown us a relatively good time–a time by far not as good, mind you, as the visionary, unattainable ideal, but a time much better than that which we would have experienced if we had spent the same eight weeks somewhere not too far north of the Alps, namely in Germany.

On the whole, life in the Bersaglieri barracks had been much less inflexible than life in, say, the Bamberg Panzer barracks. Whereas the barracks in Germany might easily have driven a man to ask for a transfer to the front lines, the Trieste barracks would not have compelled him to put in for such relocation.

During our stay in the city, there had been no need for us to fire our weapons while on patrol or on guard duty. We hadn't experienced any bombing or any air-raid alarm. We hadn't heard any shooting at all.

Apparently, not one of the Bamberg Panzer boys had had to leave Trieste, in many respects a fleshpot, with his health affected by V.D. As far as their bodies were concerned, for some–for many, indeed–the Latin "a sound mind in a sound body" of Juvenal (A.D. ca. 60–140) could easily have become, to use the cliché, wishful thinking.

Our brothel goers in Trieste hadn't much cared about the body-mind connection or the relevant aphorism in German. They would say, "Luck is what a person must have."

An age-old characteristic, the young soldier's foolhardiness is depicted beautifully by Shakespeare in As You Like It, II, vii, 149–53:

> Then a soldier,
> Full of strange oaths and bearded like the pard [leopard],
> Jealous in honour, sudden and quick in quarrel,
> Seeking the bubble reputation
> Even in the cannon's mouth.

Every young soldier had better be especially lucky–everywhere.

While in Trieste, we hadn't received any further training in our Panzer specialities. We hadn't even often marched Panzer-style–the day of the big boozing prohibition was an exception–so we hadn't sung a great many marching songs. We hadn't, however, forgotten the Panzer training that we had taken to Italy with us, and we hadn't lost our toughness.

Recalled to Bamberg, we underwent updated tank-related training. Also, we learned much from the many stories of the wounded Panzer men who had been returned from the Eastern Front to the barracks, close to which a stationary, deactivated Soviet T–34/76 forcefully reminded us of

our covenant with the men of Panzer Regiment 25 who were serving at
the Eastern Front.

Less than half a year after Trieste, we would, in north-eastern
Romania, at a place called Suceava–about 950 km east northeast of
Trieste, incidentally–make good use of all of the Panzer training we had
received; we would also, in many ways, benefit from the experience we
had gathered as soldiers in field grey in a foreign country.

The Last Respite Prior to the Ostfront

Towards the end of 1943, I left the Bamberg barracks for about two
weeks, not a long absence, but one that revealed how important training
for winter warfare was to the Army.

In the *Wehrmacht*, the incongruous expression *Gebirgsmarine*
(mountain navy) meant a nonexistent or unheard-of military branch.
After the war, if it was said of a man that he had served in the mountain
navy, it meant that he had not served at all in the *Wehrmacht*.

What about Panzer skiers? What odd breed were they supposed to be?
Well, there was no unit, large or small, composed of such soldiers;
however, small numbers of Panzer men were given at least some mountain troops training.

I never did find out why I rated the honour, but in December of 1943,
I, along with nine others, was suddenly sent from Bamberg to Oberstdorf
im Allgäu, close to the Swiss border, about 130 km southwest of
München, for some serious lessons in military-style skiing.

Throughout its duration, the skiing course emphasized safety.
Starting with instructions on how to get around on a level field in a valley,
the mountain troops instructors soon got us flat-land Tyroleans–another
incongruity–to ski up and down fairly steep slopes. Always, when on skis,
each of us carried a rucksack containing a 10-kg load.

The upper surface of our Army-issue skis was snow-white, except for a
green stripe, about two cm wide, down the middle of each ski from one end
to the other, exclusive of the binding. That band of green made it easier to
find a ski lost in the snow.

Going uphill great distances mostly meant using the familiar, but
laborious, herringbone method, in which the skier sets the skis in a form
representing a V. Another technique, the 'sidestep', would let a man gain
altitude just about as quickly as the herringbone, without the danger of
his sliding backwards.

High-gradient downhill skiing with a loaded rucksack over one's
shoulders required a sound knowledge of how to brake unfailingly. Before
starting to go downhill on skis, the instructors emphasized, take both
hands out of the leather loops at the top of the ski poles. To brake hard on
the way down, hold the poles between your legs, pushing their lower ends
down behind you. Then literally sit on the poles and lean back a bit. The

baskets at the lower ends of the poles, forced to dig into the snow, will act as a reliable brake.

For decelerating and stopping on gentle slopes, we of course used the well-known snow-plough, a technique in which the heels of both skis are pushed outward.

One Panzer guy hadn't slipped his hands out of the loops for a fast run downhill. When his right ski pole got caught on an open gate in a fence, he was stopped abruptly by being pulled down backwards. He suffered a badly injured right shoulder, something that probably more than just bothered him for the rest of his life.

Uncomfortably close to the bottom of our handiest steep practice slope in Oberstdorf stood a solid barrier–a row of hotels. At such an old, well-known resort, generations of skiers had demanded accommodation with immediate access to the main see-and-be-seen slope; hence, the high density of buildings. There, if a man skied too fast and too far, he and his striped skis, and his rucksack, could accidentally just about end up in the lobby of one of those places.

On one practice run on that hill at about the midpoint of the course, I, despite my strenuous application of the obligatory ski pole-under-the-buttocks brake, was still going fairly fast as I approached the walkway in front of the hotels. At the end of my close shave, a little old lady, seeing me seated, as it were, on my ski poles, asked me, "Is that also part of your service?" Perhaps that lady had, decades earlier, skied at Oberstdorf; perhaps she had, at that time, gone down the same hill in schuss–without having to carry a shifting, rucksacked load, and with fewer structures to stare her down. She might as well have asked me if the entire course was part of the Panzer soldiers' duty.

The course instructors were, to be precise, mountain troops N.C.O.s and, judging by their accent, natives of some of the mountainous regions in the extreme south of Germany. Near the end of our course, I had the impression that a couple of them knew that they were in deep trouble because they and we, their entire class, not having left the mountain well before the onset of darkness, had been forced to stay out the whole previous night. In the early evening, all of us had planted our skis in the snow, God knows where, and, hugging the mountainside, had followed snow-clad ledges. We had come upon an alpine meadow with a small hut on it, but hadn't stayed there very long.

Next day, in Oberstdorf, we had heard right away that the civilian mountain watch had been notified of our being overdue. So had the military.

Did the Panzer skiers exist? Yes–sort of. If some old weekly propaganda newsreel–please don't bother to look too hard, though, because the mountain troops kept all of the skis and related equipment after each course was over–shows for instance, a Panzerkampfwagen IV or a Jagdpanzer IV with skis strapped to its superstructure, chances are that at

least one member of the crew did receive a couple of weeks of ski training–
perhaps at Oberstdorf in Allgäu in 1943.

The saying "When someone takes [has taken] a trip, he can relate
something" of course pertains to each of the various trips I undertook in
1943, and to my account of each of those trips; collected, those stories are
the ones I have presented here, more than 60 years later.

In retrospect, 1943 was, for me, the calm before the storm, for in
1944 I got to know, indelibly, the real seriousness of life at the German
Eastern Front, where the sole commandment was "Kill or be killed."

CHAPTER 5

Becoming, and Being, a Panzer Gunner

Panzer Gunner, the title of this book, obligates me to emphasize, in it, important fundamental aspects of Panzer gunnery. In addition to others, many serious students of military history whom I have guided at the Canadian War Museum in the last nine years proved to be keen on learning how the optical sight for a Panzer's main gun was used by the gunner to achieve astonishing numbers of kills of enemy armour. However, because published information on the use of the telescopic main-gun sights in the Panzer IV and the Jagdpanzer IV is hardly available in popular form, I elect to use, for this chapter, some of the excellent material readily available concerning the Panther and the Tiger tanks– material that was, and still is, applicable to the Panzer IV and the Jagdpanzer IV. That I did not serve aboard the Panther or the Tiger does not preclude my offering such material to my reader.

It is definitely preferable to have the bulk of the Panzer gunner's functions explained in one chapter–this one.

In 1943, training for the position of Panzer gunner followed no prescribed plan of definite duration. Unlike, for instance, the tank driver, the gunner did not receive a couple of months of concentrated, formal training. Generally, the professional development of the gunner was of a prolonged and partly autodidactic nature. Whereas the Panzer driver was awarded a driver's license for armoured, full-tracked vehicles, the Panzer gunner received no certificate of graduation or qualification–ever.

The gunner-to-be probably would get his first taste of something like Panzer gunnery in one of the outside shooting lanes of a concrete-baffled 100-m military rifle range close to some Panzer barracks. A scope-equipped.22-calibre single-shot barrelled action clamped into a single traverse-and-elevation mechanism built into the front of a plywood turret supported by four sturdy legs at the firing line would serve as his main gun. If his Replacement Battalion trained men who were destined for its Panzer Regiment at the German Eastern Front, he, with that little.22, would shoot at the steel silhouette of a Soviet T–34 propelled by a cable operated by a crank at the firing line. The Corporal who controlled the contraption would even reverse the tank's direction for a spell, and then move it forward again, all at varying speeds. Right there and then–that early in a Panzer soldier's career–his instructors could tell if he had any feeling at all for lead. Hitting the relatively small tank silhouette was difficult. At a distance of 25m, the Kleenex-box-high T–34 appeared to be about 850 m distant. The Panzer Regiments were forced to resort to

43

improvisations like the 22 in training the men who wanted to become gunners.

By 1943, certainly, the Panzer Gunnery School, in operation since 1935 at Putlos, had neither the number of Panzers nor the vast amounts of live ammunition, AP as well as HE, necessary for large-scale, thorough gunnery training. Panzer gunfire simulation systems and blanks were not in use at that time.

Situated about 45 km east of Kiel at the south-eastern shore of the *Kieler Bucht* (Bay of Kiel), Putlos is now a suburb of Oldenburg in the district of Holstein, which should not be confused with Oldenburg in the district of Oldenburg. Oldenburg in Oldenburg lies some 210 km south-west of Oldenburg in Holstein.

Late in 1943, the *Wehrmacht* had 22 Panzer Divisions, 17 of which each had one Panzer Regiment; the other five Panzer Divisions each had only part of a Panzer Regiment. A full-strength Panzer Regiment consisted of two Battalions, each with four companies. The complement of the 1st Battalion was 51 Panthers; that of the 2nd Battalion was 52 Panzerkampfwagen IVs. In addition, there were the assault guns of the Panzer Divisions and the non-Divisional Tiger Battalions.

All that armour called for a large number of gunners. Ideally, at any given time in 1943, dozens of men, at least, should have been receiving Panzer gunnery training at Putlos, or at places like Putlos. However, as good as none were sent there. Even the instructors who evaluated men by means of the lowly.22 had never been to Putlos. The large training areas were also places that the vast majority of the Panzer fellows never got to see in 1943 or thereafter.

In 1943, although there was a lot of gunnery training conducted at the barracks of the Replacement Battalions, gunner training always stopped short of real, live gunnery practice, or of firing demonstrations.

One aspect, above all, of the swearing-in ceremony at the Panzer Replacement Battalion 10 influenced some of the attendant recruits to become Panzer gunners.

Then and there, the drawn-up Panzer IVs, turrets and all, had remained an impressive sight, making many a young man present contemplate his own coming function inside a Panzer.

Shortly after they had had their oath sworn for them, so to speak, some of the fellows said that if their role involved handling a couple of a Panzer's guns–the main gun, and the one machine gun, both belonging to the turret–well, that would be just fine with them.

At this point, mention must be made of the battle-seasoned gunners who participated in the unofficial training, in the barracks of the replacement units, of their eventual successors in the field. Those veterans, just about all of whom were recovering from battle wounds, delighted in imparting much of their invaluable expertise to the future occupants of the fighting compartments inside the Panzer turrets. Many of those vets–those,

The author in uniform 1943

especially, who had clashed, often one-to-one with the gunners of the T–34s of Ivan, or the Soviets collectively–thanked Christ that, throughout the years, the Soviets' tank optics had remained distinctly inferior to those of the Panzers. They spoke, of course, of what the replacement units had, or had not, taught them during Panzer gunnery training, and of what they had picked up subsequently in the way of turret wisdom, meaning the lore arising from life in the turret of a Panzer. Dealing with one or more of those pieces of wisdom, an informal lecture delivered in soldier's German in a barracks room was usually hilarious, notwithstanding the generally gloomy atmosphere of the whole place, and always highly informative.

Despite all those endeavours, official as well as unofficial, it seemed, by 1943, that the only sure way for the aspirant to become a full-fledged gunner was to serve an apprenticeship, even if only a brief one, as a loader at the front. There were, really, no better-qualified instructors, no more extensive firing ranges and training areas, and, for that matter, no keener fellow students, than those at the front lines. If a loader survived the battles and displayed the proper aptitude and attitude, that experience constituted a great step towards his becoming a gunner.

During the many hours that he spent in the proximity of the gunner, his main mentor, the loader would learn quite a bit about the gunner's duties. The loader would, for instance, know that in battle the main gun should be traversed past a front corner of the Panzer as infrequently as possible. He would know where to find, up on the telescopic sight, the rather secluded switch for the reticule illumination. He would know how to jab the emergency impulse generator to fire the main gun after the Panzer's electrical system had failed partially or entirely. He would know of the need to aim the main gun, before the start of a rest period or the like, at a spot from which a surprise attack might be launched at his Panzer. He would know the location of the vehicle's demolition charge.

What the loader would be a lot less familiar with, however, was how to deal, chiefly by means of the main gun, with a dangerous enemy's broadside, or 90-degree, travel, oblique, or 45-degree, travel, semi oblique, or 30-degree, travel, and head-on, or 0-degree, travel. In all such cases, it was the speedy and accurate laying of the main gun that required the ultimate in expertise of the gunner.

The gunner's proficiency certainly was not exclusively the result of sufficient classroom instruction augmented by adequate gunnery practice. In their quest for still greater personal expertise, ambitious gunners craved topflight, printed gunnery instruction, the arrestive kind that was to be found concentrated in the *Panther Primer*–a manual bearing that title had been issued to Panther crews–and in the *Tiger Primer*. Primarily, the *Panther Primer* and the *Tiger Primer* were, as far as the gunner was concerned, instruction manuals. Secondarily, they were, for him, reference manuals.

Regardless of the reason for their production, the *Panther Primer* and the *Tiger Primer* contain priceless passages pertaining to the job of the gunner in 1943, as well as thereafter in the Second World War.

Unless the proximity of his target obviated the need for the calculation of range prior to his use of the main gun, the gunner always calculated the range before getting the lead which, like the range, sometimes was not required because of the nearness of the target. The gunner's overall sight picture, acquired for his calculation of range, quite naturally yielded details useful for his subsequent work with lead.

The more conspicuous part of the reticule of the Tiger I's telescopic sight consisted of the beautifully bold outlines of a row of points; the less conspicuous part of the reticule will be discussed soon. At the midpoint of the row of points was the main point; it was also called large point. Equally spaced, three to the left of the main point, and three to the right, were the six auxiliary points, also known as small points. The main point, in the shape of an equilateral triangle, was twice the width and twice the height of each auxiliary point, which was shaped like a caret. The apexes of the main point and all of the auxiliary points were at the same level. The distance between the apexes of two adjacent points represented four mils, a figure of the utmost importance to the gunner not only in connection with his determination of range, but also with his use of lead. A measure sometimes essential in calculating range, the height of an auxiliary point denoted two mils.

The *Tiger Primer* shows, below a row of points such as those just described, a row of vertical lines representing mils. There, the long mil line numbered 0 is shown as being directly below the apex of the main point; the long line to the left of 0, as well as those to the right, are numbered 10, 20, 30, 40, and the short lines, intermediate between the long mil lines and representing 5's, are unnumbered.

The illustration reveals that, although the *Tiger Primer* gives the number of mils between the apexes of two adjacent points as four, the row of mils shows ten for that interval. Possibly the disproportionate row of mil lines was included in the *Tiger Primer* to hammer home, to the gunner, the importance of mils in his work. That thought is bolstered by the truck facing towards the left, extending–partly to the left of 0, and partly to the right–for all intents and purposes over a total of 30 mils, as well as by the exercise involving the use of those 30 mils from the outset– i.e., without the need to convert point intervals into mils–to calculate the truck's range.

Perhaps the arrangement of mils in that illustration in the *Tiger Primer* was to be regarded as a schematic of the mils in a piece of optical equipment used, for instance, by an observer to gather gunnery information for transmission, by radio, to the gunner's Panzer, although Panzers, for their direct fire, did not have to rely on information provided by observers in other vehicles. However, when confronting, for instance, well-camouflaged enemy armour, a Panzer crew had to accept as gospel whatever an observer reported to it from his vantage point concerning, say, the whereabouts of an enemy tank or two. In such cases, an observer, in conveying information valuable to the gunner would use mils.

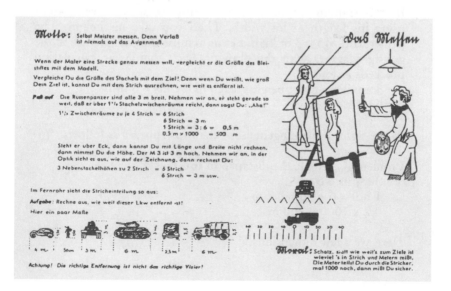

We will, next, see, with the aid of translations of the original, what the *Tiger Primer* has to say to the gunner about the determination of range solely by means of the reticle in that gem of an optical sight for the Tiger I's main gun.

The following is a translation of the preceding *Das Messen*.

Motto: Even masters measure, for they can't rely on estimations merely made by eye.

MEASURING [RANGE]

When the painter wants to measure a distance exactly, he compares the length of a pencil with that of the model.

You must compare the size of the point with the target! When you know the size of your target, you can calculate, by means of mils, how far away it is.

Pay attention: All Russian tanks are 3 m wide. Let us assume that one of them is standing at a distance at which it straddles 1½ point intervals; then you say, "Aha!"

1½ point intervals, each of 4 mils = 6 mils
6 mils = 3 m
1 mil = 3 ÷ 6 = 0.5 m
0.5 m x 1000 = 500 m

If he is standing diagonally, you cannot make your calculation using his length or his width. Then you take his height. The [American] M3 is 3 m high. Let us assume that the picture in the gunsight agrees with the drawing [*sic*]; then your calculation proceeds as follows:

3 auxiliary point heights, each of 2 mils = 6 mils
6 mils = 3 m, etc.

In the sight, the arrangement of the mils appears as follows:

Problem: Calculate the distance to this truck!
30 mils = 6 m
1 mil = 6 ÷ 30 = 0.2 m
0.2 x 1000 = 200 m

Here are a few dimensions:

Attention! [Because of the different types of ammunition], the correct distance [alone] does not constitute the correct sight [setting].

Moral: Instead of guessing just how far your target is away,
Judge, through your sight, what metres and what mils do say.
The metres then divide by all the mils you've found.
The quotient times 1,000 take, and know your range is sound.

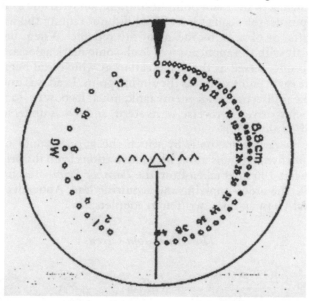

Incorporated into the reticule, but less central in position than the row of points and, hence, less conspicuous, was that part of the telescopic sight which the gunner, before giving the main gun–or, for that matter, the turret machine gun–its final aim, normally had to set according to range and type of ammunition.

Taken from the *Tiger Primer*, the drawing below shows the common range scale for AP and HE at the right, as well as the one for MG at the left. Each range is understood to be followed by two zeroes, making, for instance, the greatest distance for AP and HE 40 followed by 00, namely 4,000 metres.

If the range was relatively short, and if he was somehow prevented from applying the range-finding formula prescribed in the *Tiger Primer*, the gunner could fire his gun by shooting point-blank at a stationary tank. For that kind of shooting, he would of course have to know the initial part of the trajectory of his 8.8-cm AP shot, at least for the distance to which vital-zone-cognizant, tank-killing, point-blank shooting was restricted. Ultimately, instead of using the *Tiger Primer*'s formula to determine the range for his shooting, and instead of firing point-blank, the gunner could resort to time-consuming bracketing or, literally, knife-blade, or over-and-short shooting to establish the distance to his stationary target from his gun, in the process possibly achieving a direct hit with his third round.

With his target more than about 200 m distant and moving in any direction, practically, the gunner—we now turn to the *Panther Primer*—after having determined the distance from his gun to his target, would have to calculate the measure of lead, which he needed to fire his gun accurately.

Whereas, as has been demonstrated, the determination of range required the use of the main point in conjunction with one or more of the auxiliary points, the acquisition of lead did not require the use of any of those points, or of mils, by means of the reticule. When, however, the gunner dealt with the application of lead, some mark associated with the auxiliary points served as the demarcation at which lead began, and the apex of the main point served as the aiming point. Lead was understood to begin at the midsection of an enemy tank, not at its bow or, in the event of the tank being driven in reverse, at its stern, and it was understood to end at the tank's midsection.

There were two methods by which the gunner could obtain lead. Using a nonrhyming translation with illustrations from the original, let us examine what 106 lines taken from the *Panther Primer* teach the gunner about—note the order—applying and acquiring lead; Appendix C contains the original German lines, written in couplets.

The Mirandola Circus

The splendid family of circus riders
In blouses white as lilies,
With stripes rose-red and wide,
And kids lined up like pipes belonging to an organ,
Is here, for lack of funds, presently beginning
To sextet-dance atop a single horse.
So, circling cheerfully,
Within the circus ring,
Is, sleek and chocolate-brown, a mare
Which simply is named Mirandola.
The troupe seems to be inclined

To mount the horse by jumping onto it.
Mama runs, away and up she jumps;
You think it's much too early–O, dear me!–
However, exactly at the moment
At which she leaves the ground,
Mirandola, as if by calculation,
Approaches, so as to meet her path.
Mama jumps onto the horse in one bold leap,
And the whole crowd shouts with joy.
The horse has hardly run a few steps farther
When mama's husband undertakes to be a rider.
He, too, runs into emptiness and jumps–and look!–
He sits exactly there behind his spouse.
The action's speeded up,
And every kid jumps that much sooner.
One thinks that something will, for sure, go wrong;
However, things click every time, surprisingly.
In the end, they sit there, all O.K.,
Behind their mother on that only horse:
One has to jump as soon as the horse gets close,
Then things always will work out exactly.

If you shoot at targets that are moving,
There's the same consideration:
Before a shot gets to its target,
It needs some time–although not much.
In that short time,
The target travels, though not very far.
No matter how short the interval may be,
The shot arrives late and misses.
Therefore, simply deal with it artfully:
Shoot towards the point at which the target will arrive.
The target then towards the shot does travel.
That's why this trick's called lead.
Shoot when your target's still not there,
Then you will hit it with the *KwK*!
If something's travelling only 200 metres away,
Don't be concerned about its speed.
Aim straight for it! For the shells' times of flight
Are insignificant at such distances.
If, however, its movement is more distant from your muzzle,
There's but one solution: lead it!
The measure of the lead is found
In mils. Just how, you will below find out.
Now, calculate where, in the row of points,

The start of lead will lie.
Then, as is done the world throughout,
You hold the sight at six o'clock.
Now, see how, skimming the line of points,
The target hurries straight toward the middle.
When it has arrived at the small point
Which you selected as the start of lead,
Then fire away, and pay attention, please:
The target's midpoint is what really counts.

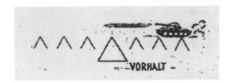

[Lead]

Thereafter, hand off the gunner's wheels!
Instead, check, with a most concerned look,
If, when you see the flash ahead,
The target exactly at your main point lies.
If so, the lead is fine.
If not, you have to make correction.
Provided that the target has gone past a ways,
You to your lead that distance add.
If, however, the target, when the shell explodes,
Is still short of the main point,
You the missing bit of distance
From your lead subtract.

[Too Far] [Still Off]

If your target's heading is not to yours athwart,
If it is oblique to your direction,
That does not affect
Your lead at all.
However, if your target speeds
At an acute angle towards you,
That requires correction:
Here you take only half the lead.

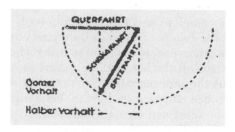

[Above Stanza Applies]

The next question, then, is this:
How do I find the lead?
Estimate only the target's speed–
That's something that everyone will learn in time!–
Then note the lead that's printed in the table
If your arithmetic is not so hot.
If you have trouble handling figures, do just that;
It's called the old way of getting lead.

[Speed of Target]

km/h	40	20	30
Pz.	3	6	9
Spr.	4	8	12

If you want to know the lead for every speed,
You'll have to do a big of calculating.
That, however, is no witchcraft:
Estimate only the target's speed, divide by three!
Then you have the lead,
In mils, for AP ammunition.
For HE shells, consider that
They are longer on the go.
The lead must be increased.
You must, as illustrated here, the lead adapt.
With HE: the speed divide by two.
That's all there's to it,
And the table is not used at all.
It's termed the new way to get lead.

[AP velocity: 3
HE velocity: 2]

To arrive at some particular complete and reticule-ready lead, the gunner, in addition to using what the *Panther Primer* calls the new way of obtaining lead–or, as far as that is concerned, in addition to using what it calls the old way–had to know, right off the bat, and, in a short supplementary calculation, make use of the indispensable fact that four mils were equal to one interval between adjacent points in his reticule; however, the entire lead calculation remained mentally feasible.

For example, provided it were travelling at 24 km/h at an angle somewhere between 90 and a little more than 30 degrees, the Soviet, tank for which the range was calculated earlier in this chapter would require, for AP,

$24 \div 3 = 8$ mils of lead

and, since four mils equal one interval between two adjacent points

$8 \div 4 = 2$ point intervals of lead

For HE, the lead calculation for that same tank becomes

$24 \div 2 = 12$ mils of lead and $12 \div 4 = 3$ point intervals of lead

A target coming, or going, at an angle of about 30 degrees or less required half of the full lead calculated for either AP or HE. Of course, a target moving at 0 degrees, or at almost 0 degrees, required no lead at all. Travelling at 36 km/h at an angle which required full lead, a target needed, for AP, exactly the half-reticule's maximum of three point intervals of lead. However, many tanks were capable of travelling much faster than 36 km/h; the Soviet T–34/76, for instance, was capable of a maximum speed of 53 km/h, which, for AP, required $53 \div 3 = 17.67$ mils of lead and $17.67 \div 4 = 4.42$ point intervals of lead, or 1.42 point intervals beyond the three intervals that were available in the half-reticule.

The basis for the official approval of the generous leads resulting from the gunner's mental calculations could be, simply, that they worked, even at long ranges. By 1943, Panther gunners were urged, generally, to fire at the enemy at increased distances; the Panther's main gun was easily capable of inflicting killing damage through the side of many a type of tank at 2,000 m. As well, possibly, the liberal lead for the Panther's gun was in part sanctioned because of the likelihood that the average gunner would fire his gun a split second before, or after, the mid-section of an enemy tank coincided with the aim-off mark at which lead had to take effect.

At the German Eastern Front, a gunner's application of lead could easily be thrown off because most of the Soviet tanks had their turrets positioned relatively far forward, just as most of the Soviet assault guns carried their superstructure and cannon well forward.

Perhaps it is, at this point, best to acknowledge wholeheartedly that there should be no doubt concerning the general validity of what stands written, with the mid-World War II gunner in mind, about Panzer gunnery in the roughly 50-year-old, authoritative *Panther Primer* and in the likewise authoritative *Tiger Primer*.

Without benefit of lead, the gunner could, under certain circumstances, fire his gun point-blank; the *Panther Primer* commands, "Aim dead centre" for the tank whose range is 200 m or less. Fork shooting, meaning three-tyne-inspired shooting, the lateral bracketing–and then, possibly, the hitting–of the target by means of AP or fragmentation-shell fire, was a method which the gunner could employ when working without calculated lead at longer distances.

The gunner of course had to be familiar with a lot more of his telescopic sight than just the entire reticule. For each Panzer, the bare-bones technical data customarily provided, under optical equipment, the model number of the turret, or main, gunsight–not much information to work with.

There were many Panzer gunners, in 1943, holding the rank of Lance Corporal, whose two chevrons signified that he had at least two full years of service. A man's reputation, mainly, would get him installed as a gunner. Rarely would the one-chevron Private First Class fill the position of gunner. Never, one might say, did a Private get the job. The requirement for the so-called N.C.O.-gunner did not exist in the *Panzerwaffe*; neither, by the way, did it exist for the N.C.O.-driver. The Commanding Officer of a larger unit might prefer to rely on an all-star crew, with a Sergeant as his gunner, and a Corporal as his driver. In a command tank, the Communications Officer doubled as the gunner–about the only time an officer served in that position. The gunner was the deputy crew commander; therefore, as, for instance, a Lance Corporal he could well give directions, if not orders, to a driver who happened to be an N.C.O.–not bad for a gunner who was, say, 19 years old.

Knowing, from his own training and experience, that the gunner had to perform much of his work mentally, the ex-gunner, in writing of Panzer battles, is frequently tempted to make use of the interior monologue, a kind of SOC, or stream of consciousness, in an effort to increase his reader's appreciation of the gunner's function. However, many interior monologues–perhaps one related to each firing of the main gun– would certainly cause those Panzer stories to suffer from a certain kind of reiteration.

CHAPTER 6

Encounters: Travels with and without a Panzerkampfwagen IV

In the spring of 1944, 17 five-man Panzer crews of the 8th Company of the 25th Panzer Regiment–I had, in Bamberg, recently been assigned to that Company–travelled about 200 km by third-class passenger train from Bamberg to the Nibelungenwerke (Nibelungen Works) in Linz on the Danube in Austria for the purpose of accepting new Panzer IVs for the 2nd Battalion of the 25th Panzer Regiment, still fighting at the German Eastern Front. By that time, the Nibelungenwerke, which had been manufacturing Panzer IVs since April of 1941, was the only remaining manufacturer of that type of medium Panzer.

Secured aboard flatcars, the Panzer IVs, 17 of them, were ready for us at the Ni-werke, as the plant was called locally. We noticed, first thing, that the fighting compartment of each new Panzer IV featured a new 9-mm *Maschinenpistole 40* (submachine gun 40), as well as a new *Kleinempfänger* (midget radio) with a bakelite housing. That receiver was the little brother of the *Volksempfänger* (people's radio), an inexpensive radio presented practically free of charge to Germans of limited means.

We could appreciate why the MP40s were there, but we couldn't figure out why the 220-volt radios were included with the Panzer IVs. There was no such power supply in the area to which we were taking those vehicles. No matter what, the little radios went along for the ride.

Not having seen much more of the city of Linz than the railroad siding at the Ni-werke, we travelled, by freight train, some 400 km to Przemysl (pronounced Chair-may-shill), a city in the southeast of Poland, close to the Polish-Ukrainian border. During most of the Second World War, the name of that place was known to many German soldiers because of its huge *Entlausungsanstalt* (delousing facility). Militarily, Przemysl was the hub of German railroad traffic into and out of the southern part of the Soviet Union.

Without having to be deloused, we Panzer men, still living in the Panzer IVs on the flatcars, rode the railroad another 200 km, approximately, to our destination. After a total of something like 800 km of train travel, we finally delivered those full-tracked armoured fighting vehicles to our Regiment at Chernovtsy at or about the end of March 1944. On that occasion, I, with 17 months of service in the German Army, was welcomed as a newcomer at its *Ostfront* (Eastern Front).

The trip had required the 17 Panzer IV crews–85 men–because, for instance, the Panzer IVs could, without being unloaded, have been used to repulse raids on the railroad by partisans, especially east of Przemysl.

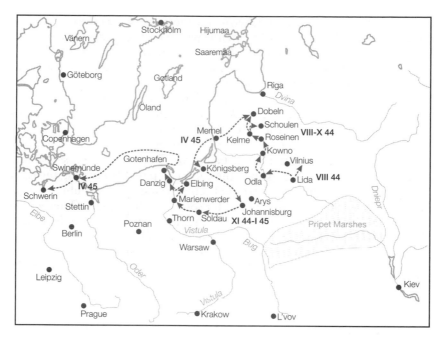

Map 2   Combat path of the 7th Panzer Division, Eastern Front July 1944–May 1945

Skeleton crews could not adequately protect a train consisting of a loco-motive, nine platform cars, eight of which each carried two Panzer IVs, and two boxcars. At the end of March, 1944, Soviet troops captured Chernovtsy (Romanian *Cernauti*, German *Czernowitz*) close to the foot-hills of the Carpathians.

Today, Chernovtsy is located in the Ukraine, not far from the south-eastern border of Poland, the eastern border of Czechoslovakia, the north-eastern border of Hungary, and the northern border of Romania. Taking my cue from the fact that there exists many a three-country corner or place where three countries meet, I submit that Chernovtsy presently lays in the proximity of a kind of–I repeat a kind of–five-countries corner. Before it was taken by the Soviets in 1944, the city lay in a territory belonging to Romania; it was, even then, close to my dreamed-up five-country corner.

Perhaps one week before Chernovtsy was captured by Soviet spear-heads on March 30, 1944, to be exact, we had arrived in that city, which then had, and possibly still has, an overpass spanning the multiple rail-road tracks leading, as far as we were concerned, to and from part of the front, which, by then, might have been described, looking northward, as lying to the left of us, to the right of us, ahead of us, and, farther away, even behind us.

Making that overpass in Chernovtsy memorable was the elbow bend at the bottom of the rather steep incline which we had to descend immediately after crossing the overpass. One after another, each of our Panzer IVs, in the lowest of its six forward gears and proceeding as gingerly as possible, crawled down that cobblestoned incline to the tight 90-degree left turn. There, each driver, using his left steering brake, had to disengage, and then brake, his left track, allowing the right track to propel his tank leftward, away from the concrete barrier at the outside of the bend.

Something like 25 tons of Panzer IV moving on cobblestones requires deft steering. Take it to the left just a bit too much in a case like that and the right rear could swing against the concrete, possibly severing the right track. Lose a track and a tank would become essentially immobile. To get moving again, the crew would be in for some very hard work. They would have to drive out some of the pins in the more than two tank lengths–a Panzer IV was close to six metres long overall–of lost steel track, drag the manageable shorter pieces in front of, and in line with, either the first or the last of the eight road wheels, and re-pin the track without joining its ends. Then they would have a buddy tow their Panzer IV onto their laid-out, re-pinned track. After that, they would lift the ends of the 99-link track and pull them over the return rollers, making sure that some links were engaged by the drive sprocket at the front and the idler at the rear, and drive in the one final pin to join the ends of the track. Slow, hard, rotative work. Dangerous as hell in combat. Bad, too, in a small bottleneck, as at a bridge. If many a horse, as the saying goes, was lost for want of a shoe, many a tank was lost for want of no more than a track.

All of our Panzer IVs got past that concrete wall at the bottom of the hill and out of the city all right. The last vehicle that I saw crossing that bridge was a half-track towing a quadruple-barrelled 2-cm antiaircraft gun, its barrels pointing rearward. The four men aboard the half track had fear in their eyes, and were in a hell of a hurry. Maybe they had lots of fuel and ammunition, maybe not.

Normally, all of our new Panzer IVs would have been in battle in a matter of a day or two, if not sooner. Not this time. A couple of Panzer IVs and their crews were in for some sport with an ally of Germany. Mine included.

The Romanian Army in the area wanted a dozen of its foot soldiers to be made fearless of going up against enemy tanks. The twelve had been farm boys, obviously, and were under the command of a swarthy, bullying sergeant.

Even after all these years, I wonder about that one day of training they carried out with our help. On a field of the previous year's grass, we would drive, by the hour, our Panzer IVs on a course resembling a narrow rectangle perhaps 50 m long. A crude attempt at spring ploughing was what the ground looked like.

Side view of Panzerkampfwagen Ausf H. (The Tank Museum)

Front view of Panzerkampfwagen Ausf H, note spare track used as additional armoured protection on the front glacis plate. (The Tank Museum)

The Romanian boys, one at each pass of a Panzer IV, would jump up alongside it and, throwing two stick smoke grenades, one at each end of a 60-cm long cord, would try to get them to dangle over the 12-o'clock gun barrel, at a point just ahead of the turret. They never did ignite any of those German-supplied grenades during their efforts, so there was no smoke from them.

However, the Romanians and their grenades made us think a lot about our vulnerability to such smoke. Hanging from the gun barrel, close to the turret, such grenades could emit a great deal of dense smoke, some of which would be certain to obscure the view through the telescopic gun sight, located 40 cm to the left of the centre of the bore of the 7.5-cm gun. Likewise, smoke would probably, no matter how strong the wind, reduce or cut out visibility through most of the five vision slits in the Panzer IV's cupola.

Fumes inside the Panzer IV were dispersed, in part, by air blown into the turret by the engine's cooling fans. Some of the grenade smoke reaching the stern of the hull would surely be drawn in quickly with the fresh cooling air, of which the 320-h.p. Maybach V–12 engine moved plenty, and could thus find its way into the fighting compartment. There was no heater in a Panzer IV. Drafty and cold it was inside such a vehicle, except in the daytime heat of summer.

The Romanian Sergeant wanted his tank tacklers to look alive and make progress. Once, at least, he, swinging his own steel helmet widely by its chin strap, struck a man he regarded as a slowpoke in the small of the back. Because of strict regulations, no German N.C.O. or officer would have dared to do anything of that nature.

Noon came, the gymnastics were halted, and the Romanians let it be known that they wanted to dish out a hot meal. They had had a field kitchen pull up near the ploughing match.

Our loader, a proper fleet-footed gopher, took our new mess tins and brought them all back filled with hot, meat-enriched kasha, prepared, basically, from hulled or crushed grain, and popular in eastern Europe. Because the morning hadn't been stressful, some of the crew stayed in the Panzer IV, except for going for a piss one at a time.

The Romanian cooks had plenty of kasha, and we Panzer men, who hadn't been near a generous field kitchen for a long time, just let them have our tins repeatedly for seconds. If we ate seconds, we ate thirds. Did we eat kasha at noon that day! None of our hosts seemed to know how few men belonged to a Panzer IV crew. Our friends didn't find that out until later that afternoon, long after their kitchen had left the scene. There was a kind of Trojan Horse aspect to the whole unusual affair.

For sure, the Romanians got to know our loader. It was he, I believe, who spotted their ignorance of the number of men per tank they were dealing with. A good loader could, in a hurry, sense any advantage in something like that. Outside work was his forte, and, because of it, he would usually be urged to remain a loader.

Looking, for a moment, at the rest of the crew, there was, to the loader's left, the other mezzanine man, the gunner, who, habitually, would mentally place the metallic blackness of the points of a reticule just below items in his surroundings, ready to shoot them, as it were. A man with an aptitude for what would amount, formally, to geometry and trigonometry. A man who would, for the rest of his life, use as a reticule specks of dirt on windows and windshields, always trying to aim, quickly but surely, at cars, trains, persons. Rare, by the way, was the natural gunner who held a tank driver's license.

Below, ahead of the gunner, sat the driver, ever cognizant of sounds, internal and external, through his earphone-free ear, and always endeavouring to minimize noise emanating from his big baby, all the while ready to respond immediately to the requirements of any situation. Each man aboard had a throat microphone as well as a headset with two earphones, one of which covered an ear, while the other sat above the other ear, clamped against the side of his cap.

Next, also below, but seated at the right, another keen observer of ambient sounds, the radio operator, with his grey-boxed equipment wired to a usually purposely shortened, range-reducing antenna located at the left rear of the hull. As well, he had one MG34 with a thumbscrew-adjustable, skullcap-like plastic saucer linked to the butt. Amazing how much steadiness that device, resting on the top of his head, imparted to the aiming of the hull machine gun. The radio operator's greatest worry was his radio frequencies for the day. How not to forget them and how not to divulge them. The first thing that the Soviets would demand to know of a captive radio operator was those frequencies. Their decoy tanks—captured German armour manned by so-so German-speaking *hujas*, pronounced *who-yaws*—that's Russian for *pricks*—would use that sort of information. The word was that those decoyers were members of Soviet penal battalions.

On the third level, a bit higher up in the turret than the gunner and the loader, with the breech of the main gun in front of him, somewhere between the level of his shins and that of his belly, but usually at about the height of his fly, sat enthroned the tank commander whose most important attribute was equanimity. Usually, a tank commander had experience as a tank gunner. Few tank commanders lived long enough to gain vast fighting experience in the turret's top storey. Those who did—Shakespeare's *Uneasy lies a head that wears a crown* applied to each of them— were appreciated, and adored as saviours, by the men; never did a Panzer soldier feel insecure about joining the crew of one of those heroes.

At the end of their field day, the Romanian sergeant and his boys did find out exactly how large a crew fitted into a Panzer IV. All five of us alighted to be able to say good-bye to the lot. Their helmets were off to us, so to speak, because of the enormous appetite each of us had shown for their kitchen's kasha.

We, for our part, saw them mainly as a bunch of poor buggers who would need lots of luck to stay alive. One pastel-blue egg-shaped hand grenade taken from the egg rack at the back of the inside of the turret and thrown out of the tank commander's hatch–even without the obligatory count of one and twenty, two and twenty, three and twenty, or three seconds before tossing it–would have made life extremely short for any infantryman approaching a Panzer IV, as the Romanians had so many times that day.

About 75 km south of Chernovtsy, we did, not much later, become involved in a tank battle during which we lost our Panzer IV to one turret- and gun-disabling armour-piercing shell fired at us by a Soviet T–34. With no interior explosion, and with no dead or wounded, we had time to retrieve our turret MG34 and scram with it, as well as with 600 rounds of 7.92x57. At Suceava, we retreated westward, into the Carpathian Mountains.

While viewing the interior of an abandoned roadside brewery just west of Suceava, one of our fellows–I believe his last name was Moser– found a few kegs of beer. However, our man wasn't the first soldier to venture into the place. On his back on the concrete floor, just inside the entrance, lay a young Red Army soldier with no weapon, just a bullet hole in his forehead. His pale pecker partly pulled out of his pants. A white man who had possibly paused–perhaps much too long–for a piss inside the place, and been summarily shot on the spot by his Commissar.

The one full keg that Moser lifted onto his shoulder didn't accompany him far. Neither did our MG34 go far with us. Both were probably gotten rid of at about the same time–the MG34 presented to some outfit that wanted it; the keg, by then empty or nearly so, dropped into a ditch.

Checked occasionally by patrols, especially at the railroad stations, we generally rode the rails on our way farther west. We had been given the papers we needed; it was a matter of our finding transportation. At that time, early in April of 1944, there were not yet units that rounded up soldiers to forcibly detain us. From Suceava, we wanted to travel, via a shortcut through northern Romania, into Hungary and then westward to Budapest and Vienna.

In the Carpathians, at a point about 90 km southwest of Suceava, we found out that there would be no train for us to take out of the mountains. We learned that the tracks were intact, but that there was no longer any traffic on them. We also heard that there was a long railroad tunnel ahead.

Soon after entering the tunnel on foot, we walked in total darkness. Flashlights we did not have. One arm extended sideward–for me, it was my left arm–each of us had to grope his way along what seemed like hundreds of metres of rugged, sooty and seeping rock.

What if, after all, some train were to barrel through? What if the tunnel was blasted shut at the end ahead of us, or at both ends? What if partisans were lying in wait for us at the exit? What if?

Shortly before the end of our subterranean adventure–we could, by then, see the proverbial light at the end of the tunnel–the single track curved slightly to the left, as I recall. We got out of there safely and, by various means, travelled west about 350 circuitous, tunnel-free km before reaching Hungary.

We had with us a Berlin swaggerer by the name of Stobbe, a born commentator. In one of the Hungarian towns, we saw a lovely young lady at the side of the main street. Stobbe said aloud, "You are a pretty girl; you have only one defect." The girl replied, "*Daz eez [Das ist] kein Fehler.*" She meant that being Jewish was no defect. One side of the front of her jacket exhibited the yellow Star of David. God only knows what befell that girl–and what became of Stobbe.

The remainder of our trip back to our home barracks in Bamberg was comparatively uneventful. We found them to be a sombre place. Many a suffering man sojourning there wore, along with his other medals, the wound badge in black for a wound, or for wounds, received; some wore the wound badge in silver.

That smoke-bolas-hurling squad of Romanian infantry in the vicinity of Chernovtsy, that lifeless young Soviet soldier in the brewery near Suceava, that wormhole of a tunnel in the Carpathians, and that indignant, youthful Jewess in Hungary–those encounters, because of their remarkableness, occasionally tend to overshadow, after some 60 years, the loss of our Panzer IV in our battle with some Soviet tanks at Suceava.

CHAPTER 7

Panzer Battle at Suceava in Northern Romania

Early in April of 1944

I now present my story about the Panzer battle at Suceava, upon which part of the chapter immediately preceding this one is based.

Of great concern to our unit was the fact that the Soviets had been on Romanian soil not only at Chernovtsy, since March 30, 1944, but also 175 km southeast of that city, at Jassy, since March 26. Just west of Jassy, they were as far as the Seret River, about 65 km inside the border, and only about 10 km from the main highway, which runs, for about 280 km, roughly parallel with the eastern border of Romania–an important road linking Chernovtsy with Bucharest. Then, on April 2, the Soviets broke into Romania elsewhere by crossing the Prut River east of Chernovtsy. The inevitable happened: tank-versus-tank encounters.

I don't know about the ultimate fate of all of the unit's 17 Panzer IVs that we had unloaded at Chernovtsy so very recently, and that had all crossed the railroad overpass there, but I do know what happened to ours.

Perhaps 75 km from the southern outskirts of Chernovtsy, our Company waited. A flood of Soviet tanks–more than likely T–34/85s– with mounted infantry would want our piece of the highway badly. Soggy fields. Ditches full of runoff. Not much opportunity to outmanoeuvre any of the tanks so as to kill them and their passengers when they would be broadside, more or less.

Much better, at first, would be to be in position on some side road that allowed a large zone of fire. Such a vantage point would be preferable to a spot which would force us to stand our ground directly on, or next to, the main road itself, where, for us, it would very likely be a matter of firing the main gun with its barrel over one of the front corners of our Panzer IV because that method added the advantage of slope to our vertical frontal armour, and to the vertical armour of one side of our hull. Understandably, neither the driver nor the radio operator liked that technique because of the likelihood that one or the other's hatch cover would be obstructed by the gun barrel. The two disliked it doubly–yes, hated it– because we had a full load of 87 shells, a good many of which sat in the racks immediately behind the driver and the radio operator, barring their emergency exit through the turret. At any rate, we took up our positions off the road.

"Aha! On the highway, one behind the other, 19 T–34/85s with their swarms of bees. Just as expected. First thing, kill the tanks. With that, a large number of infantry will kick the bucket. If necessary, use the machine gun." It was then about 10 a.m.

The machine gun meant one machine gun, that of the radio operator. The fact that the 7.5-cm gun was loaded with an armour-piercing shell–and would, very likely, continue to be loaded with that kind of insurance–ruled out the precise firing of the co-axial turret MG34. The Panzer IV's telescopic sight had a common scale, 0–3,200 m, for fragmentation shells and machine gun ammunition; for armour-piercing ammunition, it had two different scales–one, 0–2,400 m, for capped ballistic, and another, 0–1,400 m, for composite rigid. The armour-piercing shells we carried enabled us to reach out to 2,400 m.

Dealing with AP shells and the targets for which they were intended meant avoiding, or limiting, distractions. The gunner needed both hands for his 7.5-cm gun. For him, his foot-fired MG34 was strictly secondary. Shooting required concentration.

For our Panzer IV, things went just fine right away. From a distance of about 250 m, we nailed one T–34 at an angle of about 45 degrees. His infantry scurried off him like groundhogs off a big sun-warmed boulder as a low rifle bullet spatters their posteriors. He caught fire.

From where we stood on a side road, about 175 m from the western side of the highway, we saw, not much later, that other Panzer IVs had also done their work well. Judging by the billows of black smoke from diesel-fuelled open-air furnaces–there could, as well, have been other T–34s that were down for the count, but weren't burning–our unit had, within perhaps ten minutes, knocked out at least eight T–34s on, or close to, the highway.

Our prudent choice of positions had paid off, although we had lost two Panzer IVs, the crews of which were, however, alive and preparing to hike it–or ride it, if they could–out of the immediate area. Where planning is being done, shavings fall. We no longer saw any Soviet infantry. The survivors of the batch on the T–34 that we had destroyed were not in evidence, having probably scrambled aboard some of the unscathed T–34s that had headed south, down the highway, towards the Soviet bridgehead near Jassy.

The battle wasn't over. We knew that the maximum speeds of a T–34 and of our late-model Panzer IV were, on a hard surface, about the same–48 km per hour. Besides, the Soviets would have to be wary of plate- or disk-like antitank mines, grey metal containers shaped something like an oversize hockey puck, each about 31 cm in diametre, and containing up to 5.44 kg of TNT.

All types of anti-tank mines–Soviet or German–were feared by all Panzer IV crews. One mine would break the track of any tank; usually, it would damage or wreck the suspension as well. Another terrible effect of an antitank mine was the concussion it created, especially in the lower parts of a Panzer IV. Drivers and radio operators seated on the lowest level

of the tank had been dazed and unable to walk for hours after their tanks
had absorbed most of the full force of such a mine.

Our company commander, who must have read our minds regarding
our top speed, radioed "Pursue immediately!" Three Panzer IVs would be
involved. The other 12 would stay there, acting as the rear guard. We left
the safety of our site on the side road and joined two others for the chase
on the highway. There was no formation, only following the leader.
Plenty of ammunition. Plenty of fuel. We wouldn't have to worry about
antitank mines. If the Soviets could get past them, so could we. There
were enough T–34s ahead of us to do the nasty work of ridding the road
of any mines. Furthermore, with us not far behind them, they wouldn't
have time to plant new mines of theirs before we caught up with them.

Depending on the direction of the wind, they could have tried to use
smoke to force us to advance more carefully; they could then have engaged
us as we emerged rather slowly from their side of the fog bank. Another
thing that would have been very detrimental to us out there on the wide-
open pavement was a wave of T–34s following us after bypassing our rear
guard by using secondary roads. None of that happened.

We knew exactly what our company commander had ordered us to
do, and it looked as though it might work well enough. Attack the T–34s
wholesale from behind. A bit unorthodox, but not unfair. Remember that
the spring fields were unsuitable for any tank, slow or fast, including the
T–34 with its 50-cm-wide, low-ground-pressure tracks.

Probably our biggest advantage was that we would have our eight-cm-
thick frontal armour directed towards the T–34s, whereas each of their
tail ends would measure no more than about three cm in thickness.
However, tanks being tanks, we couldn't rule out the possibility that each
of the Soviets would make his on-a-dime turn and meet us head-on. We
would have to catch up with those roadrunners and, having spotted them,
let them have it from behind immediately.

Catch up with them–all eleven, it turned out–we three Panzer IVs did
just after a right bend in the highway, having chased them something like
five km. Probably entirely unaware of us, the unevenly spaced T–34s in
their stretched-out column moved ahead steadily within very easy range,
certainly, of our AP shells. Obviously they had posted no rear guard, not
even one on foot.

First thing would be to get off at least one volley with each gunner
aiming with a six-o'clock hold, at a large imaginary bull's-eye between a
pair of T–34 tail pipes or thereabouts. There, an AP shell would easily
penetrate the engine compartment, at least disabling the tank, and very
likely melting its white-hot way through to the crew. The idea of shooting
exactly up Ivan's arsehole was not unheard of, and it demanded a low six-
o'clock hold. Another possibility–it required the six-o'clock hold–would
be to aim at a point just above the rear deck of the T–34, so as to catch the

turret under its overhang, crippling the thing. For any tank involved in a battle, *disabled* usually meant *dead*.

The first volley of the two that we three Panzer IV had agreed upon would alert the surviving T–34s. After the second volley, it would be a matter of knocking out, possibly in some bend in the highway, the lead T–34 or one close to it, causing it to block, if possible, or slow down, the T–34s so that they could get their sloped steel asses branded *P-IV* by some AP shells.

Each of the two volleys–our Panzer IVs were stopped, and the T–34s were in a bend about 300 m. distant–sounded more like the quickest of salvos, but the effect was that of a volley in each case. Who had knocked out whom? Right there and then, nobody knew for certain. What counted was that of the eleven or so runaway T–34s, four were burning, leaving seven in the column. Later on, because we had not cross fired, we easily established whose kills they were. One was ours. Two for our Panzer IV up to that point that day.

Before we could concentrate on firing at the remaining T–34s, they were all traversing their guns to something like six o'clock, treating some of the infantrymen aboard to half a carrousel turn. The tank commanders should have charged each of the leeches a *kopeck*, the hundredth part of a Ruble, for that extra. The T–34s had made no about face, but they were shooting towards their rear while on the run–Parthian archers in 1944 Romania.

By that time–we three Panzer IVs were still halted at the start of the bend in the highway–the T–34s were about 500 m ahead of us, their guns still swung over their rear ends, and, it seemed, firing as fast as they could. So were we firing as hard as our guns could take it. As the Soviets raced away, one T–34, presumably hit and no longer firing its gun, began to burn, and veered off to the western side of the road. That left six T–34s intact and running.

The Soviet infantry was gone with the tanks; we couldn't see any heads, no matter how carefully we looked. If there were no sloggers, there would be no acts of heroism directed by them at our Panzer IVs.

Next, talk about a stroke of bad luck for us. Fired from a distance of about 650 m, one of their armour-piercing shells hit our turret glancing, well off centre and just above the upper level of the superstructure, and, although it did not pierce our steel completely, it left a 20-cm-long gouge–a kind of gigantic spot-weld–that prevented the gun from being traversed away from two o'clock. No more use of the main gun, for the time being, in our Panzer IV.

The six T–34s must have, in record time, diesel-clattered many km towards Jassy while we drove back to the scene of our first encounter of the day. Our Panzer IV was second in our three-vehicle column. The first one had its gun forward; the last was ready to take care of our rear.

About where we had left them, we found our company commander and all of his 12 Panzer IVs. With their crews keeping a very sharp lookout in all directions, the tanks had their guns trained on the highway, some to the north, and others to the south. All 12 had their outlines broken up by indigenous camouflage, branches taken from trees farther back in the small woods, at whose 170-m-long highway side they all stood under trees. Actually, there was a gravel forestry service road alongside the highway.

The Soviets would have an augmented force follow their tank spearhead. Burning tanks would be a long-lasting source of smoke, and smoke alone would tell them where the action had been, and would be. They knew that we were confined to the highway, the one that had cost them 13 T–34s so far. They might arrive with their 12-cm mortars or, if they were more aggressive, with their rocket launcher, nicknamed *Stalinorgel* (Stalin's organ)–no pun–because of the discordant sound made by its rockets in flight. The 12-cm mortar fired a 15.85-kg bomb 5.94 km. The launcher fired thirty-six 8.2-cm rockets, each carrying 3.04 kg of high explosive, to a range of 5.49 km.

Mortars it was. Their bombardment started about 30 minutes after we had rejoined our company. We couldn't see the bastards who were doing the shooting, so our Panzer IVs couldn't fire at them. A Panzer IV never was much good for indirect fire. Direct fire was what the Panzer IV and its 7.5 stood for. We were helpless against one of the nastiest land weapons of the Second World War. A reconnaissance patrol must have come up ahead of the mortars, and probably was watching us while we were being given the works.

To the rear of its turret, the top of the Panzer IV was extremely vulnerable. Extending from the back of the turret, a sheet metal stowage bin offered practically no protection for anything–not for its contents, not for the turret, and certainly not for the top of the hull, where two baffled steel gratings were located–the one at the right for fresh air to the two engine cooling radiators, the one at the left for air from them. A soft spot, a chink in the Panzer IV's armour, its Achilles heel–that's what that whole rear deck was with its two gratings, each about the size of a large doormat with a bold-lettered "Welcome" woven into it. Jerry cans and drums of fuel were taboo, especially back there. A Panzer IV was not a fuel truck.

After shooting some half dozen mortar bombs without scoring a direct hit on any Panzer IV, the Soviets ceased firing, probably wanting us to abandon our positions just inside the roadside bush. Their bombs had dropped onto the treetops. The jagged bomb fragments pestering the Panzer IVs were not particularly dangerous to our crews inside. It would have had to be a direct hit, pretty well, to cause grief.

Of course our company commander was well aware of all of these considerations. It was about 11:15 a.m. and he couldn't keep his Panzer IVs harboured at the edge of the woods. A true Panzer soldier, he decided to turn his predicament into a sortie–a good fight. Better to be the hammer than the anvil.

Before he, with a total of 14 Panzer IVs, drove away from the woods, he ordered us–because our disabled gun would be of no use in the swiftness of further tank combat–to blow up our baby as soon as their departure had gotten the Soviets' full attention. That should give the five of us a chance to clear out on foot.

All we could take out of our Panzer IV was the turret MG34 and 600 rounds of ammunition in belts, leaving something like 2,550 rounds behind. Our stowage bin was riddled by the mortars. Nothing at all in there worth taking along.

We destroyed our Panzer IV by means of our one-kilogram demolition charge, which was stored strapped to the upright support below the gunner's seat. As a matter of fact, it was the gunner's duty–my duty–to pull the igniter of the 90-second fuse. There had been no transfer of 7.5-cm shells. The vehicle–it had served us well–was blown apart, its turret lifted from the hull. A damned shame.

Good-by to that highway. We left it at Suceava, roughly, to travel the railroad–at least the railroad tracks–to Guru Humorului, and points beyond, towards the west.

For a while, as we headed for the mountains–the Carpathians–on our way out of the area, we heard the bark of tank cannon. Later–in the barracks and in the field–I never was able to find out more about those 14 Panzer IV crews–those 70 men–who facilitated our escape from the Soviets after our Panzer engagement at Suceava that day early in April of 1944.

The German main front line along the eastern border of Romania remained relatively stable from the latter half of April of 1944 until August 20 of that year, when the Soviets began their offensive to destroy the Axis forces in SE Europe. By that time–as a matter of fact, by July, 1944–the 7th Panzer Division was fighting in Lithuania.

CHAPTER 8

Tank Warfare in Southern Lithuania in July 1944

From July 2 to July 6, 1944, our Division was transferred, via Warsaw, by train from Stanislav in the Ukraine to Lida, 150 km west of Minsk, a city central to the Soviet's Bagration offensive against the German Army Group Centre that month. Lying in a partisan-plagued area, Lida was only 90 km away from the eastern border of East Prussia, Germany's easternmost province. Our Division was headed for the ill-fated Army Group Centre. The Division briefly advanced north-eastward from Lida before entering southern Lithuania. Panzer Regiment 25's Second Battalion, of which I was a member, did not participate in the Division's operations up to Dobeln in Latvia, and, after that, to Memel, Königsberg, and Johannisburg. Rather, it operated in southern Lithuania before retreating to East Prussia.

The 7th Panzer Division in World War II, pages 421–22, states:

Here [south of Kelme in Lithuania] the entire Division is at last assembled during the period from August 13 to 16 [1944] with the exception of the 2nd Battalion of the 25th Panzer Regiment. In the battle area west of Olita, the 2nd Battalion of the 25th Panzer Regiment was constantly subordinated to other battle groups and was separated from the [7th Panzer] Division. It fights with the 131st Infantry Division and the 170th Infantry Division and–after the relief of its own Division from the battle area around Olita by the 196th Infantry Division–is attached to that Division. Together with it, the 2nd Battalion of the 25th Panzer Regiment battles its way back to the border of the Reich [to East Prussia]. This Panzer Battalion constitutes the backbone of the [196th Infantry] Division and, as a "fire brigade" with constantly changing attachments, is used daily for the clearing-up of the situation at the respective focal points and, in the course of events, is employed as a rear guard. Stationed earlier in Norway for four years, the [196th Infantry] Division is by no means equal to the demands that have to be made on the Battle Group in such situations, so that the [2nd Battalion–more or less on its own–is forced to fight its way back [retreat] constantly.

We Panzer crews of the 2nd Battalion of the 25th Panzer Regiment did not, I am certain, grumble about our unit's successive attachments to the above three infantry divisions. Most of our exploits in southern Lithuania took place without our having been ordered by the infantry to carry

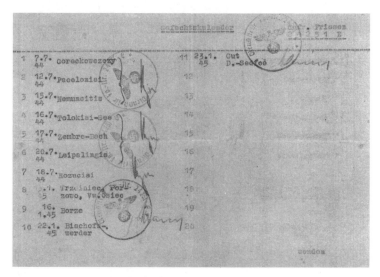

Tank battles log, or tank combat record

them out. We were separated from our Division until we rejoined it in West Prussia not long before our tank battles there took place in January of 1945.

I recall that we crew members never knew, in Romania, that in 1944 the entire 7th Panzer Division was under Romanian command from April 25 to July 1, the day before it left Stanislav in transferring to Lida. *The 7th Panzer Division in World War II*, pages 412, 414, revealed to me, decades after the end of the Second World War that our Division served under the Romanians. However, our tank battle at Suceava in northern Romania preceded April 25.

Looking at my log of tank engagements, I am reminded of a few words of the song *"Alte Kameraden"* (Old Comrades): *"Zur Attacke geht es Schlag auf Schlag ...."* (To the attack we go, blow after blow ...) The log, which I was able to retain despite many a tank battle, many km of travels, a stay in a military hospital in 1945, and, later that year, in a discharge centre, shows my name and rank as well as my field postal code, 24251E. Never will I forget that code, which stood for *8. Kompanie, Panzer Regiment 25, 7. Panzer-Division.*

It was the signature of the Company C.O. that certified every entry in my log, which shows, in part, the following list of entries:

7.7.44	Goreckowszozy
12.7.44	Paceloniai
15.7.44	Nemunaitis
16.7.44	Tolokiai-See
17.7.44	Zembre-Bach

Map 3   Tank Battles in Lithuania Summer 1944

18.7.44   Rozuciai
20.7.44   Leipalingis

That was seven tank-versus-tank engagements within two weeks. In one four-day period, there was one engagement daily.

In Lithuania, the Leipalingis area, in which we fought some of our tank battles, lay about 195 km west of the Soviets' July 4, 1944, front line, from where on that date, the Soviets launched a new series of attacks. It will have been the Soviets' broad thrust towards Grodno that we had to struggle with, starting, according to my log, on July 7, 1944. Leipalingis lies about 45 km north of Grodno, which was stormed by Soviet tanks on July 15, 1944. Let me give you an account, based on my experience, of the first engagement listed above.

Mentally very sharp, Second Lieutenant Jakob, a straight-faced little fellow, was the gentlemanly, yet most efficient, commander of our fit and well-trained Panzer IV crew in Lithuania. Judging by his regional accent, he hailed from somewhere in northwest Germany. The 2/Lt. was in his early 20s whereas each of his men, who had all been born in 1925, was 19 and a Private First Class. Our driver, gaunt-faced Johannes (Hannes) Elzer, in civilian life a long-haul transport truck driver from Andernach on the Rhine River, where his family had a trucking business, functioned flawlessly in our Panzer IV. Hannes often talked about his beautiful younger sister. Her lips, he claimed, were redder than the ripest cherry. Peter Zenner, nicknamed Lousy Zenner, or L.Z., because he seemed to attract lice quickly, was our main-gun loader and our gopher. Whenever he emerged from inside the turret of our Panzer IV, he gazed appreciatively at the sky. By trade, he was a plumber from Saxony. The radio operator, Erwin Rogge, had been taught the trade of winding coils for electric motors small or large, old or new. Occasionally, he received, from his parents, who owned a butcher shop in Bavaria, a field-post parcel containing delicious small smoked sausages. He shared those treats with the rest of the crew. About all that can be added to what previous chapters of this book say about me is that I was 5 ft., 11 in., or 1.78 m, tall.

Goreckowszozy or the Dummy Panzer IV Turrets on Opening Day

With the Soviets advancing westward again, we had a few days, at the most, in which to prepare ourselves to meet their armour. Our resourcefulness would help us do damage to *Ivan* and delay him to some extent–and save lives on our side.

The idea of partially dug-in, or hull-down, Panzer IVs came up. Overall, a Panzer IV was 2.72 m in height, 2.91 m in width, and 6.01 m in length. Two-thirds of the total height, namely about 1.82 m, could be dug in without inhibiting the operation of the turret, and thus, the 360-degree use of the main gun at its lowest-possible angle of depression. A drive-in pit, excavated out of a hillside to afford the hull and superstructure of a Panzer IV mainly frontal protection, would require a minimum depth of, say, 1.5 m; the pit would also have to have a width of slightly more than 3 m, as well as a length of close to 6 m.

These dimensions meant that, very likely, something like 12 to 14 cubic metres of earth would have to be removed from the side of the hill to arrive at a pit deep, wide, and long enough to accommodate a Panzer IV. However, earthmoving equipment was unavailable to our crews wanting to start the job of creating individual pits for their Panzer IVs. Unless a suitable slope, enough time, and, above all, enough entrenching tools were available, there was no sense in starting the work. Stymied, we had to look for some other means of helping us inflict as much damage on the Soviets as we could.

One of the men suggested an excellent solution, namely the use of full-size wooden models of turrets, set up on the crest of a ridge so as to have them appear to belong to dug-in Panzer IVs. There was, for that sort of ruse, a precedent known as Potemkin's villages. The Russian statesman Prince Potemkin (1739–1791) had sham villages of cardboard constructed along the Dnieper River, where they could be seen by the Empress of Russia, Catherine II (1729–1796), and her entourage, all of whom were travelling by boat during that stage of their journey to visit the Ukraine and the Crimea in 1787. The phony villages were the cover-up by Potemkin, a favourite of Catherine II, of his failure to colonize that area.

Dug-in Panzerkampfwagen Ausf H - representative of the type of protection time
prevented the author's unit undertaking. (The Tank Museum)

Our four new fake tank turrets would intentionally be made readily
visible to the Soviets; there would be no attempt to camouflage them, not
even partially. The Panzer IV crews would construct the turrets of weath-
ered wood, which, in Lithuania, was not hard to come by. On each turret,
a graceful log would be the main-gun barrel, and there would be a muzzle
brake at the end of it. The gun mantlet would be a length of log, and the
turret skirt would consist of boards.

Saws and other hand tools were easily liberated, or scrounged, from
farms, and the work went very well. Too well, in a way. Some of the men
had to be kept from producing, for instance, an L/100 gun–a super-gun
with a barrel 7.5 m long. Really, each turret, gun and all, had to command
respect instead of looking ridiculous. Laying eyes on our Potemkinian
turrets, the *hujas* would have to exclaim, in awe, "*Yupo twoio madj!*"
(Fuck your mother!).

Set in place, the quartet of completed phoney turrets did not look bad
at all. A couple of them even had nice touches, such as an open crew
commander's hatch. Each had, so to speak, a standard 3.6-m-long L/48
gun barrel. As a final detail, three hand grenades were fastened to the
inside of the back of each turret, not as a booby trap, but as a hit-sensitive
explosive charge. A jerry can of precious gasoline placed inside each turret
would have ensured even greater pyrotechnics.

Because we knew that the first wave of Soviet armour would, as always, be bent on seizing the land immediately adjacent to the roads, as well as the roads, we expected that our fake turrets, together with the turrets of our eight Panzer IVs peeking over the crest of our ridge, would make those *tankists* (*tankist* is a Russian word for *tanker*) leave the highway and advance towards our positions.

When six T–34/76s–an unusually small number in mid-1944–arrived in tandem just before 9 a.m. on opening day, we of course couldn't hear the *hujas* utter their favourite curse, but a few of them targeted our dummies, telling us that our trick was having some effect. Only eight of the twelve gun barrels aimed at the T–34s spat steel, something the *hujas* may not have caught onto. We stood about 350 m from the northern edge of the east-west highway running through the region.

Those six T–34s all turned off the highway and onto the July-dry fields, keeping their frontal armour directed, more or less, at our muzzle blasts, and fanning out slightly. Our knobbed ridge was a fine place on which to be in position for a battle with the T–34s, but it would have been much more advantageous had there been a substantial water barrier between the highway and us.

All zigzaggers, those six T–34s were not being driven by average gear grinders. Like toys with fresh batteries in them, they sped about spiritedly, some of them almost sideswiping one another, and then trying to fan out still farther. Undeniably, though, they were firing their main guns and coming closer to us. Still, not one of them had been made to stop on his tracks or, better, off his tracks.

One of our Panzer IVs caught a Soviet shell, reducing us to seven real guns. Damned nearly down to their number, that brought us.

We had succeeded in drawing the half dozen T–34s away from the highway; now it was a matter of making sure that they would never get back onto it–at least not all of them.

The T–34 crews had to be enticed to quit racing, so that they would present us with the opportunity to give them their licking.

Right away, therefore, 2/Lt. Jakob ordered me to fire high-explosive shells to blow up, in no particular order and at plausible intervals, our dummy turrets. Maybe the Soviets would think that their guns were killing Panzer IVs, one after another.

Above all, our exploding dummies might make the *hujas* in some of the T–34s do a double take and slow down their wild ride, probably because they would want to get off more well-aimed shots–the kind that had, they might think, already killed five Panzer IVs up on the ridge.

Our tactic worked. Four of the T–34s slowed down to a crawl, or stopped, and were promptly knocked out. Because it was hard for them to withstand a superior armoured force, the guys in the two remaining T–34s looked for a way out. They broke off their zigzag assault on our positions, turned to their right, and, as fast as they could, drove eastward, parallel with the highway. By then, both were using screening smoke.

The score on opening day: One for them, four for us. Not a great number of kills, but a great–a very great–show on their part, as well as on our part.

Although the following anecdote is not part of the above story concerning fake Panzer IV turrets, it is presented here because it does show a Panzer officer's use of a knocked-out Panzer IV as a decoy.

Aim for the killer batteries in a tank

The Panzer IV's four 12-volt batteries, each the size of a large wooden case for 24 one-litre bottles of beer, were located on the floor inside the hull, below the fighting compartment. Hardly ever thought of and seldom inspected, those life-givers were also a source of grave danger to the crew.

A low hit in the hull below the turret would usually rupture that quartet of storage batteries and tear apart the fighting compartment's steel flooring above them, allowing battery acid to splash and spray into at least the turret, and acid fumes to fill the vehicle.

One Panzer IV that I heard of had been pierced by a low side hit from a T–34 without exploding or igniting. Most of the members of the crew, with extensive acid burns to their skin, could see themselves blinded and physically tattered. With battery acid eating away at their asses, the turret trio could not be expected to continue to fight. Of course their Panzer IV was done for.

However, in their case, the crew commander was not given permission to blow up his tank. Instead, he was ordered to get his crew and himself out of there. They all headed for a water hole and some serious ducking.

The terrain which the Panzer IV had its batteries shot all to hell must, from what I heard, have resembled that of southern Lithuania. It was not smooth and uninterrupted like a serving tray; rather, it was rolling and abounding with riverine barriers.

The terrain being ideal for a bit of craftiness, their C.O. had decided to use the crewless Panzer IV as a decoy. He reasoned that, since the Soviets couldn't readily approach the tank to capture it and it would draw Soviet fire away from his intact tanks, he would, even if it couldn't return fire, temporarily allow it to stand where it was. His armour-piercing shells could see to its destruction as soon as killing it became necessary. Using a Panzer IV with shot-up batteries as a dummy was unusual. I never heard of anyone else having done so.

In the event of lesser battery trouble, with the loss of the 12-volt power, the Panzer IV gunner could fire his 7.5-cm main gun by means of a hand-jabbed emergency dynamo for electric primer. The small-diametre firing-plunger button was fixed into position ahead of the left shoulder of the gunner, out of his way, but not outside of his reach, so that he could not push it accidentally, whether or not the regular electrical firing circuit was functioning.

Any crew commander who believes that an opponent's main gun is running low on ammunition might want to get his own gunner to aim one metre or so lower than he would habitually–if that's where the other guy's batteries are. There may not be many enemy shells left to catch fire on the tank being hit, but there are always the batteries, acid-filled and crew-terrifying. Fuel–gasoline or diesel–is another big factor when the enemy's shells can be judged to have been about expended. Go for the batteries. Go for the fuel tanks. Know your adversary's construction and take advantage of it.

Paceloniai: Panzer IVs, SPWs (Schützenpanzerwagen or Armoured Halftracks for Infantry) and Anti-Aircraft SPWs Jointly Clear a 50-km Stretch of Main Highway

The 7th Panzer Division in World War II, pages 416–17, states the following:

> On July 11, while the main body of the Division blocks the Soviet crossing of the river [the Merkys River] at Varena, the 2nd Battalion of the 25th Panzer Regiment, together with Battle Group Weitzel, actually the Division's reinforced 6th Panzer Grenadier Regiment, on that day attacks alongside [not on] the highway leading to Olita and, via Daugai, advances as far as Paceloniai, some 15 km southeast of Olita.
>
> Strong enemy anti-tank gun barriers [at Paceloniai] prevent any further advance towards Olita …

The purpose of our off-road battles with the Soviets along that highway–we did secure a 50 km-long stretch of it–was to regain control of it to prevent the Soviets from cutting off, from the south, the German Army Group North.

Paceloniai is an entry for July 12, 1944, in my tank battles log. For me, that day began in a special way because six of our Panzer IVs were to be accompanied by a Battle Group with more three-ton halftracks than we had ever seen with us at one time. It had ten SPWs, the type of half-track of which every Panzer Grenadier Regiment usually experienced a shortage. Each SPW was designed to carry a ten-man squad. It was pointed out to us that two of the SPWs were not reconnaissance halftracks per se, but that their crews were trained in reconnaissance. Also, there were two anti-aircraft halftracks. Talk about a Battle Group!

Lieutenant Colonel Weitzel's armoured Panzer grenadiers were espe-cially welcome in our midst, so to speak, because most of their SPWs were armed with the 7.5-cm L/24 Panzer gun, which was no longer being installed in the Panzer IVs. Each SPW with the L/24 could carry 52 shells for that gun. We were also pleased to see the anti-aircraft halftracks. They could be used against land-based targets with excellent results.

We were compelled to fight along both sides of the highway. In July, the Soviets would have had such an important road just about paved with anti-tank mines. Also, they would have watched the highway for so-called sitting ducks, namely defunct German armour or other vehicles. Therefore, the truck-mounted, or motorized, grenadiers of Battle Group Weitzel would not be included in this action.

Before we set out, 2/Lt. Jakob, the leader of the six Panzer IVs, took about 15 minutes to acquaint us with the tactics of the attack, whose immediate purpose, basically, was to assault the Soviets' anti-tank gun defences at both sides of the highway. 2/Lt. Jakob explained that, to begin with, one reconnaissance SPW, one anti-aircraft halftrack and three of our Panzer IVs would lead, with the other three Panzer IVs, the other SPW and one anti-aircraft halftrack perhaps 100 to 150 m behind them. From the rear, those SPWs would provide fire support directed against anti-tank guns or tank-killer infantry. Via radio, they would also point out additional targets for the Panzer IVs' heavier guns.

The Panzer IVs would, if necessary, advance in steps, using terrain as cover whenever possible. The Panzer IVs at the rear would provide fire support for the leading Panzer IVs. When the foremost Panzer IVs have advanced to good firing positions, they would lay down fire to support following Panzer IVs as they leapfrog to the forward position.

The armoured infantry would assist the Panzer IVs and, in particular, destroy enemy anti-tank weapons. The Panzer grenadiers would ride in their SPWs as far as possible and dismount to destroy individual pockets of resistance. Upon neutralizing the enemy's anti-tank forces, the Panzer IVs and most of the SPWs could advance together in one assault wave. One of the anti-aircraft halftracks would precede the wave; the other would follow the wave.

After the first few uneventful km of our advance, we, travelling just off the right side of the highway, spotted the stern of a stationary SPW about 200 m ahead of us. No one about? Abandoned? Situated there by the Soviets to distract their enemy? No one could have proceeded more cautiously than we did, ready to destroy anyone or anything that fired at us.

From a short distance, the exterior of the SPW showed no signs, such as armour penetration or scorched paint, of having been involved in battle. Inside the SPW, however, a lifeless, bareheaded sergeant slumped in the driver's seat. He had been dead only a short while. No other human remains were visible.

The front of the sergeant's field-grey jacket bore several pin-on medals. One of them was the General Assault Badge, the equivalent, for the Panzer grenadiers, of the Panzer Assault Badge in Silver for Panzer men. That General Assault Badge jibed with SPW; however, the condition of the SPW and the sergeant's body in it looked damned suspicious. We left the body where it was. Later, perhaps, some Soviet would want those medals and, in ripping them off the dead man's jacket, would spring the booby trap.

I still believe that at that lone SPW the Soviets had set up their equivalent of the headhunters' practice of placing severed human heads on stakes, signifying FORBIDDEN TERRITORY. GO ANY FARTHER AND YOU, TOO, WILL BE KILLED. Nevertheless, we continued on our mission. Yep, there, out ahead, they were Soviet anti-tank guns. Not an overwhelming number of them, but each most dangerous. With a few of our Panzer IVs forcing the Soviets to keep their heads down, the Panzer grenadiers went to work, shooting, getting close to the Soviets and, for instance, throwing hand grenades into their positions. The grenadiers' score: three Soviet anti-tank guns and their crews killed; no losses for the grenadiers and for our Panzer IV people.

After advancing without incident—without being shot at, that was—for about 25 km, we received anti-tank gun fire from a bush about 100 m to the left of the highway. A couple of our Panzer IVs fired HE fragmentation shells at the spot indicated by the recon SPW by radio. In a case like that, HE fire was best aimed not to hit the trees at ground level; rather, it was best to aim at a point about six metres above the ground. The result was a far greater dispersion of shell fragments, meaning a far greater likelihood of wounding, or killing, each member of an anti-tank gun crew. There wasn't much AP fired by the Panzer IVs on that occasion. The Panzer grenadiers soon got into the act and made sure that the Soviet crews and their guns would never again endanger anyone—anywhere.

The closer we got to Olita, the more we expected to see many Soviet aircraft above the highway. That day, we did see some—a few at a time, but no more than about a dozen in all—only they were not flying at a low altitude. The anti-aircraft SPW crews knew that their single-barrel 2-cm Flak 38s couldn't reach aircraft flying at great heights. A Flak 38 had an effective ceiling of just over 1,000 m and a maximum horizontal range of 4,700 m. Its rate of fire was 180–220 rounds per minute, its barrel elevation was minus 20 degrees to plus 90 degrees, and its traverse was 360 degrees. True, Soviet ground-attack aircraft were no trouble for us as we followed the highway towards Olita, but they certainly meant, at about that time, great trouble for the troops surrounded there.

At their anti-tank gun barriers—note the plural—at Paceloniai, the Soviets may have had other surprises in store for us. They would not have had time to force slave-labour civilians to excavate anti-tank ditches, but they may very well have sewn anti-tank mines by the hundreds, and had armour lying in wait for us. At any rate, our six Panzer IVs couldn't contend against the strong anti-tank gun barriers at Paceloniai. We were ordered to advance southward from Paceloniai, towards Nemunaitis.

At Nemunaitis, Six Panzer IVs and Ten SPWs Randomly Encounter
Soviet Tanks, Ground-Attack Aircraft and Infantry

According to my tank battles log, on July 15, 1944, I took part in a battle at Nemunaitis, south of Olita. That was a few days after our Panzer IVs and the Battle Group Weitzel had left Paceloniai before entering, to the south, an area that must also have been filled with Soviet infantry and about every type of weapon that the Soviets needed to assemble in it, including artillery, mortars, Stalin organs, tanks and ground-attack aircraft.

It wasn't that at Nemunaitis our Panzer IVs and SPWs faced these unwholesome features of the Soviets concurrently. No, the whole battle was a string of events, each restricted to tanks or ground-attack aircraft of the Soviets, or their infantry. There would be action for the Panzer IVs; there would also be action for the SPWs.

The highway on which we were advancing led from Olita, via Nemunaitis, to Leipalingis, which lay about 40 km south southwest of Olita. All of our action took place on the stretch between Paceloniai and Nemunaitis.

Our first encounter with the Soviets on July 15 involved four of their T–34/85s and three of our Panzer IVs, the other three Panzer IVs being held in reserve farther back. About 200 m away from us when we first saw them, the T–34/85s were, no doubt, on their way northward to Olita to assist their hordes in throwing the German defenders out of that place. It

Knocked out Panzerkampfwagen Ausf H, note the mesh side-skirts, used to protect against light anti-tank weapons, including Soviet anti-tank rifles. (The Tank Museum)

was up to us to keep the T–34/85s away from Olita, or, better still, to destroy them altogether.

One advantage for us was that we seemed to see the Soviets before they beheld us. We didn't see any clouds of diesel exhaust that would have accompanied their shifting to lower gears in preparation for stopping. For precise shooting, a tank gun needed a solid platform. A halted tank, no matter whether it was a T–34/85 or a Panzer IV, constituted such a platform.

There was, however, one aspect of the whole encounter that was not favourable to us. The four T–34/85s were travelling in single file, with each of the first three partially hiding the turret of the tank behind it. Their single file was, of course, also not advantageous to them.

2/Lt. Jakob–I was the gunner in his Panzer IV–relied on each Panzer IV gunner to put his first AP round where it counted–right below the main-gun mantlet of *his* T–34/85. The fourth T–34/85 would get the same treatment–if he hadn't already turned on a dime in an effort to get away. Otherwise, he would get it, so to speak, into the seat of his pants, where his stern armour was comparatively thin.

No need to calculate the range. Just set the range scale at 175 m, then fire on 2/Lt. Jakob's order. Within a few seconds, 2/Lt. Jakob gave that order and the first three Soviet tanks were dead. Predictably, the last one, too, got it, killed by Manfred Kuhlmann, a fellow Panzer gunner whose experience at the German Eastern Front was greater than mine. Again, our Panzer IVs' 75-mm L/48s had done the trick.

The men in the recon SPW and the AA SPW were well trained. They had hugged the side of the highway from the time we first saw the T–34/ 85s. Thus, they had not obstructed our gunfire. If the T–34/85s had been carrying Soviet tank-riding infantry, the SPWs would have used their MG42s on them.

No more than 15 minutes after we had taken care of the T–34/85s, the SPWs to our rear opened up with their MG42s. An Ilyushin T1–2m3 Shturmovik ground-attack aircraft, flying low, was their target. It had come from behind our SPWs back there–an attack from the rear, as was to be expected. However, the pilot may not have considered the total number of MG42s there. After he got his tail ripped apart by 7.92-mm-calibre bullets, he headed over top of us and, his plane out of control, crashed onto the highway, not far from where the T–34/85s were burning.

During the last two years of the Second World War and ever since, much has been made of the Shturmovik ground-attack aircraft's armour, meaning the pilot and the rear-facing machine gunner were protected from below and from the sides by armour. However, many German ground machine gunners, including those in the SPWs, had learned to concentrate their fire on the rear portion of the low-flying Shturmovik's fuselage–its tail end.

Each of the SPWs to our rear had at least two MG42s aboard, making it a lot of bullets, many of them tracers that could be directed at the rear end of a Shturmovik at one time. Shturmoviks were not always brought down by German fighter aircraft or by German AA guns, large or small. German MG42s got their share. Imagine 8 x 1,550 = 12,400 bullets per minute aimed at shredding an aircraft's tail.

Possibly the one 20-mm Flak 38 to the rear of us had special AP ammo along. That stuff was guaranteed to down a Shturmovik.

Each Panzer IV had two MG34s, one coaxial with the main gun and mounted in the main gun's mantlet; the other mounted in the bow armour and operated by the wireless man. Consequently, a Panzer IV had no anti-aircraft machine gun at all. Also, a MG34 fired 800 to 900 rounds per minute, a lot less than an MG42. The Shturmovik that dropped dead onto the highway not far ahead of us may have expected to find only Panzer IVs without SPWs in that area.

At about midday on July 15, we had, I am certain, an encounter with three members of a tank-killer squad of Soviet infantry on the Olita-Nemunaitis highway. Our leading recon SPW had spotted a strapping fellow in what, from a distance, appeared to be a field-grey German Army uniform. He looked as though he needed a lift. There could have been German stragglers in the area, so the recon men, covering the fellow in field grey with one of their MG42s, stopped their SPW. Then they noticed two guys–each was, despite the heat, wearing a German camou-flage poncho–sitting nearby on an embankment just off the side of the road.

Realizing that they had probably latched onto a trio of Soviet Panzer killers, the recon crew called for an officer, 2/Lt. Jakob, to rule on the situation. All three had been searched. Also, armoured infantry had a close look at the spot where the three Soviets had been found.

So far, the ringleader–that's what he had to be–had not answered a few straightforward questions, such as "Have any German vehicles driven past here today?" 2/Lt. Jakob got the guy's attention by loudly commanding, in front-line Russian, "Rooky wairk!" (Hands up!). The man's hands couldn't have shot up higher. Neither could those of his two pals.

There was a lot wrong with the main man's uniform, the jacket of which was too small for him. The sleeves were far too short. Still worse, the front of his cap had on it the Army's national insignia, in which the eagle, perched on the swastika, had outstretched wings with the tips of the wing feathers tapering inward in a straight line from top to bottom. However, the jacket did not display the matching Army-style national insignia sewn in place just above the right breast pocket. No, sir, the jacket showed, on the upper part of its left sleeve, the SS-style insignia with the eagle with outstretched wings perched on the swastika, but with the ends of the wing feathers forming a curve, like parentheses. Clearly, the man was wearing an Army cap and an SS jacket. Besides, the collar showed no SS rank.

2/Lt. Jakob ruled that the armoured infantry should take the three impostors into custody as POWs–after they had been made to strip, more or less. Others in the Division would want to question the prisoners.

Those three falsely dressed Soviets must have been expected to function as decoys linked to further tank killers who were close enough to the highway and the Panzers that might come that way.

Tolokiai-See (Lake Tolokiai): Within One Hour, Two Tank Battles in Southern Lithuania

From Nemunaitis, we, with our six Panzer IVs and the grenadiers with their eight SPWs, did not proceed immediately towards Leipalingis. Rather, all of us were sent to the *Tolokiai-See*, meaning Lake Tolokiai, about 12 km west of Nemunaitis. At Lake Tolokiai, we fought in two adjacent battles that began after the Soviets attacked Olita from the west. Lake Tolokiai and the town of Tolokiai, just north of Lake Tolokiai, must have lain the path of the southern flank of the attacking Soviets.

The 7th Panzer Division in World War II, pages 417–18, states the following:

> Already at 0430 h on July 15, the enemy attacks with superior forces from the area west of Olita and, with strong support of tanks and ground-attack aircraft, throws back, in a westerly [*sic*] direction, the weak defence troops of the battle commander at Olita ....
>
> The enemy also continues his attack in the darkness and during the following night (to July 16). The battles in this sector go on with unabated fierceness and rigour on July 16 to 17 and July 18.

My tank battles log shows that I fought at Lake Tolokiai on July 16; however, it is interesting to note that the battles in the Olita area lasted until July 18.

Lithuania was far-from-ideal tank country. That nation's 65,200 sq. km is dotted with 4,000 lakes. Also, there are numerous rivers and canals. Lake Tolokiai was, and still is, the easternmost of three lakes lying fairly close together at about the same latitude. Each of these lakes is about 5 km across North to South, and about 3 km across West to East. The 1962 edition of the *Encyclopedia Americana* states that in 1939 Lithuania had 1,626 km of solidly built highways. The estimated lengths of local roads were as follows: first class, 4,160 km; second class, 8,233 km, third class (extremely poor), 18,025 km.

Naturally, in Lithuania the Soviets preferred to have their tanks travel and fight on firm ground; however, if the need arose, they did not hesitate to risk traversing low, wet areas in their movements. Having studied a topographic map, we Panzer men might be able to predict approximately where, for instance, the crew commander of a wide-tracked T–34/85 would switch from hazardous going to true *terra firma*. If we wanted to, we could very likely welcome him, his crew and his vehicle back to dry land.

Upon our arrival at the northern shore of Lake Tolokiai very early on July 16, we noticed the absence of wharves. Furthermore, there were no boats on the water, but there were houses, barns, sheds and trees close to the shore. Of course, the Soviets would hardly cross all, or part of, Lake Tolokiai to meet us in battle; they had to come overland to attack us. In that lake country, it was a question of whether our battle with the Soviets would take place on wet land or on dry land.

Hearing battle noise coming from the area to our north, we could have easily believed that the Soviets would come our way by road from up there. Still, the lake at our backs forced us to be circumspect. Before long, we discovered impressions made by two pairs of tank tracks–each impression had the standard Soviet T–34/85 track width of 50 cm–in the soft earth not far from the waterside. The two tanks had followed every bend in the shoreline.

Our topographic map showed us that the water from Lake Tolokiai flows, as a narrow river, more or less north-eastward into the Niemen River. A major river, the Niemen flows generally north-westward in Lithuania and empties into the Baltic Sea.

Just above the upper end of Lake Tolokiai, a single-lane wooden bridge spanned the little river shown on our map. T–34s must have crossed it, and other T–34s were bound to use it. At the bridge, we found no evidence that T–34s had forded the little river. We had received word, by radio, which the Soviets' broad front was still moving towards Olita; therefore, we could expect Soviet armour at Lake Tolokiai.

What if we could blow up that short bridge just as it carried a Soviet tank? Demolition charges (*geballte Ladungen*), each consisting of six German "potato masher" HE stick hand grenades fastened around the circumference of the metal head of one such hand grenade–the one whose four-second fuse had to be pulled to set off all seven hand grenades–should cause the bridge to collapse, plunging at least some Soviet armour into the water, and thoroughly distracting the Soviets. Destroying each of the bridge's four wooden supports required but one such demolition charge; in all, the demolition of the bridge would require 28 HE stick hand grenades.

Our Panzer grenadiers had crates full of stick grenades in their SPWs. They also had rolls of dark-coloured all-purpose cord. Quickly assembling the demolition charges posed no problem. Each relevant fuse would be set off by pulling a cord tied securely, at the porcelain bead, to the two cords attached to the fuse. Pulling the cord required a volunteer with another man for backup, both of them hidden not far from the upstream side of the bridge. They wouldn't want the current in the little river to tug at the cord and botch their work. A great opportunity to win at least the Iron Cross 2nd Class. Soon, a seasoned corporal of the grenadiers volunteered to blow up the bridge. With him would be a young Lance Corporal, also a volunteer.

A couple of our brick-sized *Kiloladungen*, one-kg demolition charges with 60-second fuses, each meant to be used only to destroy a badly damaged, non-recoverable or abandoned Panzer, would have collapsed the entire bridge. However, using them for such things was *verboten*.

Shortly after the grenadiers had fastened their stick-grenade charges into place on the bridge, three of our Panzer IVs–including the one I belonged to–were ordered to watch a crossroads about two km north of Lake Tolokiai. Word that Soviet armour was likely to appear there originated with one of the three SPWs that had been sent out earlier to reconnoitre the area immediately northwest of Lake Tolokiai.

The centre of attention at our new location was not only the very crossing of what could hardly be called two roads. With our main guns covering the immediate east-west stretches of road as well as the closest northward stretch of the north-south road, our Panzer IVs were in position on dry land featuring dozens and dozens of evergreen trees, the finest concealment available in the area. Hidden by those trees, we observed mainly the stretches of road and the adjoining terrain.

Officially still out on reconnaissance, our three SPWs, coming from farther west, soon arrived at the intersection at which we, in our Panzer IVs, stood, waiting and watching. Immediately, their skeleton crews took our advice and positioned their vehicles among the evergreens. Then they reported that they had outrun about half a dozen T–34/85s, some with tank-riding infantry aboard, and that, because there were no other east-west roads in the area, those T–34/85s had to, before long, reach our barrier of Panzer IVs, reinforced by their SPWs.

About 15 minutes later, the T–34/85s were at the crossroads. Seven of them. Obviously unaware of our presence there, the Soviets seemed not to be in a hurry to drive past the place and the evergreens. We realized that such an ideal opportunity for us to wipe out that many T–34/85s relatively easily would not recur soon. Directed at me, 2/Lt. Jakob's "Fire!" initiated the process of annihilation of the Soviet tanks. The firing of our main gun told the other two Panzer IV crew commanders to order their gunners to commence firing, and to continue firing, the very sequence I had started seconds earlier.

The SPW men first of all had to machine-gun the Soviet tank riders, including those that had dismounted. Then they had to switch to their stubby 75-mm guns to help us kill all of the T–34/85s, even if they, in doing so, could not refrain, as much as possible, from using undesirable confusing crossfire.

After each of our Panzer IVs had fired just a few rounds of AP, we had three Soviet tanks ablaze. At that point in the battle, with the Soviets in their remaining four tanks still returning our fire, the only damage our group had suffered was a gouge in one frontal corner of the turret of a Panzer IV, and the radiator and engine riddled, probably by machine gunfire, in one of the SPWs. The crews had heard and felt that damage being done to their vehicles.

In the end, the T–34/85s, all seven of them still at the crossroads, had been destroyed. Also killed, from what we could tell, were about 20 tank riders. Our entire tank-versus-tank battle had lasted only about ten minutes. Then it was time for us to rejoin our three Panzer IVs and our five SPWs at the bridge at Lake Tolokiai. We hit the road, hoping that we would continue to be fortunate in Lithuania.

Four days earlier, at Paceloniai, we found out that the Nemunaitis area, which included Lake Tolokiai, harboured much Soviet infantry and many different kinds of Soviet weapons. When we were again only about a dozen km west of Nemunaitis, the part of the German Panzer doctrine that states, "After a victory, always prepare for a counterattack," turned out to be true.

As we got closer to the bridge at Lake Tolokiai, we saw that it was the scene of a tank battle in progress. Three of the new IS–2, or Joseph Stalin–2, tanks were there on behalf of the Soviets, who may well have thought that the three Panzer IVs and the five SPWs they were attacking were the ones that had just defeated seven of their own a short distance farther north.

Again, we, in 2/Lt. Jakob's small group, were in an advantageous position. This time, the enemy was thoroughly distracted and had his left side exposed to us. Even if the IS–2s, without turning their frontal armour towards us, directed their 122-mm main guns our way, each Panzer IV would get a couple of rounds off in the time it took an IS–2 to fire one round of its slow-loading two-piece ammo.

Right from where we had stopped on the road, we fired at the IS–2s from about 200-m. The Panzer IV was a wonderfully stable platform for its main gun, contributing to its excellent accuracy. Six Panzer IVs and the SPWs proved to be too powerful a force for the vengeful IS–2s to overcome. They were all destroyed, the machines and the men.

When some of 2/Lt. Jakob's men saw three T–34/85s burning at the bridge, they let each one catch an AP or two, just to be certain that they were all defunct. A little later, after the battle, we certainly heard the reason for the T–34/85s' being on fire. Regrettably a number of us–Lt. Jabob's men–hadn't witnessed the demolition of the bridge and the simultaneous destruction of the three T–34/85s.

Indeed, the Soviets may have dispatched the three IS–2s to Lake Tolokiai in retaliation for their losses, on dry land, at Lake Tolokiai and at the crossroads with the pines. Closely associated, those two places are together referred to as *Tolokiai-See* in my tank battles log.

Two SPWs and six members of their crews–the others were outside their SPWs at the time–were killed at about the midpoint of the 15-minute battle. We regretted the deaths of those six Panzer grenadiers who, like the rest of them, had become dear to us. Those fellows were excellent soldiers, always ready to stand by their brothers, the Panzer men.

Regarding each of our dead comrades, we could do little more, it seemed at first, than take with us the lower half of his identity disk after breaking it from the upper half, which we had to leave attached to his remains.

However, with the exception of the men who had to stay as lookouts in the driver compartments and turrets of the Panzer IVs, and in the corresponding places in the SPWs, we had the manpower to dig, quite quickly, six shallow graves–one for each body–and to lay all of the bodies to rest. Thus, the corpses were not left to putrefy in the open in a strange land.

I believe that every man who was present during the improvisation of that little cemetrey thought of Ludwig Uhland's words to the haunting and appropriately mournful German song *Der Kamerad* (The Comrade), in which a soldier recounts how his best comrade and he marched side-by-side into battle, and that a musket ball, aimed their way, indiscriminatingly dropped his comrade. The song culminates in the soldier, still fighting, expressing himself as follows:

> *Will mir die Hand noch reichen,*
> *Derweil ich eben lad'.*
> *Kann dir die Hand nicht geben,*
> *Bleib du im ew'gen Leben*
> *Mein guter Kamerad.*

Although it lacks metre and rhyme scheme, the following translation conveys the meaning of the above five lines:

> You crave to place your hand in mine
> While I right now reload.
> I cannot stretch my hand t'wards you;
> Remain my finest comrade
> Throughout eternal life.

Like the surviving soldier in *Der Kamerad*, we battled on. Next, we proceeded from Lake Tolokiai to Nemunaitis and the highway south.

Zembre-Bach or the Fuel Dump Past Zembre

The part of Lithuania in which we operated between, and during, tank engagements was dotted with many bodies of water, not all of them natural. One rather large rural communal pond, actually a flooded gulch, had at its outlet a four-metre-high broad backed, weather-beaten wooden dam measuring about three Panzer IV lengths–that was about 18m– overall bank-to-bank. Away from the backwater, upstream as well as downstream, the stream itself was much too deep to be forded by a tank.

If I were asked to tell you of the most hazardous structure that I ever saw a Panzer IV drive across, I would unhesitatingly describe our small unit's crossing of the rickety wooden bridge atop that ancient and shaky Lithuanian dam which, for sure, had long shown symptoms of partial incontinence. It wasn't so much the skimpy width of the one-lane bridge that was worrisome; it was its agedness that caused us to have great concern.

It took a member of our crew, walking backwards–in itself a dangerous act on the warped, fissured top planking–to hand-signal to the driver, the only man aboard the Panzer IV for the occasion, which way he had to steer to keep his tracks equidistant from the rounded and splint-ered brinks of the railing less bridge.

Had the dam and its bridge collapsed, and the 25-ton Panzer IV plunged the four metres, the driver–he had the hatch to his private entrance to the tank wide open–would, very likely, have been washed downstream alive, and his baby inundated for quite a while, to remain stuck, thereafter, in the swollen creek at the bottom of the gulch.

We could little afford not to have all of our Panzer IVs make it across. In the end, we had individually coaxed every one of them–a total of five– to the, for us, advantageous side of the wide creek that any Soviet commander would surely have considered to be a barrier to Panzer IVs.

I can say, because I was present at that dam-bridge crossing, that I learned the meaning of a memorable line from the Panzer song (*Panzerlied*) – " ... for ourselves, we scout out passes that no one other-wise found." Come to think of it, the stream we managed to cross that day may well have been known as the *Zembre-Bach* (Zembre Creek), a name shown in my combat log, and part of the locale in which tank combat involving our Panzer IVs took place on July 17, 1944.

It was the *Zembre-Bach* that we had crossed with a great deal of anxiousness, not for the purpose of having it lie between our Panzer IVs and something undesirable, such as Soviet pursuers, but to enable us to penetrate beyond it to something very desirable–the eradication, by means of fairly long-range 7.5-cm fire, of a Soviet advance dump that had sprung up at a spot on the east-west highway during the previous few days. There, T–34s would, like drop-ins, come and go, refuelling, stocking up on ammunition and, maybe, even on rations. Where food was concerned, those gents were frugal. They did like their vodka, though.

Having crossed the Zembre, then, we could come at the Soviets from their rear. Let me use an analogy and say that we could thereby avoid the hassles associated with visiting a popular drive-in theatre–a line-up, a box office, and a ticket taker, all guaranteed to be unfriendly to the nth degree towards us. No, sir, we would surreptitiously enter their theatre, and get to view their giant screen from a hill that, according to 2/Lt. Jakob's topographic map, commanded the area right down to the highway and beyond. If we could help it, we would create the action down there, and it would be lively.

Judging by the map, the range would be about 1,500 m, meaning that we could use AP shells as well as HE shells on the job, depending on what we would spot in the place.

As far as Soviet pursuers were concerned, it was generally prudent to have an appreciable body of water between them and the Panzer IVs. However, if–and I say *if*–we were to be pursued by T–34s after shooting up the dump, we would be unable to cross the Zembre without a lot of delay, although we had left the old dam and bridge intact–well, we had left it standing, at least.

We would, of course, do well to stay away from the Zembre altogether and see where fate, with some stiff resistance on our part to that something called fate, would steer us. A man had to be highly adaptable if he wanted to ride in a Panzer IV. He also had to be firm. He, like few others, had to be able to take it as it would come.

Without having to cross as much as a small stream, we drove about one km from the *Zembre-Bach* Bridge to our designated hill, but not onto the top of it. On foot, 2/Lt. Jakob and a couple of others, including the Company C.O., went ahead for a scrutiny of the highway, and the Soviet dump and its environs.

2/Lt. Jakob told us–we, his crew, had still not pulled up for a look– that three T–34s stood down there for refuelling by means of hoses connected to hand-operated pumps inserted into fuel drums rolled next to the T–34s, which stood broadside to our hill, as if at the average service station for cars. Also, there were, he said, two large trucks parked near the refuelling area, and perhaps 15 men present.

After I had made sure that my gun sight was set to 1,500 m for AP, we pulled our Panzer IV forward, so that I could see, for myself, what 2/Lt. Jakob had spoken of. Next, we turned off the engine to eliminate vibrations. Also, for such delicate long-range work, the electrical firing of the main gun would afford me a great advantage.

Next in importance to the three T–34s came the rows of fuel drums, not all of which would be empty. Destroy the T–34s and the fuel in the drums, and our front line could breathe a bit easier. Take out more than that–the two trucks and the men standing or walking around, the majority wearing padded leather helmets–and our success would be phenomenal. Our company wouldn't often get to see such a concentration of standing and presumably unmanned T–34s, along with a lot of *Sprit* (pronounced *shpreet*, and soldiers' slang for fuel, diesel or gasoline, as well as for alcoholic beverages, such as vodka) for them and others of their ilk. Everything looked good for our raid on that dump.

To reduce the risk that some individual targets in the assemblage might be fired at with undue delay, our selection of targets would, as always, be governed by the no-crossfire rule.

Although the fuel drums were next behind the T–34s in priority, there was to be no deliberate shooting at them before the men and the trucks had been worked over with HE. The fuel, because its burning could obscure some targets, had to go last, oddly enough. One Panzer IV would use HE shells, starting with the men, then switching to the trucks, and, finally, to the fuel drums, which were lined up about 20 m from where the refuelling was being done.

The five of us began firing at about 1:30 p.m. Despite the fact that none of us had used his gun at more than about 1,000 m, our AP shells hit where they were supposed to. After I had fired two shells–each of the other three firing AP will have used about that number up to that point– two T–34s were on fire. With one T–34 left, we continued to use AP.

The flash of HE impacting could not be mistaken for AP impacts. The Soviets had been kept away from their T–34s by HE fire from one Panzer IV, that of the Company C.O. Already there were fewer men to be seen. Presently, another T–34 was burning, making it all three that would no longer be attractive to their crews. On the side, the trucks received a few of the Company C.O.'s HE. His fire kept the trucks from being moved or driven away; in fact, his shells had rent them badly.

In all, I had fired a total of three AP. Assuming that each of the other three Panzer IVs using AP had fired about as many shells as I had, our average expenditure was something like three shells. No complaint there. Some workers in one corner of the armament industry must have had a good day when they sighted-in our 7.5-cm guns.

How many HE shells the Company C.O. had fired I don't know, but he had the Soviets thinned out and the trucks burning before we switched to his type of shell for a shot or two at the fuel drums.

Soon, the Soviets' entire advance dump, with its visiting T–34s and its trucks, had been destroyed, although some of the men, because they had taken cover, must have escaped. We truly felt that the *Zembre-Bach* and the advance dump had been great experiences–one great experience, actually–that would be talked about for a long time at 24251E.

However, a saying "One should not praise the day before the evening" held true. Three T–34s, driving east–not west–on the highway, came into view about 1,000 m west of the fresh ruins ahead of us, making their range about 1,800 m. Likely low on *Sprit*, the three were coming to drink diesel by the drum.

A Panzer IV had, in keeping with the austerity of its interior, not much of an instrument panel for the driver to consult. It had no fuel gauge, just as it had no speedometre and no odometre. Time to refuel was signalled by a sudden weakness of the starving engine–that engine weakness could come at a very inopportune moment–demanding that the driver instantly flick a three-way valve to tap the reserve-tank fuel, good for perhaps another 50 km of road driving. Total theoretical road range of the latest Panzer IV was 301 km; cross-country, it was 182 km. Total fuel–gasoline–capacity was 603 liters. It was a Panzer IV engine's second, and final, falter that spelled *died of thirst*.

Assuming that the T–34's reserve diesel fuel capacity differed not vastly from that of the Panzer IV, we could believe that prompt refuelling was essential for a T–34 running on reserve. If the fuel dump was *pasholl* (pronounced *pa-sholl*, and meaning, in Russian, *gone for good*), the T–34 wouldn't–couldn't–drive much farther.

Seeing *pohade* (pronounced *pow-haw-day*, and meaning *much* in Russian) smoke from diesel-fuelled fires in the distance must have caused, first thing, all of the four men in each of the three T–34s to outdo one another in uttering, with the greatest of earnestness, their choicest bit of obscenity–"Yupo … !" Considering that those vexed guys could see a total lack of fuel and food ahead, they had to express their three-word vulgarism far more earnestly than they would have in response to a less provocative situation. Those 12 men would be in trouble, no matter where they turned. Running out of fuel on a highway was bad, but usually not as bad as in the fields, away from a compact surface.

On the highway, towing a stalled Panzer IV was relatively easy mechanically. The ends of two steel tow cables would be attached to the shackles at the front of the Panzer IV to be towed, and then crossed, and the free ends attached to the two shackles at the rear of the towing vehicle. Towing with the cables crossed kept the Panzer IV that was being towed from wandering.

More like tank recovery, mired-tank towage–possibly the consequence of having run out of fuel–might, for at least a short distance, require two tanks as towers. The alternative to two tandem tanks harnessed in front of, or behind, the to-be-towed tank was the yoke of towers, with one tow cable linking the right front shackle of the load with the left rear shackle of the tower on the right; the other cable went from the left front of the load to the right rear of the tower on the left. To achieve maximum straightforward pull, the two towers had to be relatively close together and parallel to each other without, of course, touching.

Under fire, preparing to tow a tank, as well as towing a tank, was a very dangerous undertaking because the tanks involved, either standing or moving very slowly, were of necessity in close proximity to each other, or to one another.

The T–34 was equipped with shackles and tow cables; we can assume that it would have had to be towed much the same as a Panzer IV.

Having stopped their three T–34s on the highway about where we had first spotted them, the Soviets, after their initial formulaic, obscene solemnities, must have continued to express sober thoughts, amounting to what is so well expressed in Falstaff's following line: "The better part of valour is discretion … " Those crews, hardly legalists even in the presence of a Commissar, will have opted collectively to exercise their power or right to decide or act according to their own judgement. They about-faced and drove west, and out of sight. Word would surely get around that everything they had expected to find available at the dump was, like the dump, *nyema* (Russian for *no more*).

Had the T–34s discovered us on the hill above their blasted dump, and had they fired at us, and we at them, there would have been a good chance that at least one T–34 would have escaped to tell his world, just as some survivors had already told theirs, of the most recent whereabouts of our Panzer IVs. It was just as well that there had been no indication of their having spotted us, and no shooting on the part of either side. Where, exactly, might they, with their fuel paucity, be?

Time for us to execute relocation. It was 2:15 p.m., three-quarters of an hour after we had begun to annihilate the dump, and we were still on the hill, 1,500 m off the highway. Hours and hours before sunset it was, and a lot could still transpire that day.

About four km west of the blackened half acre on the highway, there lay, 2/Lt. Jakob's topographic map showed us, an interesting intersection of the highway and a secondary road, which could become the hub for some sniping activity à la Lithuania on the part of our Panzer IVs. The intersection would be not too far away from the front line, judging by the sound of sporadic gunfire, and not too close.

Starting at an angle of about 45 degrees to our left from where we had stood, all five of our Panzer IVs proceeded from the hill towards the highway, expecting to hit the pavement about 1,500 m west of the scene of the fire. We would, in a way, have to slip onto the highway, and over to the intersection we had in mind before traffic on the highway picked up. We were surprised that not even one entire westbound Soviet convoy had shown up during the time we watched the stretch. The Soviets would not have put in an advance dump a few days back without expecting to generate sufficient traffic to warrant its existence. We were convinced that the highway would not belong to us alone for long.

Still two km or so away from the intersection, we got the chance to think hard about doing some more sniping. It was our five Panzer IVs against–guess what?–their three T–34s, the very ones we had seen shortly before. Obviously tied to the immediate area, they had, we were certain, little or no fuel left; however, they didn't know that we had knowledge of their extreme vulnerability. Any tactical movement on their part would, we knew, be very limited, very feeble. We wondered if their engines were still running. An animate tank, when engaged, almost always had its engine idling, at least, especially in the presence of enemy tanks. In the presence of meant within reach, or range of the main guns of the enemy.

The three were firing at us from just off the highway, where they stood, only half hidden by immature trees. No sense trying to slug it out at length while we were bunched on the highway. To hell, though, with going at them impetuously. Instead of rushing them hundreds of metres—everything was part of a very dangerous game—our quintet of Panzer IVs would want to see what those desperate T–34 commanders would do about evading a move of ours that might appear to them to be a diversionary manoeuvre. We had no rear guard, so things had better quickly work out well for us. The guys about half a km down the road wouldn't be going anywhere before getting fuel. We, however, were off in response to a plan.

The Panzer IV's sole reverse gear was rather slow, but it was strong and sure. Many times that gear had allowed a crew to back away from real trouble, so as to allow it a subsequent different approach. Now, five crews were backing up—not backing off or backing down—a few hundred metres, well past the next gentle bend in the road. The move called for screening smoke, which we didn't have. Hidden by the bend, we would drive into the fields north of the highway. Thereafter, in one long sweep, during which we would take advantage of low ground, we would get set to do what we had in mind for the intersection a couple of km away. Half hidden and protected by a hill, or hills, we would ease our Panzer IVs into position for sniping at the three T–34s.

No sooner said than done applied to our arriving at a suitable location, and to our successful sniping, from about 500 m, at all three T–34s standing broadside to us. I pitied the doomed guys who were cooped up in the three crematories.

Our crossing the *Zembre-Bach*, our devastating the Soviets' advance dump including three T–34s, two trucks and God knows how many men, and our later destroying another three T–34s–and all that in the hours before evening–had made July 17, 1944, an eventful day, one that we could honestly praise after all.

Rozuciai

For many a season, Sergeant Beizinger was one of those N.C.O.s under whom it would have been an honour to serve in a tank. The last time I had a good look at Beizinger was after he had been lifted aboard our Panzer IV and propped up against our turret girdle for a ride after an engagement of ours with Soviet tanks in the Leipalingis area. He sprawled there on the deck like a man barely alive. I looked hard to assure myself that the guy we had aboard was the formerly ebullient Beizinger.

With precise vertical demarcation running in line with the bridge of his nose, the right side of his face and neck had been burned to a brown crispness, his skin there resembling that of a fried chicken; furthermore, that half of his face had been deeply and profusely dimpled by fragments, giving it the appearance of a piece of much-tufted upholstery. His wounds were probably not confined to the right side of his head and neck.

When Beizinger was aided off the back of our Panzer IV, I doubted that he would ever again have anything to do with a Panzer. His face had been disfigured grotesquely as the result of a hit in the side of the turret. Since he had apparently been wounded above the shoulders, it may have been his commander's cupola that was penetrated by something extremely nasty.

"And if faithless luck lets down our small band ... " is how the beginning of the fifth, and last, stanza of the Panzer song rationalizes bad luck of the sort that Sergeant Beizinger had experienced.

Leipalingis or the Sniping Panzer IVs

Through the years, whenever I have been reminded of the mutilated face of Sergeant Beizinger, I have thought of the words of Samuel Johnson (1709–1791): "There, but for the grace of God, go I." Let me tell you why I have, once again, quoted Dr. Johnson.

In rural Lithuania, tank warfare had, from our point of view, turned out to be largely a matter of our having to fight T–34s as if they were hedge-concealed snipers.

2/Lt. Jakob was good at using his service binoculars; often, having spotted a target, he would give me a approximate target, at the same time placing one hand on either my left or right shoulder, depending on which direction he would want me to traverse the turret. Once I had the Soviet tank in my gun sight properly, I would let loose a 7.5-cm armour-piercing shell or two. Our success with that spy-and-shoot technique was not great, although we did account for one slowly snooping T–34, knocked out at about 400 m in broad daylight.

After that sort of shooting, it was usually relocation, with 2/Lt. Jakob scanning intently all the while. We were lucky that our crew commander, as an officer, carried binoculars. He also had a topographic map of the area, the very thing I wish I had today, as I write of our Lithuanian exploits.

We, with our tanks, were, once again–it was July 20, 1944, the day of the attempt on Adolf's life–in the process of relocating so as not to present a stationary target. With only extensive fields of ripening grain on both sides of the country road we drove on, we did not have the best of cover. Far from it. However, we were trying to take advantage of the rolling terrain, and would drive up the side of a hill far enough to be able to study, by means of the binoculars and the gun sight, what lay beyond its crest. If things looked *korosh* (Russian for *fine*), we would carefully proceed.

The T–34s were playing hide-and-seek with us, just as each Panzer IV was with them. One could, at any time, expect to be fired at by a well-hidden, sniping tank; although I was inclined to believe that at least one Soviet antitank gun was in the vicinity of the road. Something damned inconspicuous just about wiped out our Panzer IV there.

Looking through my 2.4-power sight mounted 40 cm directly to the left of the axis of the gun barrel–I could observe, within a generous entire angular expanse, whatever lay in line with the barrel, which was at 12 o'clock. That I was doing when, lightning-fast, a horizontal jet of large, white sparks whisked noiselessly, from right to left, across the middle of my field of view–like a stream of molten metal it looked, blown by an invisible, oversize acetylene torch momentarily cutting steel.

Something wicked had at least nicked us, and we were forced to move away fast before we received another taste of this medicine. Only one way to go–over the top of the hill. Possibly the sniper couldn't see us there. We had to assess the damage to our Panzer IV.

Well ahead of the mantlet, at an angle of about 90 degrees, the bottom of our gun barrel had been gouged by an armour-piercing shell. Had it struck about four cm higher, the shell would undoubtedly have severed the barrel. However, the missile had, apparently touching the bore, taken a perfectly curved bite out of the steel.

Clearly, our gun barrel had been dealt a blow by a missile from something in the order of our own 7.5-cm gun, possibly a Soviet 8.5-cm tank cannon. Still, our enemy's *modus operandi* smelled of antitank gun, in that they had remained hidden so much better than the average tank in action.

Be that as it may, had the Soviets managed to hit our Panzer IV 2.5 m. farther back–given the opportunity for a subsequent shot, they very likely would have penetrated our turret dead centre, so to speak–I would not be writing this account. If our turret had been perforated, I would, at the very least, likely have immediately acquired a ghastly appearance akin to what Sergeant Beizinger had suffered no more than two days earlier.

So, you see, it is because of our having been spared, on the day on which our Panzer IV was struck in the gun barrel, that I, before I continue my story, again quote Samuel Johnson: "There, but for the grace of God, go I."

Back to our Panzer IV with the five of us inside it, facing downhill on the country road amid the grain fields, but drawing no more fire. We knew that our main gun was useless except, possibly, that we could use it to scare shit out of some T–34 crew members by laying it in their direction–definitely a suicidal undertaking. Perhaps we could look for suspicious vegetation and spray it with an MG34 or two, hoping that a Soviet antitank gun crew would be in there somewhere to get their hides holed.

We could, if we were insane, go to three o'clock and back up the hill, towards the crest behind us, looking for Soviets that might have just come out from behind their camouflage, and hose them down with the co-axial MG34. We had to banish all such wild thoughts from our minds. We had to think and act rationally. We had to see what our pals were doing. Above all, we had to find out where they were relative to our position. We needed their help before we could move, or do anything at all.

For us, radio silence was not mandatory. Urgent messages could be transmitted within the four-Panzer unit. However, our report to the Company C.O. would have to be couched in language unintelligible to any listening Soviets. 2/Lt. Jakob, in radioing, would best use Panzer IV-related, but esoteric, vernacular. He would also best keep in mind *Fasse dich kurz* (keep your message brief), a dictum abounding on signs at the public telephones in the *Reich*, and adopted by the *Wehrmacht*.

Our predicament would keep us from sending anything like a basic report, structured in accordance with the answers to five questions prompted by the *a e i o u* series, in which *a* stood for *wann?* (when?); *e*, for *wer?* (who?); *i*, for *wie?* (how?); *o*, for *wo?* (where?); and *u*, for *was tue ich weiter?* (what will I do next?).

Not many days before, it had happened that one Panzer IV crew commander had hinted at his enjoying *Zigarren* (cigars, meaning 7.5-cm shells of both kinds). A voice with a decidedly Russian accent had butted in, and said, "We are bringing [will bring] cigars." Their own brand, no doubt. One had to be careful on the air. *Feind hört mit* (the enemy listens in), a caution seen for years on myriad posters in public places inside the *Reich*, also had validity in the field.

Our message was phrased something like "We don't have anything to lock into place." The gun in the Panzer IV could, for long road marches or for transit by rail, be locked at +16 degrees by means of a quick-release internal crutch, mounted along the inside of the turret roof.

Our call to the Company C.O., which he promptly answered with "understood", was the first of several messages back and forth, none of them unimportant. The crew commanders were pros. They deduced what our needs were. They also knew where danger lurked nearby because 2/Lt. Jakob had provided them with the approximate bearing from our Panzer IV to the Soviets who had deeply creased our gun barrel; he had based that figure on the direction of the rounded groove across the bottom of the barrel, and on his topographic map.

The commander of one of our Panzer IVs, some 250 m behind us, let it be known that he would use the road to venture our way with extreme caution. Why not? He knew, from us, a lot more about the lay of the land than we had known—and he had a bearing to watch. We could, by then, hear his engine and cooling fans. Based on the word that he would be approaching, we had turned off our engine. If we had heard a diesel engine start, we would quickly have driven farther down the road or into one of the grain fields, turning to face whatever would come.

Presently, one shot. Not from somewhere to our right, more or less, but from behind us. It turned out that the Panzer IV commander there—he was perhaps the most experienced of the four, including ours, in the area—had literally stuck his neck out just prior to driving close to the top of the hill before the one on whose down-grade side we still waited. As a matter of fact, he, acting as a sort of periscope, had, with his black cap off, practically stood on the top of the turret of his Panzer IV to get a good view, mainly to his right, without exposing one mm of his turret above the hilltop. Then, the gunner, virtually on target after getting, with the driver's help, the muzzle of his 7.5 clear of the crest and the adjacent grain, had fired fast and unerringly.

So, 2/Lt. Jakob could claim an assist. His directions had resulted in one T–34 being "cracked," as a nut or a vault. About 200 m away, at the far side of our large grain field, in a clump of trees of pyramidal shape—that's where the well-camouflaged T–34 had caught an AP shell.

The waist-high grain front of the T–34 had made the vehicle's overall height appear much lower than its actual 2.41 m, as though it had been dug in. Interestingly, in the event of too-low an elevation in a Panzer IV's aim, uncut, mature grain would, for instance, afford the half-naked members of a Soviet crew busy with cracking lice in the sun outside of their tank a fair degree of protection against HE shells which, fired into the plants, would burst, although I doubt that the main man in the T–34 had been aware of that fact. One Panzer IV crew that I knew had experienced a bad scare when one of their HE shells shot mistakenly into ears of ripened grain at the side of the road, had exploded not many metres in front of the muzzle brake of their gun.

What gave the T–34 away was one Soviet sap out in the grain field, acting like an athlete on an oversize ball diamond trying to steal from third base to home plate. Before he had time to finish his run, home base was ablaze. He was likely the only one of his crew to survive, and he must have run in the Lithuanian fields for a good while. Maybe he had been sent out to see what we were up to on the road.

There were, we knew, no tank tracks through the grain, indicating that the T–34 had not been driven into position from the stretch of road we were on. The Soviets had had a fine ambush set up—until one of our Panzer IVs, because they had almost gotten us, got them. Maybe they, too, should have relocated after singeing us. Mind you, for us it was good that they hadn't moved at all. Their commander had been more of an occasional or pot-shot sniper than a deadly accurate, true sniper. There was a difference.

In the presence of excellent 7.5-cm protection, we drove off, our most recent victor in the lead. He was now the point tank, just as we had been before he arrived to help us. So far, there had been no talk of our bailing out and blowing up our Panzer. About half a km farther back, on the same road, our other two Panzer IVs followed us. Maybe we'd be O.K. for a while, even though our Panzer IV had only the MG34s and us our P38s. We had been ambushed, according to 2/Lt. Jakob, about four km away from the main highway, where we hoped to be able to do some real damage. Lots of Soviet military traffic on a road like that. Maybe we could put some tracer bullets into unarmoured vehicles, making them catch fire. Our guardian could concentrate on the armour, as could the other two, after joining us.

We hadn't covered more than a couple of km when, compared with what we had just experienced, we got into what appeared to be a far worse situation, a move popularly described as "from out of the rain to under the gutter," the equivalent of "from the frying pan into the fire". We had identified a proper barrier, intended, no doubt, to keep us from getting any closer to the highway.

Again, the rolling terrain was favourable for us. Gunfire from the main component–several Soviet tanks–of the barrier, 300 m straight ahead, wouldn't be able to touch us because we were taking advantage of the hill just before the one they were on. This time, there was no grain field to our left; to our right, there was, however, a large one.

Of course the T–34s–that's what they had to be–were not in view, but to each belonged a head wearing the distinctive ribbed and padded Soviet *tankist's* leather helmet, reminiscent of that worn by a boxer's sparring partner taking pains to keep himself from becoming punch-drunk. Taking turns, almost, at least four Halloween-pumpkin heads would peek over the hill frequently. Apparently, two T–34s sat off one side of the road, and two off the other.

The bastards had an additional, intimidating weapon set up somewhere not far from the scene–mortars, but not the 12-cm calibre. What the T–34s couldn't do just then, those mortars were trying to achieve by laying down four-shell barrages without getting closer to hitting us.

For some good reason, there had been no mention of our trying to bypass the Soviet barrier. In the fields, one wide, lazy Lithuanian creek, for instance, could stop us. The topographic map told our commanders why we needed to stick to the road.

Not wanting the stand-off to continue, I suppose, the Soviets suddenly had two diverging T–34s coming at us simultaneously, one in each of the fields, like the jaws of wide-open, crocodilian vice-grip pliers wanting to take the life out of us with one fast squeeze. Nothing in the world would have come in handier for us than a new 7.5-cm gun barrel, fitted, sighted-in, and ready to go. Ammunition was plentiful.

We had lots of spunk left, especially after our two trailing Panzer IVs got into the act. No longer anything like 500 m to the rear of us, they had come to join the fight. The first sign of their presence was a solid hit on the T–34 to the left of the road. Half of its crew jumped out of the top hatch of their dead tank and played it smart–they did a fade-out in the long grass.

All 2/Lt. Jakob and I, as well as the driver and the radio operator, had been able to do was observe the happenings. Our loader had, all the while, felt like a guy listening to a ball game on the radio instead of watching it on TV.

Facing great odds, the second T–34 continued to charge at us. Three Panzer IVs with good guns faced only him, now that his pal had been made junk of. Of the three, the two rearmost Panzer IVs had a good view of the underdog, and let him have both barrels, killing him in the field of grain. No one escaped there. The Soviets' vice-grip pliers had become not even a minute alligator clip.

Two concerns remained unresolved–the remaining duo of T–34s and the mortars, all of which had stayed quiet since their two compatriots had ventured forth. Time, now, to play an empirical Panzer trick on the Soviets. Every Panzer IV I ever heard of retained a generous stock of fragmentation shells, simply because armour-piercing were used so much more in the business. Our trick would give us the opportunity to use at least a few of the HE shells.

What we had in mind was a variant, actually a simplification, of fork- or prong-shooting, meaning zeroing in on a target by firing left, right, and centre, or right, left, and centre. Our plan was to use, in unison, only the middle tine of the fork when the Soviet crew commander off the right side of the road showed his helmeted head above the grain. The best coordination on the part of our Panzer IVs would be required for the performance of our trick.

We had the Soviets' range–300 m–so there was no need to even think of knife-blade shooting, zeroing in on a target by firing one long, one short, and then the hit; at any rate, that technique could best be done on more or less level terrain, not the kind on which the T–34s stood.

It would be a matter of getting our HE shells to fly unobstructed above most of the grain on the hillside facing us, and to explode among the stalks and ears just ahead of the T–34 commander's face. Lots of shell fragments should do the trick. Sniping it would be, yes, but with the 7.5. Our expert gunners were, I knew, up to the job.

Experts also, our drivers were keen on playing their role in the plan. Each of them, directed by his gunner, would–after 'Leather Helmet', having had another look-see, had ducked–use his Panzer IV's crawler gear, lowest gear, or first gear to inch, without undue engine howl, upgrade to a point from which the gunner could definitely see–I repeat see–that the muzzle of his aimed gun was unobstructed and well above the crest just ahead of him. The gunner, more than anyone else in his Panzer IV, would have to observe the words *Immer soviel [so weit] wie notwendig, und nie mehr [weiter] als genug* (Always as much [as far] as necessary, and never more [farther] than enough), a maxim imparted to me, by the way, by 2/Lt. Jakob on some such occasion during the time I was his gunner in Lithuania.

We in our wounded Panzer IV might get in on the action with our MG34s if some of the T–34 crew wanted to exit from the top hatch. A T–34 had no side hatches in its turret. A couple of the crew, at least, simply had to use the hatch at the top of the turret. If they wanted to escape after being hit, that is where they would show up, moving fast, like a couple of cottontail barely ahead of a bloodthirsty ferret at the tight mouth of a burrow.

Everything was in place and, sure as hell, the split second in which to do some precise shooting came when the leather-clad head of the T–34 commander, definitely the one on the grain field-side of the road, poked up for a visual survey. Three HE shells instantly went his way, each arriving in the grain something like one-third of a second. His leather helmet did him no good to ward off multiple, lightning-fast swats of that magnitude.

There was no frantic scramble for the uppermost exit from the T–34 just rendered leaderless, so our drivers, under the direction of their crew commanders, backed their Panzer IVs downgrade a bit, to where they had stood, roughly, before moving forward to form a firing squad.

Maybe it was the sound of our backing off ever so slightly that gave the stricken Soviets the idea to bolt from the hill. Maybe it was because of an order they had received. Anyway, a series of loud snorts from their diesel, accompanied by track clatter, told us that the penultimate T–34 was *dawai* (Russian for *gone*), and certainly not heading towards our hill.

In the field, the standard test of the accuracy of a Panzer IV's 7.5-cm gun was one HE shell fired at an intact window, or a closed door, of an abandoned building from about 1,000 m, that figure being the distance for which the gun had supposedly been sighted-in before delivery. Convinced that his gun was sighted-in according to specification, a good gunner might want to refine his shooting; he could, for instance, calculate, by means of mental arithmetic, that, to hit the Soviet's head at 300 m, he would have to hold 28 cm, or 1½ times the width of that head with helmet, to the left. Here, however, it had been a matter of hitting the grain at the exact elevation, not the man's head directly. Besides, in this case, being a bit off centre horizontally would result in better dispersion–a far greater number of fragments in the target.

Probably because he had become demoralized by the demise of his two buddies out in no man's land, and, perhaps more so, by the killing of his close neighbour, the last T–34 blue-stinkingly accelerated away from behind the hill, beating it towards the mortars. He probably took with him a new one for his Commissar–a story about a new curved-barrel cannon in the Panzer IV.

The discussion of Panzer IV ammunition supply arose. We, of course, were the ones with the most of both kinds of shells. Transfer of ammunition would be feasible if the mortars continued to be quiet. We undertook the job, not bothered by the two smoky next-door T–34s, and gave away our shells through our loader's hatch. Our commanders had two Panzer IVs at a time maintain watch while a third got its share of our shells. We also handed over all our 7.92 x 57 machine gun belts. Our Panzer IV had been degraded; it had become a defenceless, exhausted munitions carrier.

Our Company C.O. wanted to get close to the highway, the aim of his mission. Fuel was, apparently, no problem. Next–and we had felt it coming–came the Company C.O.'s order for us to use the one-kg demolition charge on our Panzer IV, and to report to our unit somewhere to the west as soon as possible. We were to wait until the three other Panzer IVs were well down the road before performing our sad chore.

So it came to pass. Pulling the fuse of the charge made me think of Suceava. There, it had been a jammed turret and, hence, a disabled 7.5; here, it was the gouge in the bottom of the gun barrel. There, too, I had to do the blowing-up of an otherwise perfectly good Panzer IV. The job could break the heart of a gunner, even if he had to do it no more than once in his career as a Panzer man.

Not about to go for a stroll down the road, 2/Lt. Jakob and I, with the others following us at relatively long intervals because of the mortars, ran into the grain field to our right. We were used to surprises, but what we damned nearly got ourselves into only a few metres off the side of the road was about a dozen piles of human shit, sun-simmered and fly-infested. For me, those shit piles have remained a kind of minor mystery compared, for instance, with the major mystery of the dead Red Army soldier in the Suceava brewery.

Although there were no telltale scrapes on the surface of the road, or near the road, maybe the four T–34s had, much earlier, stopped at the place we had just left, but had decided to go back one hill–after doing all their dumping. Getting our guys past the crap piles was like guiding them through a minefield. Speaking of mines, that was one bad item that we hadn't encountered while in our Panzer IV on the road, and that we didn't need now that we were on foot.

The mortars had become active, blazing away at the field that we hadn't yet cleared out of. Any movement of persons through unreaped grain is conspicuous, even if those moving through it are close to the ground. We were fairly low, believe me.

Creeping along, I found 2/Lt. Jakob's officer's pistol, which, unlike his binoculars, was a personal belonging of his, lying where he had crept. Jakob never gave a guy a hard time, and it was a real pleasure for me to be able to hand him his 7.65-mm pride and joy.

Despite the fact that the mortars tossed many a shell into that large grain field, we all made it out of there. How, you might ask next, could we ever carry out the second part of our Company C.O.'s order–to get back to our unit? Yes, how did we get back to 24251E?

We stayed away from the highway for many a km, eventually approaching it carefully according to 2/Lt. Jakob's map, so that he could look, through his binoculars, for an intersection manned by military police and showing signposts. Eventually, we came to an intersection at which we recognized a sign in the form of a left-leaning rhomboid about 20 cm wide overall and about 10 cm high, namely the tactical symbol for Panzers. Soon thereafter, we located signs that read *8/25*.

Soldatenklau hadn't detained us along the way and fairly soon we were back with Sergeant Stenger et al. Stenger, the kingpin, was genuinely glad to welcome us, especially those of us who had been with him at one time or another, acquiring reputations as gentlemanly foragers–to complement, of course, our reputations as fine fighters at the front.

Indeed, after living through the intense series of engagements shown in my tank battles log, all of us needed a good steward to help us recuperate.

Because the word *Soldatenklau*, familiar to many German veterans of World War II, recurs in this work, the reader should be aware of its denotation. *Soldaten*, the first part of *Soldatenklau*, means *soldiers*. A German slang expression, the second part, *klau*, short for *klauen*, means, in English slang, *to hook*, or *to steal or seize by stealth*. Therefore, *Soldatenklau* translates into *hookers of soldiers*, or *seizers of soldiers*.

The English expression *press gang* comes close to being the equivalent of *Soldatenklau*. *The Random House College Dictionary* defines *press gang* as follows: "a body of men under the command of an officer, formerly employed to impress other men for service, esp. in the navy or army." Of course, whereas *Soldatenklau* targeted soldiers, a press gang targeted civilians.

CHAPTER 9

In the Land of the Lithuanians: Panzer Men Away from the Front

In Lithuania, any Panzer soldier belonging to 24251E who had lost his Panzer IV and lived to tell the tale, but couldn't head for the home barracks because the remainder of the unit continued to operate, was bound to become a member of Sergeant Stenger's usually squad-size body of foragers.

Like so many members of Panzer Regiment 25, Stenger was a Bavarian, and, like so many N.C.O.s in that regiment, he was a 12-point buck, a man who had signed up for 12 years of service in the *Heer*.

Sergeant Stenger wore the black Panzer duds, but no one, I think, had ever seen him inside a tank. Not a lean man, he was at heart probably a gourmet cook of sorts.

He would line up his foragers, perhaps 12 or 15 of them, and tell each two or three men what to bring back from their foraging. For instance, he would say–not order–"You three go and fetch carrots."

Foraging under the sponsorship of Sergeant Stenger didn't mean that we were out of touch with our regiment. We received our regular rations, meagre as they were, and canteen goods, as well as uniforms, or parts thereof, as required. Foraging meant supplementing our diet; foraging meant getting extra eatables.

Stenger was known to have some ideas about aesthetics. One day, he had a few of us build a latrine next to a wood farm shed that stood at the top of a small hill. Knowing that Stenger would object to our layout of the latrine, we dug a two-metre-long trench, and purposely put the rail into place in such a way that anyone using the facility would have to face the wall of the shed.

Making his inspection of the job, Stenger quickly spotted the ass-backwardness of the whole thing. He lectured us at length about how beautiful a landscape could be viewed from the hill, whereupon we moved the perch to the other side of the pit–and things were fine, just fine.

Kunisch's Quest for Maslov

A fellow by the name of Kunisch (pronounced *Koon-ish*) and I, both of us at the time Sergeant Stenger's men, were out to scrounge *maslov* (Russian for butter, oil, lard, or the like) from neighbouring farms in southern Lithuania.

Let me tell you a bit about Kunisch before I relate the deplorable episode at the Lithuanian farm at which we had just arrived.

103

Along with his other decorations, Kunisch wore the medal for the winter campaign in Russia 1941–1942, nicknamed frozen meat medal. The ribbon was as red, basically, as the *krasny* (red) of the Red Army, into whose face Kunisch and others like him had been spitting since at least that cruel winter about 2½ years earlier. Sad-eyed and balding early, Kunisch seemed not to know the meaning of fear.

Kunisch had been down and up a lot of the lines of the Eastern Front, and had lived through the tides of tank battles. He was the longest-serving Lance Corporal I ever got to know personally.

Actually, Kunisch had been a front-line soldier far too long, and had, in the process, become handier with his drawn P38 than with the driver's controls of a Panzer IV, at which he was damned good. He had, to quite some extent, become brutal. Ruthless he could be, moreover.

I never saw Kunisch smile, not even on the day he came to be in possession of an entire set of silverware for six. I'll tell you about him and that silverware, but first allow me to get back to that particular farm in Lithuania.

In the land of so many wooden structures, such as dams and all sorts of buildings, we came upon, after we had walked through an opening in a wood fence surrounding a wooden house, a wooden bench with a little girl perhaps eight years old seated on it.

The blue-eyed child, her fair hair done up in two braids, held, on her lap, an open German-language primer. Obviously the kid had been put there by the farm's folk as a token of their good will. No one else was in sight.

Wanting to get right down to the business of foraging, Kunisch asked to see the head of the household. Papa appeared outside the house, showing his friendly disposition towards us. Kunisch, however, having enquired about the availability of bacon, perhaps the most common form of pork in those parts, became increasingly insistent.

I don't know how Kunisch got the idea that the farmer's bacon would be hidden in the barn, but that was where he steered the man. Damn it! I could hardly believe what happened next. Kunisch drew his P38 and threatened to shoot the farmer if he would not let him have some bacon immediately. What Kunisch did is called putting a pistol to the man's chest – a bad move. Fearing for his life, the farmer came across with a basketball-size smoked ham which he pawed out hurriedly from under the hay in the mow.

Never before did I see such rough treatment of a friendly civilian, and never again. I was ready to draw my P38 to bring Kunisch to his senses; however, the man was in a rage, and might well have killed the farmer and me.

Sure, Kunisch got the *maslov* he though he had to have so badly, but at what price? I wouldn't be surprised if that Lithuanian farmer and his family, including his little daughter, became partisans that very day–just because of Kunisch. Taking his function as a forager far too seriously, Kunisch had violated the forager's unwritten code of conduct, which stated, in a nutshell, that the forager must never use force, or even threaten to use force, while foraging, and that the forager must never deprive any locals of their sustenance.

Kunisch's Silverware

The silverware, a heavy, made-to-last-for-generations, full set for six, resplendent in its matte black box damned nearly big enough to stow an MG34, had somehow come into the custody of Kunisch in Lithuania not long after the *maslov* incident.

As often as he could, Kunisch would check his black case, at the same time probably trying to figure out how to keep it from falling into the hands of others of his kind. However, there were no others of his type at 24251E. The German soldier, even when serving with a mechanized unit, was not one to lug booty about with him. Besides, having alleged souvenirs in one's possession was prohibited. In more ways than one, Kunisch departed from the norm; that's why I write so much about him after all these years.

Carrying the black case and its contents, Kunisch reminded me of a cagey old mutt with a prize bone in its mouth, but no secure and secret place in which to stash that bone.

Naturally, the guys would have their fun with Kunisch about the silverware. Some suggested that he present it to a Lithuanian dame who would appreciate some glitter in her days of drabness. Others suggested a consolidation of sorts, a melting of the silver without the knife blades. Kunisch was opposed to any nonsense they suggested. He wanted the silverware intact—as a set, in its box.

The other guys were far too smart to covet anything as bulky as that set of silverware. We always had to travel light. A good four months earlier, at Suceava in north-eastern Romania, a guy by the name of Moser had, for a short while, been inseparable from a keg of beer he had liberated from a small brewery. Eventually, Moser abandoned the keg. Most guys were, they jokingly stated, better off looking for women, each weighing, say, a hundred kg to fondle rather than polishing silverware.

Kunisch himself noticed, as he went along, that the black case was awkward to transport and stash. Chucking the fine matte case, he bundled the silverware according to items. All the large knives in one bundle, the small knives in another, and so forth.

Even rolling and tying his goodies into pieces of fabric did Kunisch's nerves no good. With many stashes for the bundles of silverware to look after, he behaved like a squirrel during prime nut-gathering time in late fall.

Right after he had gotten hold of the silverware, Kunisch was, I know, tempted to play the contrabandist eventually. However, his black case wouldn't have fitted into the external stowage bin at the rear of the Panzer IV turret. Later, just one of those bundles smuggled into his cramped driver's compartment could, for instance, have become wedged behind the clutch pedal, preventing the clutch from functioning and disabling the vehicle.

Inevitably, Kunisch's fortune in silver began to dwindle. The bundles became fewer, perhaps by one bundle daily. In the end, Kunisch had kept only one item, a hellish big silver soup spoon, neatly swathed and tucked away in the big breast pocket of his tunic–a different kind of black case for his spoon–next to his beloved P38.

Because it did take the place of knife and fork, a soup spoon was called *universal* spoon. There was also the non-issue, galvanized *universal* pail, used for washing, doing laundry, and so forth, hanging from the back of the Panzer IV's hull.

The German soldiers' appreciation of the spoon as the most essential eating utensil was insincerely expressed by "*Jesus sprach zu seinen Jüngern: 'Wer keinen Löffel hat, der fresse mit den Fingern'.*" (Jesus to His apostles did speak: "Whosoever hath no spoon shall with his fingers feed".)

Since Kunisch's big spoon was much longer than it had to be to allow him to scrape the bottom of the inside of his mess tin with it, he probably eventually chopped the engraved handle to about two-thirds of its original length, making the spoon much more pocket-stashable. The use of an item by a soldier usually resulted in the speedy and fair evaluation of it. Often, a modification was required, or more than one.

With regard to things flashy, some guys, Kunisch included, had to learn in slow stages the wisdom of the saying "Bauble, bauble is creation from the hand of man" from Theodor Fontane's ballad *The Bridge Across the Tay*, with allusions to Shakespeare's *Macbeth*.

Let's hope that Kunisch, before the end of war, drew his silver soup spoon, or what was left of it, far more frequently than he did his *Pistole 38.*

Pig Killer at Work

Along the Eastern Front, there were two ways to get extra *maslov*–by scrounging for it, as Kunisch had so crudely and so embarrassingly, and by butchering. Butchering involved, first of all, not doing the job outside of a 50-km-wide zone on one's own side of the front line. Because of happenings at the front, the boundaries of the 50-km zone could fluctuate wildly, something the military police strove to take advantage of by often trying to confiscate the pork, dead or alive, for their own use.

The second requisite, of course, was a competent butcher. Stenger happened to have one such man, a friendly blond Bavarian built like the proverbial brick backhouse, and ready to put his strength to the test anywhere, anytime. I wouldn't say the man had a strong back and a weak mind, but what I saw at the beginning of one butchering job he had undertaken made me realize how a man could get carried away by the work he loved to do.

Bending his knees, our pal, in the presence of about ten men, got the left side of his body down low, close to the front half of the pig, and put his left arm around the animal's neck–like a true friend. Unable to run away, the pig stood still, more or less, whereupon our butcher's right hand, with his own P38 in it, came into play. One 9-mm bullet and the pig was ready to be worked on. So, it appeared, was our pig killer.

He had, in adopting a good, solid, low stance, placed his left foot below the swine's head, and caught the slowed-down full-metal-jacket bullet in his foot. Off came his left boot and sock. There was the shiny slug, sticking, literally, between the big toe and the toe next to it. Not much blood. No fracture. Pure luck.

Lots of fresh pork for the pots after the medic's meat inspection. Having a sample of the meat inspected by the medic was actually the third requisite for field butchering pigs. No one was happier about the fortunate outcome of the incident than Sergeant Stenger, for he, and we, needed the blond boy's expertise for butchering pigs in Lithuania.

The Schwimmwagen Group

Southern Lithuania was ideal *Schwimmwagen* (amphibious Volkswagen) country. Temporarily, our company operated one such vehicle. *Geerbt* (inherited). The boys never got to try it out; one or two of the officers and a few senior N.C.O.s would play with it by the hour on a steep-banked pond.

With egg hand grenades thrown well away from their tub, they tried fishing. However, their catch, a few stunned carp, was no good. No one even suggested taking such coarse fish to Sergeant Stenger's kitchen.

Watchful Willi and Alex, the Adviser

Willi Scherb so impressed me as a character that I remember his first name. He was a bantam, stocky and quarrelsome. Like Kunisch, Willi had been at the Eastern Front for a relatively long time, all of it, as far as I could tell, as a tank driver. As such, he had a fine reputation.

Willi was known for his seriousness on the job, a trait which had, no doubt, contributed to his longevity as a Panzer soldier. When he was on guard duty in the street of some hamlet, at night, he would specialize in poking, in the belly, with the muzzle of his watch-supplied 98k rifle, those he challenged, including his buddies. If his demand, "Password!", was not answered immediately, Willi would get tougher with "Hands up!" and the like. Catching an officer who was slow to respond would make Willi's night.

Of course Willi knew the Russian equivalents of his scare-the-shit-out-of-people German commands. *Stoi!* (Stand!), *Rooky wairk!* (Hands up!), and *Issy soodaw!* (Come here!) was a series he knew well, but could not use for fear of being taken for a Soviet by his pals and being shot at. Also, Willi, who had been around long enough to be able to compare advance with retreat, and who knew the signs of the bad times that accompanied especially the latter, could come up with a short "Russian" poem of anonymous German authorship, such as the one entitled "*Woyna*" (War): *Nyema koori, nyema yeika, / Nyema matka, nyema bala-laika.* (No more chickens, no more eggs, / No more women, no more music.)

One of Willi's best friends was Alex (pronounced *All-yex*), a *Hiwi* (pronounced *hee-vee,* and a contraction of the word *Hilfswilliger,* meaning someone willing to help the enemy, or "collaborator"). Alex had served in the Soviet armed forces. Clothed in the German field-grey uniform, but without insignia, he and two other *Hiwis* were assigned to our repair personnel. Unfortunately, Alex had no expertise regarding Soviet tanks, although he was eager to advise us in matters of which he had knowledge.

Often, big Alex–two of our three *Hiwis* were named Alex; the younger one, smaller than Willi's buddy, was known as *malyenki* (small) Alex–would accompany Willi on a two-hour watch late in the evening. Willi would do the catching, and, having said his piece and waved his rifle a bit, would turn his detainees over to Alex for a three-minute lecture on how to remain undetected when moving about on foot at night in, or close to, enemy territory.

Alex would look dead serious by the light of the moon–if there was moonlight–and lift his index finger to seal his lips, indicating that absolute silence was the first requirement. Pretty soon, he would go on to tell the boys, among other things, how *Russki* (Russians) would move along the outside walls of buildings, and not in the middle of the street, the way *Nyemetsky* (Germans) did. Alex made his point every time. Too bad, as I said, that Alex had not been a *tankist.* His advice in that regard would have been of even greater value to us than it was in a general way. For one thing, I would have asked him what a T–34/76 or a T–34/85 carried in the way of fragmentation shells. I never saw either model of tank use them.

Willi Scherb, the epitome of trustworthiness, trusted our three *Hiwis.* So did I.

Now, what would life behind the German lines in Lithuania have been like without Old Stenger, Crazy Kunisch–yes, I have to include that old bastard, although I would, in one respect, rather not–the blond butcher, the *Schwimmwagen* set, and Willi Scherb with his shadow, Big Alex?

A lot less stirring, that's what.

CHAPTER 10

Commentary on the Battle-Line Avowal of the Soldiers of the 7th Panzer Division

Distributed relatively late in the Second World War–certainly following the attempted assassination of Adolf, the supreme commander–the paybook-size, loose sheet, illustrated in this chapter, summarizes the ideal battle-line mentality officially demanded of members of a Panzer Division.

The wording of this avowal can, of course, be viewed as nothing more than a Division Commander's glorious pep talk, an exhortation, put into the mouth, so to speak, of each of his men.

However, because of its emphasis on National Socialism, the avowal can also been seen as constituting a kind of reinforcement, but not a superseding, of the oath of allegiance sworn by members of the Army, the Navy and the Air Force.

The *Waffen-SS* had its own oath of allegiance, which began with "*Ich schwöre Dir, Adolf Hitler* ...." (I swear to you, Adolf Hitler ...). The informal *Dir* was meant to emphasize the strong bond between the SS-men and the *Führer*.

On July 21, 1944, the traditional military salute of most of the Armed Forces–I say *most* because the *Waffen-SS* already was the exception–was replaced by the Nazi salute, which consisted of lifting one's right arm as for the military salute and holding one's fingertips at the height of the crown of one's head instead of having them touch one's right temple. There can be little doubt that, during roughly the last ten months of the war, the commander of a Panzer Division had to deal with a vastly different breed of superiors breathing down his neck.

Perhaps the avowal reflects a kind of attempt to politicize the non-*Waffen-SS* units of the *Wehrmacht* without actually incorporating them into the *Waffen-SS*. A sure sign that the avowal was sanctioned much higher up and produced at a facility far behind the front lines is the quality of the paper on which it was printed. No common, fuzzy orderly-room typewriter paper for that job.

At that time, the appearance, in the field, of a perfect piece of printing or typing was rare indeed. Many units had long before resorted to having some 'orderly room Joe' pound out, as best he could, certificates of awards, using a battered portable typewriter with a limp, war-weary, and recalcitrant ribbon. In stark contrast, the crisp lettering of the avowal shows no asymmetry of the parts or other shabby layout or workmanship.

The usually poorly typed orderly-room documents invariably had, in addition to the signature of the commanding officer, one redeeming feature affixed to them–the official seal of the unit. Oddly enough, the avowal bears no such stamp, nor does it bear the generally omnipresent national insignia, meaning the Reich eagle with swastika.

The avowal appeared at a time when many unit commanders were trying to outdo one another by utilizing a dirty practice that soon became well known as *Soldatenklau*. For instance, a tank crew, or what was left of it, could, only a few kilometres down the road away from the front line, where it had just lost its tank in battle, encounter a checkpoint manned not by military police, but by a primed-up, raring-to-go *Oberleutnant* (Lieutenant) or *Hauptmann* (Captain), not necessarily from the Army, with a dozen or so of his men: *Soldatenklau*.

Despite their various ranks and the medals they wore, and perhaps despite the wounds some of them had so very recently suffered, the tankers could be greeted by *Soldatenklau* with sneers and insults. *Shirkers* and even *deserters* were the kinds of appellations heaped upon the fellows. Next would come their rude relegation to a brief spell of service as infantrymen in the immediate area.

To have the misfortune to run into *Soldatenklau* almost always constituted an extremely degrading experience, an instance of man's

Battle-line avowal of the 7th Panzer Division

inhumanity to man. Maybe the SOBs of *Soldatenklau* had been issued an avowal still more potent than the one given to the 7th Panzer Division?

In parts of the Eastern Front, near the Baltic States, a field marshal by the name of Schörner became notorious for having numerous *Soldatenklau* roadblocks set up.

It was a time, too, when, for instance, the soldiers' simple saying "As the rations go, so goes the movement, or the war effort," if overheard and reported by a zealot, could promptly result in the death sentence against the man who had uttered that saying.

Yes, looking at a rare copy of that old front-line avowal of the men of the 7th Panzer Division does evoke many a thought in one of the veterans of that division—me. I easily recall, for instance, that none of us Panzer men shed tears after we heard the report of the attempt to kill Adolf on July 20, 1944, at his H.Q., called the Wolf's Lair, near the East Prussian town of Rastenburg, about 160 km west of Leipalingis in Lithuania.

My translation of the Battle-Line Avowal of the Soldiers of the 7th Panzer Division reads as follows:

BATTLE-LINE AVOWAL of the Soldiers of the 7th Panzer Division

I BELIEVE

in Germany. By my exemplary conduct and by the spoken and written word, I will do everything to maintain and strengthen the German population's spiritual ability to offer resistance at the front and at home.

I BELIEVE

in the German people united under National Socialism, and in victory for its righteous cause.

I BELIEVE

in my leader, Adolf Hitler, because I am a National Socialist soldier.

I AM DETERMINED

to devote, during the course of the present decisive battle for the life of my people, all of my energy, my blood, and my life, and to fight fanatically, and with unflinching tenacity for every foot of German soil.

NEVER

will I desert my comrades.

NEVER

will I forsake my weapons, which my homeland has forged for me under the greatest sacrifices.

NEVER

will I yield my tank, my vehicle, or other war material. If an order requires that weapons or other materials of war have to be left behind, I will ensure that nothing falls into enemy hands without having been destroyed.

I ACKNOWLEDGE

that I belong to the battle-line comradeship of my division.

CHAPTER 11

Narrations Associated with Panzer Men and East Prussia

Having fought, and then foraged, in Lithuania in the summer of 1944, the men of 24251E later that season moved, perforce, to the southeastern part of adjacent East Prussia, a German province which had remained largely untouched by the Soviets in their 1944 summer offensive.

In East Prussia, during the remainder of that summer, we did not much more than perform physical exercises and report to Sergeant Stenger.

Soldatenklau temporarily made life damned miserable for us in East Prussia in the fall of 1944, an experience that contributed–for me at least–to an already multifaceted collection of memories associated with the area.

To the west of East Prussia lay West Prussia, where some of our men, by then reequipped with amour, would become involved in engagements with the Soviets right after January 12, 1945.

Our Medic Was an Asshole

One day, in the latter part of the summer of 1944, another guy and I were in the orchard of an East Prussian farman orchard with many beehives in it. One goddamned bee stung me in the lower eyelid. Off I went to the medic, who took an eyedropper full of grasshopper-juice-coloured eyedrops–I recall that the name of the medicine was *Targesan*–and, squeezing the bulb of the eyedropper, caused a trickle of brown to go down my right cheek, and onto the front of my relatively new green summer weight uniform jacket, leaving a stain that couldn't be removed. Really not that much of an incident to relate, except that it showed that our medic didn't much care about the men he was supposed to help. There's far worse to tell about the man.

In East Prussia some of the guys would get in solid with female refugees, resulting in a fucking frenzy at night. Next morning there was cock inspection, conducted by our medic. Any redness of the knob, of the foreskin, or of one's entire penis was considered proof that this fellow had had sexual intercourse recently. There were severe penalties for self-mutilation, which included venereal diseases. Practically every one of the men, the medic was prepared to testify at every short-arm inspection, had been sexually active not more than a few minutes ago.

Only once did I hear a fellow in our company object to being called a fucker because his *Genusswurzel* ('pleasure root' or 'pleasure tuber') happened to be a bit red at an inspection. Quack was the man's name, and, I believe, he hailed from Trier on the Moselle River. Quack had guts, and he got away with telling the Sergeant Major, in the presence of a line-up in the hallway of the men's billet, that the N.C.O.s and the officers of the unit were as much fornicators as the men, and that our superiors, too, had their ladies among the refugees.

I knew that Quack was right about N.C.O.s and even the Company C.O. getting lots of screwing. Sergeant Major Fettköter on one occasion ordered me to escort, to the nearest railroad station, two 20-year-old lookers that he and his boss had dallied with the night before.

For an hour or so, those two girls and I travelled together in a boxcar. One asked me, "Have you ever been in love?" Maybe she meant that she thought she had been, or still was, in love with either the Sergeant Major or the Company C.O. after the one-night stand. I can tell you that almost any guy in our unit, had he been escorting those two girls, would have tried damned hard to get both of them in love with him quickly–right there in the rattling, rolling boxcar.

Quack was a righteous fellow who, for his age, had received a fairly formal education before getting into Panzers. He was just the opposite of the medic, who was the damndest 'yes man' the company ever had in my time.

Building Bunkers in East Prussia

It wasn't only his sloppiness with the Targesan while dealing with a man's bee sting, or his dishonesty as an infallible detector of dick chafe that branded our medic as unpopular. He alienated himself from the men to an even greater degree when, later on, in the fall of 1944, *Soldatenklau* made us carry tree trunks that were being used in the building of East Prussian bunkers.

Any old East Prussian head forester would have shed tears at the sight of his straight, tall pines, each a minimum of about 40 cm in diametre at the base of the trunk, being felled and debranched, but he couldn't have wept more, in a way, than we men of 24251E did regarding our plight. Certainly, carrying tree trunks of various lengths in East Prussia was the hardest physical work I have ever performed. I was 19 years old at the time. It was a good thing that Old Stenger had seen to it that we were in reasonably good shape physically before *Soldatenklau* laid its hands on us.

How did all that slavery affect the medic? He touched not one of those hundreds of large logs. He hung around, letting everyone know that he was the medic, and that, in case he had to ply his trade, his hands had to be clean. Well, he wouldn't have had any treatment for a badly injured back. That's about what some of the labouring men and N.C.O.s could have gotten because of their Herculean task.

I would rather have seen a chaplain standing there in place of the medic, watching the slave labour. Most unusual, by the way, was that the slave-driving officers of *Soldatenklau* let the medic get away with his act.

There wasn't a man in the company who would have helped that medic out of any kind of trouble with the Soviets. His name was shit everywhere.

Pleasant Memories of a Somewhat Earlier East Prussia

The gulag-like *Soldatenklau* logging operation cannot have been located more than about 35 km northeast of Lyck, a town in the south-eastern corner of East Prussia. About 1½ years earlier, at the beginning of 1943, I had received a couple of months of tank driver training at the Army tank driving school at Lyck. Peaceful, snow-covered fields and little-used roads through forests had made for delightful driving despite the fact that our driving school tank, without its turret, was open at the top. There were, in 1943, other pleasant aspects to the Lyck area.

In one village–the time had come to change drivers–we pulled up diagonally, facing a white picket fence. The man who took over the controls there was flustered, and, wanting to back up, ran the right front corner of the steel tub into the fence.

The owner of the neat, little place to which the fence belonged was a very kind, forgiving old gentleman who invited all of us–our instructor and his four trainees–in for a chat and tea. He served us one huge loaf of white bread and plenty of butter with it. He knew what young fellows could put away, especially when they were exposed to winter weather.

Saying that his family had been resident in East Prussia for generations, he told us sorrowfully that his son, then serving in the *Wehrmacht*, had had his name changed legally. "It's no longer good enough for him." He was referring to the family name, Jiditski, pronounced *Yiditski*. Probably the junior Jiditski had disliked the sound of the first three letters as much as, if not more than, the last three.

Those Farting Tank Drivers

To be respected within the fraternity of the tank drivers, a man had to master, more or less, the tank drivers' fart. Whenever drivers got together in good times, they would, sooner or later, stage a special kind of contest–a tank drivers' farting contest.

Preparation for a good Panzer driver's fart required the kind of food and drink that were guaranteed to generate the required flatus. Well prepared nutritionally, each contestant would be seated on a chair–at the tank driving school he would sit on a standard four-legged stool–and extend his legs so that his heels rested, ahead of him, on the floor.

When his turn came, each man would, next, pretend to depress the clutch pedal with his left foot, and, letting a short fart, move his right arm and hand in imitation of shifting from neutral into first gear, thereafter releasing the pressure on the clutch pedal. Without–and this was one of the strict rules–waiting, he would, after using his right foot to press his imaginary gas pedal for the imaginary acceleration of his imaginary training Panzer Ia, repeat his declutch-fart-shift-clutch series in going from first gear to second gear, and so forth, his aim being to go into fifth gear without–another rule–missing a fart or a motion.

The traditional Panzer driver's fart required the visualization of exactly six forward gears, as found in the transmission of the good, old Panzer IV, which, incidentally, also had one reverse gear. The Panzer V (Panther) had seven forward gears and one reverse gear; the Panzer VI (Tiger), eight forward gears and four reverse gears. Connoisseurs awarded extra points to contestants whose hand movements reflected the Panzer IV's double-H shift pattern for forward gears.

Usually, a Panzer driver's fart would come about spontaneously rather than in connection with a competition. The impulsive performer, standing on his right leg, would lift his left foot, and, after pretending to disengage the clutch by moving his left foot downward, would release a short fart, and use his right arm and hand as if shifting into a higher gear. Thereafter, he would lift his left foot, simulating the engagement of the clutch. Of course, he couldn't use his right foot on the imaginary gas pedal to accelerate his chariot; thus, he had to omit accelerating to the top of the gear's range before shifting to the next-highest gear, an important requirement in the actual driving of a heavy vehicle, especially a tank.

Tank drivers able to fart their way into sixth gear demonstrated that their food was adequate–perhaps a bit better than that–and that they weren't being taxed too much. The soldiers' saying "Whoever has nothing to bite also has nothing to shit" could, as far as the Panzer driver's fart was concerned, have been rewritten to read "Whoever has much to bite also has much to shit".

It took considerable mental and physical effort to perform the Panzer driver's fart properly. What would have been one long, room-clearing fart had to be divided into six minifarts, each–yet another rule–audible.

The whole exercise was also known as a tank drivers' shit, although that name might have implied wet farts or even a turd expelled involuntarily.

Any tank driver who often thought of, and practised, his Panzer driver's fart would be that much more adept when seated at the controls of his Panzer.

Yes, sir, the Panzer driver's fart was a training aid as well as a pastime.

CHAPTER 12

Reminiscences Regarding Soldiers' Songs, Marching Songs, and Decorations Day

Nothing, it seems, instantly elevated the troops' spirits more than the singing of an innocent little marching song. As well, the performance of marching songs could, and would, bring other surprising and most welcome rewards in time of war, as the following story shows.

It began at a time when most of the men of about one-third of a fresh-out-of-fighting-vehicles Company of Panzer men were taking turns manning a string of tripoded and sandbagged MG34s near a railroad station—was it Sonnenwalde?—close to a small town chock-full of refugees, mostly German-speaking, who, barely able to stay ahead of the advancing juggernaut hordes from the East, were dead tired from trudging towards safety somewhere, anywhere, in the West.

The rare Russian low-flying aircraft tended to hunt directly above the railroad, usually disregarding the roads dotted and splashed with sitting-duck-targets—fleeing people and their horse-drawn wagons, all somehow suggestive, as they trekked wretchedly, of faltering Morse signals, and of kilometres-long permutations of... – – –..., namely, of SOS.

Even the infrequent 'sewing machine', a small, slow, and old Russian reconnaissance aircraft that sounded much like a flying, foot-operated sewing machine—hence the term sewing machine— paid far more attention to the rails than to the roads, probably because new Panzers were expected to arrive close to the front by train. If Ivan was on the lookout for tanks, so were the dispossessed Panzer crews, who yearned to be able, under cover of darkness, to unload, from always none-too-wide flatcars, their brand-new Panzerkampfwagen IVs or Jagdpanzer IVs. Until that would happen, they and their MG34s had to stay close to the railroad station.

For sure, it was a time when this unit of survivors needed a change of scenery.

At the first opportunity, an impressive column—black-clad, *Pistole 38*-equipped, snappy in the military sense of the word, and genuinely glad to get away briefly from those railroad tracks and those boxcars, their alternate wheeled homes—marched into town, and onto the crammed streets, singing their extensive medleys including, no doubt, the song known as "*Mann an Mann*," which contained these lines.

Mann an Mann marschieren wir,
Einerlei wohin,

Irgend in ein Feldquartier,
Frisch mit frohem Sinn.

Singen wir ein schönes Lied
Vom dem Schätzelein,
Herrlich ist es auf der Welt
Und schön, Soldat zu sein.

(We are marching, three abreast,
Briskly, in fine mettle,
Knowing neither where we'll rest,
Nor where, for long, we'll settle.)

(A lovely ditty let us sing
About a sweetheart true;
A soldier's life for sure's the thing
In this world's wide and lovely view.)

The first three lines of the original will have been understood by the audience consisting of refugees and persons undergoing resettlement.

Certificate for my *Panzerkampfabzeichen in Silber*

Shortly after the 30-odd men had marched back to the railroad yard and to the sticky, stinking ties and rusty rails of the siding, their Company C.O. received word that the Division Commander had learned of the whole town's elatedness, brought on by the marching and singing of some of his Panzer men. The General expressed his gratitude for the success of the event; moreover, he actually had a special allowance of food and drink delivered to the antiaircraft machine gunners at the tracks.

After a few days, the unit, armoured once again, pulled away from the railroad station, never to return to the close-by town of its triumph.

In retrospect, the completely unsolicited and spontaneous marching and singing which started that short sequence of happy events must have occurred at about the time when the men had taken note of their new Battle-Line Avowal, part of which required that each soldier pledge, in effect, that he would do his utmost to maintain, even boost, the morale of the civilians by means of the spoken and written word. As it turned out, a great boost was achieved in town that day by the singing of marching songs, although nothing in the Avowal referred to words sung.

For various reasons—ignorance, indifference, insensitivity or ingratitude, for instance—there are those who, believing that remembrances of any and all soldiers' songs are of no earthly use, might well parrot the following bit of triteness: "For that, I can't buy anything for myself."

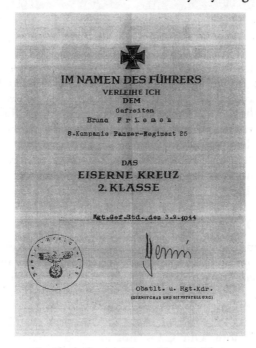

Certificate for my *Eiserne Kreuz 2. Klasse*

All of my medals

Others, including, of course, the author, will, however, declare that reminiscences regarding Soldaten and marching songs of over half a century ago have led to the realization that the lasting usefulness of those songs lies in the fact that they are instrumental in recalling the kinds of formative experiences that have influenced many veterans of the worst of times–war–to lead exemplary lives.

Probably no more reliable mnemonic device exists than the songs readily associated, by the former soldier, with many of the instances of good or bad which, so long ago, taught him so much so quickly.

Decorations Day

My performance as a gunner in Lithuania–we had not been officially credited with our Panzer engagement at Suceava in Romania much earlier in the year–was deemed worthy of the *Panzerkampfabzeichen in Silber* and the *Eiserne Kreuz 2. Klasse*, both awarded to me on September 3, 1944, in East Prussia.

With regard to the *Eiserne Kreuz 2. Klasse*, the awards ceremony gave rise to an anecdote. Our C.O., not at all popular with the men, in addressing a row of recipients–a number of Panzer IV crews were being decorated–said, "In the name of the Führer, I award to you the Iron Cross

2nd Class 2nd Class." Had he adhered to the formula, he would have used the following words: "In the name of the Führer, I award to you the Iron Cross 2nd Class."

The blokes were quick to catch on that the C.O. had committed two errors: he had colloquially abbreviated *Eiserne Kreuz 2. Klasse* to *EK II*, and had tacked on the by-then-redundant *2. Klasse*. For a while, some of the boys indulged in finding fault with the C.O.'s shitty German. There was talk of their having been awarded a fictitious class of the Iron Cross, below that of the *Eiserne Kreuz 2. Klasse*.

Naturally, the grumbling subsided, and each of the men proudly wore his ribbon to his *EK II*.

A decoration, the *Panzerkampabzeichen in Silber* (tank battle badge in silver), for tank crew, was authorized on December 20, 1939. On June 22, 1943, the *Panzerkampfabzeichen mit der Einsatzzahl* (tank battle badge in silver with the number of engagements) was introduced. The

Denazified version of three of my medals (no *Eiserne Kreuz 2. Klasse*)

Panzerkampfabzeichen in Bronze, for support units, was authorized in the same grades, and on the same dates, as the silver version.

By the middle of 1943, there were, of course, Panzer crew members who had been involved in 25 or more certified tank battles; however, I can tell you that any man who attained 25 or 50 or 75 or–Christ!–100 engagements was protected by supernatural powers. At any rate, the large numbers were something a lot of the guys would strive damned hard to achieve.

A snazzy decoration–far more than a campaign medal–was a mighty inspiration.

CHAPTER 13

The Jagdpanzer IV

This chapter and the one immediately following it are based largely on wide experience that I acquired, starting in 1943 with an eight-week course at a Panzer driving school, followed by service in the field with the Panzer IV in 1944, and with the Jagdpanzer IV in 1945. Complementing my wartime experience with German armour are my nine years of service, starting in 1997, as a volunteer in the armoured vehicles galleries at the Canadian War Museum in Ottawa.

Introduced in 1944 as a defensive tank destroyer, the first model of the Jagdpanzer IV (*Jagd* means hunt or hunting; therefore, *Jagdpanzer IV* meant *Hunt Tank IV* or *Hunting Tank IV*) basically consisted, as did the two subsequent models, of the chassis and hull of a late-model Panzerkampfwagen IV and a 7.5-cm gun.

Such a tank destroyer—low, well-armoured, fully enclosed, turretless, full-tracked, self-propelled, and mounting a limited-traverse, high-velocity 7.5-cm gun—was known, to Panzer crews, as the Jagdpanzer IV; throughout any Panzer Regiment, the vehicle's designation was strictly Jagdpanzer IV.

The *Panzerabwehrkanone* (*Pak*) troops, who themselves were known as *Panzerjäger* (*Jäger* means hunter; hence, *Panzerjäger* means *Tank Hunter*), called the vehicle under discussion a *Panzerjäger*, a word that has, in much of the post-war literature on the subject, displaced the name Jagdpanzer IV.

The original model of the Jagdpanzer IV carried, in a modified Panzerkampfwagen IV hull with a special superstructure, the 7.5-cm *Panzerabwehrkanone 39* (*Pak 39*) L/48. This vehicle was also known as the *Panzerjäger*.

Produced, but only in small numbers, was a transitional Jagdpanzer IV with the bow and vertical-face upper hull of the Panzerkampfwagen IV, and mounting the 7.5-cm *KwK* (*Kampfwagen-Kanone*) 42 L/70 Panther gun. This combination was known as the Jagdpanzer IV A. It was produced by the Altmärkische Kettenfabrik in Berlin. Hence the A in IV A.

The latest Jagdpanzer IV, with its lower and upper glacis plates as well as the other prototype-inspired modifications to the Panzerkampfwagen IV hull, also mounted the 7.5-cm *KwK* L/70. Made by the Vogtländische Maschinenfabrik A.G. in Plauen in Saxony, it was known as the Jagdpanzer IV V.

In the remainder of this discussion, consideration will, first of all, be given to some aspects of the field use of the main gun and all of the optics of the latest Jagdpanzer IV, after which its chassis and hull will be commented upon. Shown in Appendix D, the photograph of the Jagdpanzer IV with the tabulation of its technical data leaves room for the disclosure of little-known, but important, features. For instance, in this chapter blind spots are discussed, as well as many other vital characteristics of the Jagdpanzer IV.

Field use of the 7.5-cm KwK 42 L/70

By opting for a limited-traverse, hull-mounted gun rather than a rotating turret, designers found it consistently possible to mount a larger gun than that carried by the equivalent tank. Ultimately, a larger gun meant, for the Jagdpanzer IV, the installation of the Panther 7.5-cm *KwK* 42 L/70, which, for instance, gave a 15-lb. (6.80 kg) *Panzergranate* (AP projectile) a muzzle velocity of 935.13 m per second (3,068 ft. per second), compared with 750.11 m per second (2,461 ft. per second) achieved by the Panzerkampfwagen IV 7.5-cm *KwK* 40 L/48 firing the same 15-lb. projectile. The 7.5-cm *KwK* 42 L/70 was designed to meet the demand for a Panzer main gun capable of penetrating 14 cm of armour at 1,000 m.

The 20-percent increase in muzzle velocity--which translated into longer range, increased accuracy, and greater armour penetration--was the result of two features of the *KwK* 42: its 5.25-m barrel length, increased by 1.65 m over that of the *KwK* 40 L/48, and the markedly greater propellant charge capacity of its *Hülse* (case), compared with that of the *KwK* 40. The following table shows the German estimates of the effectiveness of the *KwK* 42 75-mm gun against some enemy armour at the end of May, 1944:

German estimates of the effectiveness of the *KwK* 42 75mm L/70 gun against enemy armour as at 30 May 1944:

Russian T–34
Front   800m
Side   2,800m
Rea   2,800m

Russian KV series
Front   600m
Side   2,000m
Rea   2,000m

Russian JS-I
Front   600m
Side   2,000m
Rear   2,000m

British Churchill III
Front   2,000m[1]
Side   2,000m
Rea   2,000m

US Sherman
Front   1,000m
Side   2,800m
Rea   2,800m

1. This is clearly a mistake in the presentation of the estimate, and the same side and rear figures could hardly apply if it was not. 800m frontal and 2,000m flank and rear penetrations are more realistic.
Cited from Bryan Perrett, *The PzKpfw V Panther*, p. 17.

In its application to the Jagdpanzer IV, the potent *KwK* 42 L/70 did not require a muzzle brake, although in the Panther, which had a smaller fighting compartment, it was equipped with a double-baffle brake.

Limited gun traverse, in the Jagdpanzer IV, meant a maximum traverse of 20 degrees, 10 degrees left, and 10 degrees right. Maximum elevation of the *KwK* was 15 degrees, and maximum depression was five degrees. These three figures are important in a discussion of the field use of that gun.

Cradled in the upper glacis plate of the superstructure, the 5.25-m-long barrel of the Jagdpanzer IV's 7.5-cm gun extended 2.5 m ahead of the front of the hull. At 1.42 m firing height, or distance from the ground to the centre of the bore at 0 degrees elevation–the firing height of the Panzerkampfwagen IV was 1.96 m–the barrel also lay relatively close to ground level. The projection of the long and low gun barrel was of great concern to the Jagdpanzer IV crews inasmuch as such a barrel could collide far more easily, vertically as well as laterally, with objects in the Jagdpanzer IV's immediate environment–far more easily, that was, than the turret-mounted L/48 barrels on their Panzerkampfwagen IVs could.

The gun barrel's elevation had to be monitored closely when the Jagdpanzer IV was being driven over uneven terrain, and especially when it was crossing ditches and the like. Gun damage avoidance required the closest cooperation between the crew commander and the driver, or between the gunner and the driver. A collision between gun and ground could render the gunner's controls useless. An obstructed bore meant a barrel burst on firing.

Making the Jagdpanzer IV even more vulnerable to self-inflicted damage than the ultra long barrel's propensity to dig in at the muzzle in uneven terrain was its tendency, when the vehicle was being turned, to fail to clear nearby lateral obstacles such as trees and walls of buildings, resulting in damage to the gun's mounting to the extent that the gun would not respond at all to the gunner's traverse and elevation hand wheels, but would be suspended unsteadily in the upper glacis plate.

There was no buffer or override mechanism to absorb the shock of a collision, vertical or horizontal, between the barrel and a substantial object. Severe damage of course resulted more easily if a collision occurred close to the muzzle of the barrel, increasing the wrecking leverage.

The Jagdpanzer IV's driver certainly had no use for a turret-gun warning indicator in the form of, for instance, two blue bulbs, one mounted on the left side of his compartment, the other on the right. Such an indicator, fitted on earlier production models of the Panzerkampfwagen IV, was tripped automatically when the gun was traversed over the side of the vehicle, and the corresponding lamp lit up, warning the driver to allow extra room if the tank was, for instance, passing between trees or buildings. Failure to leave extra room would result in the barrel striking an obstacle and causing damage to the gun mounting.

Although the long gun barrel of the Jagdpanzer IV with its 20-degree limited traverse did not require a turret-type lateral warning indicator, a different type of indicator, warning of possible damage to the gun because of the vehicle being turned prematurely, would have been most welcome to Jagdpanzer IV crews. Such an indicator would have helped to prevent Jagdpanzer IVs—note the plural—from becoming self-destructive when fast action prevented the crew commanders or gunners from making gun-clearance-relevant observations, and giving corresponding instructions to their drivers to allow for muzzle clearance.

As noted, a mount damaged by any external gun-barrel-and-large-object collision meant a total loss of the gun's response to the gunner's hand wheels; therefore, such damage meant a disabled main gun, possibly leading to a disabled Jagdpanzer IV, one that ultimately very likely had to be destroyed through the use, by the crew, of its own one-kg demolition charge.

Unlike, for instance, the taller Jagdpanther, also known as the Jagdpanzer V, and the Panzerjäger Tiger Elefant, the Jagdpanzer IV had no large hatch in its rear armour, through which the main armament could be removed for repair, and reinstalled. That task, it seems, had to be accomplished through the opening in the upper glacis plate, back of the mantlet and the protuberant armour.

Projecting above the Jagdpanzer IV's roof, and protected by a hood of steel, the objective of the gunner's SflZF telescopic sight was positioned about 50-cm above, and about 65-cm to the left of, the bore axis of the gun at 0 degrees elevation. Actually, the sight's tube fitted through a hole in a flat, arc-shaped steel cover, which was restricted, by means of welded guides, to sliding in conformity with the arc-shaped cutout in the roof armour below the cover. Lateral movement of the cover was by means of a linkage with the gun traverse mechanism below.

In addition to being tantamount to a bad leak in inclement weather, the curved cutout, situated in the front third of the roof, constituted a soft spot in the Jagdpanzer IV's armour.

An excellent side profile of a prototype Jagdpanzer IV/70 (V). This vehicle is fitted with *Schürzen*, or armoured side-skirts, aimed at protecting it from anti-tank weapons, including the anti-tank rifles still used by Soviet forces in 1945. (The Tank Museum)

Front view of early production Jagdpanzer IV/70 (V). (The Tank Museum)

Rear view of early production Jagdpanzer IV/70 (V). (The Tank Museum)

Close-up view of front of early production Jagdpanzer IV/70 (V), with gun barrel
locked in place. (The Tank Museum)

Close-up view, side-on, of the gun mantlet of early production Jagdpanzer IV/70 (V). (The Tank Museum)

Interior shot, showing the breech mechanism of the 7.5-cm *KwK* 42 L/70 within a Jagdpanzer IV/70 (V). (The Tank Museum)

Two more interior shots within a Jagdpanzer IV/70 (V), the former showing empty racking for ammunition. (The Tank Museum)

The Jagdpanzer IV's elevation and traverse hand wheels for the main gun were arranged vertically, their hubs facing the gunner; the upper wheel was for elevation, the lower one for traverse. The Panzerkampfwagen IV had a vertical elevation hand wheel as well as a horizontal traverse hand wheel, the latter provided with the trigger for the electric primer. The Jagdpanzer IV gunners regarded the Panzerkampfwagen IV arrangement of hand wheels as being much better than that of the Jagdpanzer IV.

To facilitate external observation by the crew, the Jagdpanzer IV offered, in addition to the gunner's telescopic sight, the following five optical devices:

Crew commander's non-rotatable scissors stereoscope
Crew commander's rotatable periscope (episcope)
Crew commander's non-rotatable periscope
Loader's non-rotatable periscope
Driver's vision slits

Provided the small instrument hatch cover just ahead of, and abutting on, the crew commander's hatch cover had been opened by flipping it towards the right, the crew commander's unidirectional scissors stereoscope could be extended to a height of about 25 cm above the roof. His fully rotatable periscope, about 61 cm to the rear of his scissors stereoscope, was built into his large hatch cover, which was hinged to open towards the rear of the vehicle. Like his scissors stereoscope, his rotatable periscope was about 74 cm from the left edge of the roof, with the rotatable periscope creating a relatively large blind spot to the left of the Jagdpanzer IV. His non-rotatable periscope was about 22 cm from the left edge of the roof, causing a smaller blind spot to the left than that made by the rotatable periscope.

At a distance of about 31 cm from the right edge of the roof, and about 79 cm farther forward than the crew commander's non-rotatable periscope, was the loader's non-rotatable periscope, accounting for a somewhat larger blind spot to the right than the crew commander's non-rotatable periscope allowed to the left.

Other than through the crew commander's rotatable periscope, there was no means of observing towards the rear from inside the Jagdpanzer IV. Vision through the driver's vision slits was strictly towards the front; moreover, the gun mantlet, immediately to the right of the slits, created a blind spot in that direction.

Blind spots were indeed a valid complaint among Jagdpanzer IV crews. The upper part of each periscope, rotatable or non-rotatable, sat, protected by an arched bar of steel, fairly close to the roof, a height of 6.3-cm above the flat roof armour seems to have been par for the upper prism, so that, with all hatch covers closed and without the scissors stereoscope in use, the following blind spots will have existed:

Direction of View	Device Used	Distance to limit of blind Spot
Left	Commander's non-rotatable periscope	6.5 m
Left	Commander's rotatable periscope (episcope)*	21.8 m
Right	Loader's non-rotatable periscope	9.1 m
Rear	Commander's rotatable periscope (episcope)*	58.2 m
Front	Driver's vision slits	2.6 m

*Same instrument rotated 90 degrees

Prominent Modifications to Chassis and Hull

Generally, the Jagdpanzer IV incorporated what was basically the chassis and hull of the Model H, the second-last model of the Panzerkampfwagen IV, a proven design that had culminated, in 1944, in the Model J, also referred to as the Model I because of the alphabetical position of *I* immediately after *H*. I and J were identical in earlier German alphabets. The Panzerkampfwagen IV was introduced before the war and underwent continual modification and improvement throughout the war. Continued production of the Model J (I) throughout 1945 was planned.

A prominent change to the Model H chassis was the reduction of the number of track return rollers from four to three; most Jagdpanzer IVs were built with three return rollers as were, by the way, some late-model Panzerkampfwagen IVs.

Its transformation from the Panzerkampfwagen IV completed, the final model of the Jagdpanzer IV featured two near-prototype glacis plates–the plates had become somewhat more inclined than those of the prototype–one below an almost horizontal ledge at the front of the hull, the other above that ledge, resulting in the bottom of the upper glacis plate being set back 0.7 m with respect to the top of the lower glacis plate.

Clearly, the frontal ledge was essential because of the three hatches that had to be built into it. The transmission access hatch in the ledge was flush, screwed in place; the steering brake access hatches, one to either side of the transmission access hatch, were hinged and projected slightly above the shelf.

Also, the superstructure's side armour was redesigned on a sloping configuration to give better armour protection.

The armour thicknesses of the Jagdpanzer IV were changed from those of the Panzerkampfwagen IV as follows:

	Panzerkampfwagen IV	
Armour of Tank	Model H	Jagdpanzer IV
Front	80 mm	60 mm
Side	30 mm	40 mm
Rear	20 mm	30 mm
Roof	15 mm	20 mm

The front 2/5 of the length of the belly armour of the Jagdpanzer IV was 20 mm thick; the rear 3/5 of the length of its belly armour was 10 mm thick. Interesting, in connection with the above data on armour thicknesses, is the fact that Appendix D gives the weight of the Model H of the Panzerkampfwagen IV as 25 tons, and that of the Jagdpanzer IV as 25.8 tons.

Whereas each of the five crew members in a Panzerkampfwagen IV had his own hatch, the four- or five-member Jagdpanzer IV crew had but two hatches, both in, and flush with, the roof the vehicle.

The driver's single-window, hooded visor in the vertical part of the frontal armour of the Panzerkampfwagen IV hull became two relatively narrow, side-by-side, unhooded, horizontal vision slits in the upper glacis plate of the Jagdpanzer IV.

Some Jagdpanzer IVs were built with two loopholes for defensive, close-combat weapons. One such hole was above, and to the left of, the driver's vision slits, the other to the right of the main gun. Each of these openings was equipped with a round shield, pivoted into place from close to the right side of the hole. All of the other Jagdpanzer IVs had one loophole with shield, to the right of the gun.

The latest model of the Jagdpanzer IV, such as the one at the Canadian War Museum in Ottawa, can easily be identified by the following four characteristics:

1. It has the upper and lower glacis plates.
2. It has the 7.5-cm *KwK* 42 L/70
3. It has three track return rollers.
4. It has no loophole and shield above, and to the left of, the driver's vision slits.

In the afterword to his 48-page *Jagdpanzer: Jagdpanzer IV– Jagdpanther*, which consists largely of black-and-white photographs, Horst Scheibert, the author of a number of books on German armour of World War II, writes as follows in the translation from the German:

From a combat point of view, the way of using chassis of the heavier battle tanks IV, V and VI to build tank destroyers was a mistake and an extravagance. Heavy armour was and is not so important for a tank destroyer; protection against shrapnel and handguns is sufficient. More important are a robust, proven powerplant, a low silhouette, great mobility and a strong, long-range weapon …. The path to more and more heavily armoured vehicles in World War II was necessary for offensive weapons, but not for the tank destroyers that stood and waited for their targets

CHAPTER 14

Driving the Jagdpanzer IV: Avoiding Transmission Abuse

In addition to revealing much of what the Panzer Private was taught during tank driver training, this chapter offers, for instance, information on the turning radii of the Jagdpanzer IV, and on track extensions for eastern-front Jagdpanzer IVs, items not covered in the tabulations of technical details in Appendix D.

What I have to say regarding the Jagdpanzer IV will be of great interest to its driver. I want to talk, in particular, about the Jagdpanzer IV's transmission, and the driver's proper use of it. Most of what I will tell you reflects some of my Panzer driver training, as well as some of my experience as a crew member in the Panzerkampfwagen IV and the Jagdpanzer IV.

Horst Scheibert in *Panzer in Russland ... 1941–1944*, p. 33, states that, beneath their thick armour, Panzers are technically complicated, and, to a certain degree, weakly constructed; the complicated chassis, the greatly stressed transmissions, the engines, the optical equipment, and the weapons and their mountings, require special maintenance. Note the words *greatly stressed transmissions*.

Let's see how the driver of a Jagdpanzer IV could avoid overstressing the transmission.

Inherently, a tracked vehicle is greatly subject to a factor known as rolling resistance, or resistance to rolling. During manual gear changing, or shifting, a tracked vehicle's momentum drops off sharply because of the resistance to rolling offered by the tracks themselves. A non-tracked, or wheeled, vehicle, on the other hand, will roll on with negligible loss of momentum during a manual gear change.

Throughout our discussion, we will have to bear in mind that the Jagdpanzer IV's Maybach HL 120 TRM V–12 engine delivered 265 hp normal output, at 2,600 rpm, and 300 hp maximum output, at 3,000 rpm.

The Jagdpanzer IV's manual transmission, the ZF SSG 76 Aphon, built by the Zahnradfabrik Friedrichshafen in Friedrichshafen at Lake Constance, featured six forward gears and one reverse gear, or, if you like, six forward speeds and one reverse speed. Because of the way in which it was laid out for the six forward gears, the transmission shift pattern was known as *double H*. Gear shifting required precise timing based on the interrelation between the engine and vehicle speeds, and therein lay much of the Jagdpanzer IV driver's skill.

Long before he had finished his two-month-long driver training–I won't simply call it driving school–any grinding of gears on his part branded him inexpert and undesirable as a crew member. If a potential Panzer driver repeatedly caused the transmission gears of a driver-training Panzer to clash, he would, very likely, be ordered to lug the vehicle's big brute of a jack a hundred metres or so, while jogging behind the Panzer. That minor punishment was called carrying the vehicle's jack while trotting behind the tank.

Let's first look at the use of the six forward gears.

Before shifting up, the vehicle had to be accelerated so that, during the process of changing from one gear to another, particularly over difficult ground or on a steep incline, it would not slow down unduly or come to a halt. The rule of accelerating the vehicle to the top of a gear's range had to be complied with before shifting to the next-highest gear.

The Jagdpanzer IV's turning circles for its forward gears were as follows:

Gear	Turning Circle in Metres
1st	5.92
2nd	13.0
3rd	21.3
4th	35.5
5th	50.9
6th	72.2

The figures shown above for the second to sixth gears are approximate. The turning circle for the reverse gear will have been about the same as that for the first gear.

To understand the reason for these vast differences in the sizes of the turning circles, we have to consider the Jagdpanzer IV's steering mechanism. The drive shaft of the Jagdpanzer IV ran forward from the engine, through a tunnel at the bottom of the fighting compartment, and, via a three-plate clutch, to the transmission. Bevel gears and the steering mechanism were flanged to the front of the transmission. The complex clutch-type steering mechanism, produced by Krupp, was a Wilson design. From the steering mechanism, two drive shafts, one left and one right ran to the two steering brakes and, thence, to the two final drives. It can be said, too, that the steering of the Jagdpanzer IV was achieved by means of a mechanical planetary steering gear and mechanical steering brakes, operated by two steering levers.

The transmission and steering mechanism access hatch was bolted onto the middle of the near-horizontal ledge above the lower glacis plate of the Jagdpanzer IV. The vented steering brake access hatches, one to either side of the transmission and steering mechanism hatch, were

hinged and projected slightly above the shelf. Preferably, the servicing of
the transmission and the steering mechanism, as well as the adjustment of
the steering brakes, was performed by field workshop personnel, although
many Panzer drivers were professional automotive mechanics.

Pulled about one-third of its total travel by the Jagdpanzer IV's driver,
a steering lever operated a clutch in the steering mechanism. Pulled
farther–past about one-third of its total travel–that same lever applied one
steering brake. Feasible only with the transmission in its lowest forward
gear, or in its reverse gear, the so-called on-a-dime turn was achieved by
promptly pulling one steering lever all the way, so that one track was
immediately braked fully. Clutched and unbraked–in other words, fully
engaged–the other track propelled the Jagdpanzer IV in a very tight turn–
a small turning circle.

Of course, the higher forward gears of the transmission entailed
greater vehicle speeds. With those gears and the corresponding vehicle
speeds, full braking so as to cause the vehicle to turn abruptly was out of
the question. With the higher gears, rather gentle high-speed turns, or
greater turning circles, resulted from the steering lever being pulled only
far enough to operate one steering clutch. If an abrupt turn was desired,
the vehicle had to be decelerated greatly, often a decided disadvantage in
battle, and a much lower gear engaged.

An abrupt turn, rather than a gradual turn, was often required
because of the need to have the thick frontal armour, and the main gun, of
the Jagdpanzer IV directed quickly towards the enemy, from whom
armour-piercing fire would come. Any attempt to turn the Jagdpanzer IV
sharply while driving it at high speed invited transmission damage. Top
speed of the Jagdpanzer IV was, by the way, 35 km/h, which is 9.7 m/sec,
or about 32 ft/sec.

At this point, a bit of the history of the Wilson design of the
Jagdpanzer IV's steering mechanism:

Regarding tracked, armoured vehicles, as much work went into
steering and transmission development during the years between the
world wars as went into engines, suspensions, and tracks. By transferring
power from one track to the other, the designers tried to do away with
steering achieved by means of the power-robbing outright braking of one
track. Gradually, these efforts led them to incorporate the steering mechanism, the differential, and the transmission into one unit.

In 1928, Major Walter Wilson used the 16-ton Vickers A–6 tank as
the vehicle for his epicyclic, or planetary, steering mechanism–a very
important advance in transmission and steering design. The Wilson
mechanism did much to dispense with the loss of power when steering. Its
design completed by January of 1934, the first Panzerkampfwagen IV,
namely the model A, appeared in 1936; it employed what was termed the
Krupp-Wilson clutch steering mechanism. Most subsequent models of
the Panzerkampfwagen IV carried that same type of Wilson steering

mechanism, as did most of its variants, including the Jagdpanzer IV. The only three Panzerkampfwagen IV variants that did not have the Krupp-Wilson steering were equipped with what was called the Daimler-Benz-Wilson clutch.

It is worth noting that, just as the various planetary steering mechanisms for tracked, armoured vehicles were named after their designers, the planetary gear systems for automobile automatic transmissions were named after their devisers, e.g., Simpson and Ravigneaux.

When shifting down the Jagdpanzer's forward gears, double clutching, was obligatory. The purpose of double clutching, or double declutching, was the momentary attainment, with the transmission in neutral, of an engine speed suitable for the smooth engagement of a lower gear.

Rolling resistance was at work whenever the Jagdpanzer IV was being driven. Often, in having to go to a slower vehicle speed because of a somewhat sharper bend in the road, a moderately steep hill, or a bad road, the driver had to select a gear two gears lower than the one already engaged. A driver was trained to avoid steering, if possible, when his Jagdpanzer IV was climbing a steep slope.

The Jagdpanzer IV could safely climb a 30-degree grade. It could also–and this figure is not known generally–descend a 40-degree slope in safety. The vehicle's low centre of gravity made such relatively steep ascents and descents possible. However, particularly with regard to steep descents, the overhang and elevation of the main gun had to be considered. Regarding the choice of gear required for the negotiation of a steep slope, the rule was to use the same gear for downhill as for uphill.

Reliable braking was important, especially when descending a steep slope. The driver was permitted to use the engine, at 2,200–2,400 rpm, as a brake. He could, of course, use his foot brake, which acted simultaneously on both steering brakes.

Driving in snow and mud increased resistance to rolling, which the driver had to take into account in his use of the transmission. At the German Eastern Front, lateral track extensions known as *Ostketten*, or eastern tracks, were in use on some Jagdpanzer IVs during mainly the winter months to increase traction. *Ostketten* were also fitted at other times because of operations in terrain unfavourable for tracked vehicles. Applied, an *Ostkette* increased, so to speak, the width of the regular 40-cm track by roughly 58 percent.

Each rectangular extension of a link of the regular track–there were 99 such extensions to each regular track of the Jagdpanzer IV–bore down on an area about 23 cm x 8 cm, or about 184 sq cm. Much of that added steel projected past the outer edge of the regular track, on the side away from the hull of the vehicle. Because of such pronounced asymmetry, *Ostketten* were often shed during turns and maneuvers at relatively high speeds.

Let's look at a few more important aspects of the Jagdpanzer IV's *Ostketten*. Consider that the Soviet T–34/76C and the Jagdpanzer IV each had a combat weight of 28 tons. In addition to having wider regular tracks than the Jagdpanzer IV, the T–34/76C had a greater part of the length of each part of its track in contact with the ground. For the T–34/76C, the track ground contact length was 3.71 m; for the Jagdpanzer IV, 3.52 m. The T–34/76C, with its regular track width of 50 cm, showed a ground pressure of 0.71 kg/sq cm. The Jagdpanzer IV, with its regular 40-cm-wide tracks, exerted 0.9 kg/sq cm ground pressure. With *Ostketten* fitted to its regular tracks, the Jagdpanzer IV had a ground pressure of only 0.67 kg/sq cm. Therefore, *Ostketten* markedly reduced the ground pressure exerted by the Jagdpanzer IV, making it more favourable than that of the T–34/76C. Decreased rolling resistance was the reward for the use of the *Ostketten*.

Conversely, the weight of the *Ostketten* added to the Jagdpanzer IV's rolling resistance. A regular 99-link Jagdpanzer IV track with all the Ostkette extensions in place weighed 1.93 times as much as the same track without the Ostkette.

A disadvantage of the wide *Ostketten* was that they prevented a Jagdpanzer IV fitted with them from crossing, aboard a railway flat car, German military railway bridges. Removing and refitting the *Ostketten* because of such bridges was a laborious undertaking. All in all, the *Ostketten* were regarded, especially by the drivers, as a stopgap.

The Jagdpanzer IV's regular track links incorporated ice grousers. Skidding and sliding, and the spinning of tracks, on ice were, therefore, not generally a problem for the driver.

One of the greatest abuses of a Jagdpanzer IV's transmission occurred when the attempt was made to use the vehicle to recover a tracked vehicle that was, say, in the Jagdpanzer IV's weight class. The standard earlier tank recovery vehicle of the Army, a large 18-ton halftrack made by Famo, had become overtaxed by the weight of the medium armoured vehicles, such as the Jagdpanzer IV, to say nothing of the heavies. Besides, the recovery halftracks were generally nowhere around when they were needed in a hurry, especially in a defensive campaign, a euphemism for retreat. The later recovery Panther, a variant of the Panther tank, was equipped with a winch that could exert a 40-ton pull, but that vehicle was found primarily with the Panther-equipped part of a Panzer Regiment, not with the Jagdpanzer-equipped part. During a defensive action, there could hardly be any waiting for a recovery Panther. It was advisable to use the combined pulls of at least two Jagdpanzer IVs to recover one 28-tonner.

Towing a Jagdpanzer IV on fairly level ground imposed far less stress on the Jagdpanzer IV's transmission than recovery work did, provided that the disabled vehicle's running gear was functional, and that the vehicle was attached properly to its tower. *Attached properly* meant the use of two crossed tow cables, to prevent the towed vehicle from wandering.

For a Jagdpanzer IV, there were many opportunities, within one's unit and elsewhere, to tow vehicles of all sorts. On one occasion, our Jagdpanzer IV was towing an out-of-gas, sidecar-equipped motorcycle, with its rider steering it, and his buddy resting in the sidecar. For us, the going was slow on the highway because of a bottleneck ahead. Put up to it by others of the crew, our driver suddenly caused our Jagdpanzer IV to shoot forward half its own length, pulling the bike away from under the biker's backside. Cursing, the man sat on the ground briefly before remounting his bike. He needed our tow badly, so he elected to stick with us. That particular tow job certainly was easy on our Jagdpanzer IV's transmission, although it was hard on the guy that landed on the road.

More than anyone else in the crew, a Jagdpanzer IV driver was responsible for keeping the vehicle in top mechanical condition. One of his just rewards–a very tangible reward, indeed–for his hard work was that he was never required to stand, or sit, any two-hour watches in the fighting compartment when the vehicle was, shall we say, parked for the night between engagements. Almost all experienced tank drivers, enjoyed, within their units, a fair measure of fame, much of which they acquired by means of their virtuosity with their well-cared-for manual transmissions.

CHAPTER 15

The Jagdpanzer IV in Winter Warfare in West Prussia

Our unit–*8. Kompanie, Panzer Regiment 25, 7. Panzer-Division*–received its first, and last, Jagdpanzer IVs in early January of 1945 in West Prussia for use, shortly thereafter, at the front in the Bischofswerder area, about 300 km west southwest of Leipalingis in Lithuania.

The 7th Panzer Division in World War II, pages 433–34 states:

> On December 23 [1944] 17 new Panzer IVs arrived for the 2nd Battalion of the 25th Panzer Regiment, and on January 10 [1945] ten new long-barrelled Panzer IVs [L–70-gunned Jagdpanzer IVs]. The latter are only an expedient because they have no traversable turret, so that the cannon has only a small zone of fire. However, the 2nd Battalion of the Panzer Regiment is now completely equipped with Panzers [and Jagdpanzers].

Please see Appendix D for technical details of each of these two vehicles.

Beginning a major offensive all along the front from the Baltic Sea to the Carpathian Mountains on January 12, 1945, the Soviets launched, as one of many, a thrust that began at Rozan, a highways junction on the Narew River, about 75 km north northeast of Warsaw. This basically north-westward thrust continued, via Mlawa and Bischofswerder, to a point on the Vistula River, about 65 km south of Danzig.

The total length of the thrust from Rozan to the Vistula was about 215 km; the distance from Rozan to Bischofswerder, about 150 km. An entry in my tank battles log shows that we met the Soviets at Bischofswerder on January 22, 1945.

Actually, we had been in action against the Soviets in West Prussia as early as January 15, three days after they had undertaken the particular thrust that we became caught up in. In fact, my log shows three engagements for January 15, 1945: Trzciniec, Porzowo, and Vw. Osiec.

West Prussia was bitter cold, 'Eastern cold' in the winter. Like the Panzerkampfwagen IVs, the Jagdpanzer IVs had absolutely no heating in them.

If the Jagdpanzer IVs were cold at that time of year, so were our various billets. Imagine searching for a couple of tables of roughly equal height, and then trying to sleep on top of them, just to get off the ice-cold, often earthen, floor. Never a mattress. Perhaps a bit of straw. A jacket in lieu of a blanket. For months, I had cold sores just above my upper lip.

1944 names given, with present names in brackets where different

Danzig ●

Graudenz (Grudziadz) ✠ ✠ Lessen (Lasin)

Poznan ●

Berlin ●

WEST PRUSSIA

● Warsaw

Gut D-Selice (Sulislawice) ✠
Porzowo (Podgorz) ✠

Bischofswerder (Biskupice)

Krakow ● ✠

Prague ●

Vw. Osiec (Osieczany) ✠
✠ Trzciniec (Trzciana)
✠ Borze (Brzesku)

Vienna
● Bratislava

Map 4   Tank Battles in West Prussia 1945

To this day, I am thankful for the toque and the reversible winter uniform that were issued to us. If this same winter wear were available today, I would hurry to buy some.

The toque, a sleeve of field-grey woollen material open at both ends, was worn by being pulled on over the head, one end around the neck, the other around the face. No steel helmet was required to put it under. Instead, each of us wore it partly over his black field service cap.

Completely reversible, the two-piece winter uniform, especially, was our salvation. Mouse-grey on one side and white on the other, the jacket and trousers were of a comfortable fit and warm, and were worn over our black uniforms. The jacket even had a hidden, adjustable waist belt and a drawstring at the bottom edge. The trousers had sewn-in braces of white webbing, adjustable to one of three positions.

Dressed thus, although still not adequately, we didn't have to resort to keeping, or trying to keep, ourselves warm by placing old newspapers and straw between our long underwear and uniforms, as the winter troops in the east had been advised to do before the reversible winter uniform was first issued in the winter of 1942–1943.

Sadly, our footwear was a different matter. Ordinary uninsulated lace-style boots was what we wore throughout the winter, just as during the rest of the year. We never were given the special heavy-duty winter footwear of compressed and moulded felt, or of a combination of thick felt and leather. True, they were bulky, and no one would have wanted to wear, inside a Jagdpanzer IV, footwear still bulkier, like the insulated overboots for sentries, made of the thickest of felt, open at the back, and stepped into with one's regular boots, then buckled shut. However, the high, leather-trimmed felt boots looked damned appropriate for our job, and would have served us well, along with the reversible winter uniform and the toque.

Poorly designed, overly loose winter clothing could have killed us. We had to live with the manhole-size hatches in the roof the Jagdpanzer IV. Slipping into, and out of, manholes were not for clothes-obese individuals, just as it never was for potbellied blokes.

Serving as the prelude to actual winter warfare – or was it already part of the warfare? – was the waiting in hedgehog position night after night, always one man in the vehicle, in a succession of West Prussian hamlets. One night, the son of a bitch who was supposed to relieve me just didn't show up, making me do four hours straight in the ice box.

We were becoming nicely acquainted with our Jagdpanzer IVs, but we always had some concern about how the baptism of fire–not ours, but that of the Jagdpanzer IV–would go. We knew what the Panzerkampfwagen IV's 7.5-cm *KwK* 40 L/48 was capable of. We wanted to find out how the Jagdpanzer IV's 7.5-cm *KwK* 42 L/70 would perform. All we could do until the day, the hour, the minute and the second of the test was move about a bit.

All that waiting took place before January 15, 1945.

Trzciniec, Porzowo and Vw. Osiec: On One Day, Three Encounters with Soviet Anti-Tank Forces

On that sub-zero January 15, something extraordinarily strange happened to us: we encountered Soviet anti-tank guns and Soviet tank-killing troops which were, no doubt, in the area to help repel an expectable German counterattack at Bischofswerder. Our first counterattack in a long time.

Instead of accompanying their front-line tanks, Soviet anti-tank guns generally followed behind, albeit not much later. Therefore, our Panzer men had not run into Soviet anti-tank guns at our front lines in that part of Europe.

When our Jagdpanzer IV–the first of three such tank killers in our group–rounded a bend in a sideroad well after daybreak on January 15, I was surprised to see, about 50 m ahead of us, a Soviet soldier running obliquely across the snow-covered road. He carried, on the shoulder of his padded winter jacket, a single shell, probably the kind used in their T–34/ 76. Were we close to an anti-tank barrier?

We certainly did not stop our Jagdpanzer to investigate. Well memorized by us, our relevant Panzer tactics flatly prohibited such stupidity. Instead, we hurriedly withdrew to a point well back of the bend in the road.

The Soviets' splendid workhorse 7.62-cm heavy anti-tank gun–the German Army converted and used all of them that they captured–was easily camouflaged. The top edge of its shield was about one metre above ground level, or about the height of the average man's navel. The gun's maximum range with high-explosive fragmentation (HE) ammo was about 13,500 m. Traverse was 60 degrees, and elevation was minus 6 degrees to plus 25 degrees. A hellishly efficient weapon. Its armour penetration was 98 mm at 500 m. The Jagdpanzer IV's frontal armour had a thickness of 80 mm.

Our Panzer tactics demanded that, in the kind of situation we were confronted with, we observe the following three rules:

1. When facing anti-tank weapons at long or medium distance, first return fire before moving against them. First, halt to return fire effectively, and then commit the bulk of the company to move against them whilst leaving one platoon to give supporting fire.

2. If anti-tank weapons are encountered at close range, it is suicide to stop! Only immediate aggressive attack at full speed and with all guns firing can be successful and reduce losses.
3. In action against anti-tank guns, never allow a single platoon to attack alone, even with strong covering fire. Anti-tank guns are not deployed singly. Remember, lone tanks in Russia are lost!

In addition, we had to observe another tactic, this one regarding a Panzer's entry into a developed area. To avoid becoming a sitting duck on a road near a village, our Jagdpanzer IV had to take advantage of a diversion, or of diversions. So, each of our two fellow Jagdpanzer IVs, ready to fire HE, would position itself at its chosen side of the place. It was their job, too, to interdict Soviets wanting to head out of the hamlet, possibly towards the next group of houses.

We knew, for sure, that our HE fire, which probably could not be precise because the target would not be distinct, might not kill the entire standard Soviet anti-tank gun crew of five. Wounded or not, some crewman could aim and fire the still-loaded gun. Accurate AP fire, on the other hand, would surely destroy the anti-tank gun. However, hitting a relatively low, well-camouflaged target would be chancy. Besides, there probably were two or more Soviet anti-tank guns in the vicinity of where I had seen the ammo lugger running. The German Army's standard practice for a Panzer engaging an anti-tank gun was to fire AP and HE rapidly and alternately.

Allowing our other two Jagdpanzer IVs to do their parts in accordance with our tactical rules, our Jagdpanzer IV shot two 7.62-cm heavy anti-tank guns and their crews all to hell. Each of the Soviets' guns had fired but one shot, after which they were spotted against the snowy background. Soon, we drove into Trzciniec, the first of three localities which, according to our map of the area, lay close together, and which were of interest to us.

Our tactics for getting into the next hamlet, named Porzowo, were the same. However, instead of anti-tank guns, there were Soviet soldiers standing around, at least two dozen of them. Apparently, they had not been alarmed by the cannon fire a short time earlier. Since our three Jagdpanzer IVs did not have the manpower to escort prisoners who had surrendered, we used our radio to summon armoured infantry, called *Panzergrenadiere*, who would, no doubt, arrive in their armoured halftracks. For the time being, we ordered the Soviets, with their officers well separated from the other ranks, to stand, with their hands clasped behind their heads, in front of what was probably the largest shack in the hamlet. Our Jagdpanzer IVs had their MG42s trained on the bunch. The whole lot of those fellows knew better than to try to outdraw three MG42s that could each spit out up to 1,500 rounds per minute.

In some of the houses, we found various kinds of infantry anti-tank weapons, among them at least a couple of dozen German hollow-charge *Panzerfausts*, or 'Armoured Fists', of three types: 30-m range, 60-m range and 100-m range. Each type was supposed to be able to exceed its stated range by 50 percent.

A couple of dozen empty vodka bottles indicated that Molotov cocktails were to be concocted there. It was the sort of weapon which, after it was made, did not lend itself to being transported over great distances.

Also of German origin were the stacks of anti-tank mines, with rolls of washline-like cord close by. Tied to the first of, say, a string of four or five anti-tank mines, the cord would serve to pull them, when needed, across a road. Using the mines in such a manner spelled mobility for the tank-killing troop. There was no need for it to dig into the frozen ground to lay the mines. Also, friendly traffic could be let through by withdrawing the mines.

There were also about 15 PPSh Soviet submachine guns with their 71-round ammunition drums. Not much later, when the armoured infantry arrived in two halftracks, they expressed their special appreciation for the submachine guns and the thousands of rounds of ammo that went with them.

Contrary to the fact that they had surrendered, our Soviet prisoners had, very likely, been trained extensively in the destruction of German armoured vehicles. In view of the overall quality of their equipment, we were surprised not to find any *Hafthohlladungen*, funnel-like hollow charges with a powerful magnet at the end of each of three spacing extensions welded, 120 degrees apart, to the outer edge of the cone. The wide part of the cone was about the diametre of the span of a man's hand. The whole thing had to be planted on enemy armour, making sure that two of the magnets lined up horizontally close to the uppermost part of the funnel, and that one magnet was close to the bottom. Applied that way, the hollow charge, which could defeat 180 mm-thick armour, was unlikely to shake loose and drop away from its armoured victim, especially if the victim was moving. The *Hafthohlladung* had a 7½ -second delay fuse.

Those tank busters–that's what the captured Soviets had to be–had three Soviet-manufactured Jeep-like GAZ cars with trailers. Except for their anti-tank guns, these chaps would be highly mobile. Oddly enough, the snow on the single road through the hamlet showed no tyre tracks. Right there, in Porzowo, the experts had been lying low, no doubt for days.

With our infantry in charge at Porzowo, we still had to capture the third hamlet, Vw. Osiec. A German abbreviation, possibly, *Vw.* means *Verwaltung* (administration); perhaps some German administration had been stationed there.

Again, the tactic of distracting any welcoming committee waiting for us at the entrance to the place worked well for us, and we moved our Jagdpanzer IVs down the road inside the hamlet, at the other end of which stood two 7.62-cm anti-tank guns with the barrel of one of them pointing, more or less, our way. When we arrived at the guns, we saw tracks in the snow that told us that the Soviet crew, or crews, had manhandled that gun's some 3,800 pounds, trying to put it into position to fire at us. As things stood, the crews, with their hands held high, stood nearby, but far enough from what had been their guns to keep them from acting foolishly. Our MG42s saw to that.

On the whole, it looked as though the Soviets were, at that stage, using outlying anti-tank guns to cover their storage facilities in Porzowo.

It was senseless for the two halftracks, which had remained in Porzowo to be loaded with the booty found there, to try to tow away the two captured anti-tank guns. Who would want to use such guns in the highly fluid situation in which the 25th Panzer Regiment found itself? Therefore, we destroyed both guns and their ammo.

On our way back to the terrain closer to the highway, we delivered two anti-tank gun crews to the armoured infantry, and destroyed the GAZ cars. The Soviets were lucky; they were being treated humanely at a time when both sides disliked taking prisoners.

Although our L/70s had performed well against anti-tank guns, we would have to fight full-fledged Soviet armour to find out what our gun's ultimate qualities were.

Throughout the years since that exceptional day, I have often wondered if our three Jagdpanzer IVs were dispatched to the three villages in response to a request from Divisional Intelligence. What we found there looked like a lot more than pure luck. We have to remember that a German counterattack did begin the area on January 22.

Borze: Three Jagdpanzer IVs Capture a Soviet Rocket Launcher

At daybreak on January 16, we were informed that a message, radioed a few minutes earlier from a unit of armoured infantry to our Panzer unit, pertained to a Soviet BM–13–16 rocket launcher that was moving westward on the east-west highway, termed *Rollbahn*, on which trucks and other military vehicles rolled to and from the front-line area. Maybe the armoured infantry from whom the alert came included the fellows who had inherited the Soviet submachine guns the day before.

The BM–13–16 was a truck-mounted rocket launcher; its carrier was, therefore, not a cross-country vehicle. The *16* in BM–13–16 meant that the launcher had 16 launch rails, each of which could be loaded with an M–13 rocket, whose fragmentation warhead had a maximum range of 8,000 to 8,500 m. Other types of M–13 warheads included AP, used to break up tank formations, and flares for night illumination, as well as incendiary and signal. Each M–13 rocket had a 132-mm diametre, and a length of 1.41 m. Its propellant weighed 7.2 kg, and its explosive 4.9 kg. Overall, it weighed 42.5 kg. Loading the rockets onto the rails of the BM–13–16 launcher took place after the launcher had been moved into position for firing.

The BM–13–16 launcher had no traverse and only limited elevation adjustment, and was laid by pointing the carrier vehicle towards the target. Actually, the launcher's elevation could be adjusted between 15 and 45 degrees. At 15 degrees, the range was 3 km; at 45 degrees, it was at its maximum.

Half a year earlier, the restricted elevation had led to a very unusual incident involving a BM–13–16 launcher and a couple of Panzer IVs. The crews of those Panzer IVs, believing that the truck carrying the BM–13–16 launcher couldn't leave the highway for the purpose of lining up rockets to fire at their vehicles, felt that they could, under the circumstances, never be harmed by M–13 rockets. Well, their reasoning was by no means correct. Suddenly, the front wheels of the truck were purposely steered into the fairly deep ditch at the side of the highway. Of course, that gave the entire launcher a much lower angle of elevation–maybe not an angle of depression, but a lower angle of elevation. Just before the truck changed direction, some of the rocket launcher's crew must have hoisted an M–13 rocket onto each of the lowest rails on the far side of the launcher. Without covering the windshield of the truck, the Soviets were ready to fire those war rockets. Damned if they didn't let fly their quartet of M–13s. Ultrafast, those rockets streaked not far above the Panzer IVs standing perhaps 200 m off the highway. In the end, the Panzer IV crews involved could recount how they used AP and HE, in that order, to kill the maverick BM–13–16. They also got a BM–13–16 ammo resupply truck.

With that anecdote in mind, our Jagdpanzer IV crews wanted to meet a BM–13–16, called *Stalinorgel* (Stalin's organ) by the German soldiers.

Of course, it was winter and all the ditches were full of snow-covered ice. We would, however, still have to be very wary. A launcher in the Bischofswerder area surely prefigured a fray big enough for the Soviets to call in a weapon of such might, which could swamp, in a period of less than ten seconds, a large area with high explosive. If we could help it, we would prevent the launcher already out on the highway from doing its dirty work in the very near future. We, in three Jagdpanzer IVs, were off to Borze, expecting to intercept the launcher there–at, or on, the highway.

At Borze, we went into hiding alongside some deserted farm buildings about 100 m south of the highway. After a while, there it was! The launcher, under a tarpaulin, was carried on a 2½-ton 6x6 truck, undoubtedly obtained by the Soviets under Lend-Lease, which sent them tens of thousands of American trucks. Also in the convoy were other trucks, surely loaded with various types of rockets for the launcher. It was not an entire launcher battery. At the head of the column were two T–34/85s.

Before we made up our minds to fire at the launcher and its accompanying tanks and trucks, I couldn't help thinking about the crews of the out-of-fuel T–34s that we had easily destroyed at the *Zembre-Bach* in Lithuania half a year earlier. Then it hit me: could we not capture the BM–13–16 and its attendant vehicles intact? We could kill the two T–34/85s and machine-gun a couple of the trucks immediately ahead of the launcher, causing them to burn. In the absence of Soviet air cover, we could probably force the launcher crew to abandon its truck, its launcher, and what was left of its rockets. We could then take the works into Bischofswerder; there, the artillery experts could take over. Our crew commander, Sergeant Starke, liked the idea. He let his two colleagues know via radio. Before all that could happen, we would ask the armoured infantry to assist us. We figured they were not far away.

It was high time for us to create a traffic jam big enough to stop the launcher, carrier and all. Amazing, the way our L/70s did away with the T–34/85s, and how those MG42s, firing lots of tracer bullets caused the Soviets to scramble out of the two targeted trucks just ahead of the one carrying the launcher. Each of the T–34/85s was very likely destroyed by AP shot that penetrated the low part of the side of its cast-steel turret. Cast steel was not as strong as rolled steel. After some hesitation, the launcher crew alighted, as did other Soviets. They all vanished into thin air as if they heard us commandingly shout, "*Verschwinde, wie der Furz im Winde!*" (Vanish, like a fart in the wind!) We had the *Stalinorgel* and other vehicles, but we still had to get them into Bischofswerder. Thank God that some of the infantry gents volunteered to drive the vehicles into town.

The armoured infantry at Borze was the same bunch that had helped us the day before. Their share of the booty from Porzowo, especially the Soviet submachine guns, made them very chummy.

The fact that we captured the rocket launcher in daylight on January 16 indicates that the Soviets were in a hurry to get it to the Bischofswerder area. Otherwise, they would have transported it at night. Had there been much more traffic on the highway at Borze that day, we could not have captured the launcher.

The 7th Panzer Division's Counterattack at Bischofswerder

The 7th Panzer Division in World War II, page 438, tells us that the Division, having arrived at Bischofswerder on January 22, began its counterattack south of Deutsch-Eylau, which lay 15 km northeast of Bischofswerder. Therefore, it is likely that the counterattack originated about 10 km east of Bischofswerder. At any rate, according to an entry in my tank battles log, I, on January 22, fought at Bischofswerder.

General Hasso von Manteuffel, a former commander of the 7th Panzer Division and the author of the above work, writes, on page 438, "The [25th] Panzer Regiment ... in these days [at the start of the counterattack] again had more than 20 Panzers in action." That number may have included Jagdpanzer IVs, although there was an important difference between them and the Panzer IVs, or the Panthers of the Regiment's 1st Battalion. All along, it was understood that the Jagdpanzer IV worked best from an ambush, and that, because it had no 360-degree main-gun traverse, it was less effective out in the open than the Panzer IV.

General von Manteuffel also writes, on pages 438–39, "In the encounter with the enemy southwest of Deutsch-Eylau on January 23, a tank-versus-tank battle ensues ... 13 Panzers were–it turns out later–surrounded because of lack of fuel, and were, after firing all their ammunition, blown up, and the crews overpowered by the enemy." That loss of the majority of our Regiment's Panzers blunted the Division's counterattack, reducing it to a two-day effort.

George Nafziger states, in *The German Order of Battle: Panzers and Artillery in World War II,* page 69, "In a major battle on 23 January 1945 near Deutsch Eylau the 25th Panzer Regiment engaged the Russians with 20 combat vehicles against 200. It was obliterated ... "

Because of the importance of Bischofswerder to the history of the 25th Panzer Regiment, I have chosen to rely, this far in my story, largely on the above two sources. What follows is the record of my own experience at Bischofswerder.

I remember that on January 22 we Jagdpanzer IV crews, without having been informed that we would not be fighting at the focal point of the counterattack, sensed that we would very likely see action somewhere at its fringe. There, the battle could, however, easily be as intense as at the midst of the counterattack. As was the norm, developed in the course of our long retreat from the Lida area, each of our Jagdpanzer crews could be expected to fight on its own to the greatest extent.

Our first concern was to find an ambush, a concealed site, close to which we would, very likely, have the opportunity to surprise Soviet armour. Primarily, our Jagdpanzer IVs were tank killers; so were we, their crews.

We drove our Jagdpanzer IV into the abandoned flat agricultural area about five km east of the town of Bischofswerder. Because the ground was frozen, we couldn't consider the hull-down mode of going into position. Therefore, we decided to hide our Jagdpanzer IV and ourselves in a large barn with thick walls of stone and large doors. Behind the barn was a large orchard into which we could, if necessary, escape. For that, its rows of trees were sufficiently far apart. We did not want to position our Jagdpanzer IV inside that orchard, or at the edge of it.

From inside our frigid Jagdpanzer IV in the barn—we kept one of its large doors open—I, using my main gun's telescopic sight, surveyed the large sector of snow-bound land to the east of our position. In doing so, I envisioned Soviet armour sneaking westward after travelling to some point south of our Division's counterattack. Thereafter, that same armour would move northward to get to the rear of our eastbound Panzers. Those sneaky Soviet tanks would probably be our targets on their way westward.

At midday, I could see, well within the field of view of my main gun's sight, one Soviet SU–85, a dedicated tank killer, moving nearly head-on, or at about zero degrees, to us at a distance of at least half a km. It was the first SU–85 that we encountered in all of our travels. In January of 1945, the Soviets no longer had many SU–85s in the field. Since the winter of 1943–1944, they were using newly produced 85-mm guns for their T–34/85 tanks.

Seeing an SU–85 in the area in which we stood could have meant, as far as mobile battle was concerned, that the Soviets rated their SU–85 much the same as our Division rated its Jagdpanzer IVs. The SU–85, too, was handicapped by the limited traverse of its main armament.

Only I was inside our Jagdpanzer IV when I spotted the SU–85. First thing, I called Sergeant Starke, our crew commander, to tell him what was going on. He got aboard fast. Hearing what I told Starke, Seppel, our loader, jumped on board and slid onto his seat to the right of me, at the other side of the gun's breech. Whenever the possibility of an encounter with the enemy arose, the loader was no longer the crew's gopher. He was, instead, the man who loaded the main gun with the specified types of ammo. In action, the gunner couldn't do without his loader, at least not after the first round had been fired.

Our driver and our wireless operator also appeared at their stations. To be fully effective, we needed everyone in the crew at his place.

Next, with the SU–85 coming closer, I quickly did something basic. I calculated the SU–85's range:

1½ point intervals, each of 4 mils = 5 mils

5 mils = 3 m
1 mil = 3 ÷ 5 =.60 m
.60 x 1,000 = 600 m

The range would, of course, change, but 600 m was okay for a start. We would use AP, with which our gun was already loaded. The SU–85's frontal approach did not require lead.

If the SU–85 didn't veer off to either side, it would be best for me to get our first round to hit the front of it dead centre, provided it wasn't carrying 50 cm-wide track links fastened there as armour reinforcement. A weak spot was the area close to either side, or at the top or bottom, of the hatch incorporated into the SU–85's frontal armour to the left of its cannon. Placing an AP projectile close to the edge of any hatch in an armoured vehicle resulted in 15 percent better penetration. Another thing: on the SU–85, the gun's ball mantlet was of cast steel, which was known to be 15 percent weaker than rolled steel. A hit the width of one's hand below the bottom of the SU–85's gun mantlet would do a lot more than deprive its gun of its vertical or lateral movement. On the whole, though, the SU–85's 45 mm-thick frontal armour worked in our favour. Ours measured 80 mm. Frontal fire was trickier than fire at the side or rear of the enemy. A Panzer, or Jagdpanzer IV, gunner had to use his knowledge of weak spots a lot faster than it takes to write it down.

Aiming our main gun–it was designed to enable the German heavy medium Panzer V, or Panther, to drive an AP projectile through 14 cm of enemy armour–at the area just below the SU–85's ball mantlet; I pulled the trigger, firing the electric fuse of the shell in the breech.

Immediately, I saw, a closer 400 m away, a flash on the SU–85's frontal glacis, indicating a hit. I quickly let it have another AP through its front. No one had shown up at, or on, the roof the SU–85, where the crew hatches were. The thing didn't seem to be burning. Maybe some of the crew had still been alive.

There, at last, the smoke of burning diesel fuel, confirmation of the destruction of a Soviet SU–85. I believe its crew never knew of our location in the dimness inside the barn. Should we relocate or not? One knocked-out SU–85 couldn't necessarily betray our position inside the barn, especially if we closed its door partially. No Soviet crew commander would suspect the presence of German armour behind a barn door that wasn't open far enough to allow a full field of view. So, we stayed in the barn. We could always open the door completely if we got further company courtesy of the Soviets.

For hours, we waited in vain that barn. We had time to reminisce regarding the effectiveness of our 7.5-cm L/70. Just before sundown, Starke used our radio to call the three Jagdpanzer IVs that had to be in the area. Where, exactly, we didn't know. We hadn't heard any tank-gunfire at all. However, Starke's buddies told him that they had some success. Above, all, none of their Jagdpanzer IVs had been damaged in any way.

All night long, there in that barn, all of us, except our driver, took turns sitting, one man at a time, inside our Jagdpanzer IV. Damned, was it cold! Seppel and Karlchen, our wireless operator, searched the farmhouse in vain for anything that looked like a blanket or a comforter left behind by the Germans who had vacated the farm.

In the morning–it was January 23–Starke radioed the other three Jagdpanzer IVs to arrange for a rendezvous, which, all of us attended.

At Gut D.-Sedice, Our L/70 7.5-cm Gun Gave Us Excellent Results– Luckily Before Its Mount Was Accidentally Ruined

To show you again how well the L/70 did work for us, I will next go to our third-last engagement with the Soviets, namely the one on January 23 at Gut D.-Sedice. *Gut*, short for *Gutshof*, means *estate* or *farm*. Possibly, *D.* stands for *Deutsch*.

Not one of our West Prussian engagements, by the way, was fought in town. The T–34s didn't have to use the roads, of which there were many. They took to the frozen fields; so, naturally, did we.

At least one of the three Soviet crew commanders who directed their T–34/85s westward across some of the wintry fields near Gut D.-Sedice may have thought that the farm buildings ahead would give him and his men, and their accompanying infantry, shelter and warmth during a break. The three T–34s were obviously travelling together.

Our fire caused, first, the T–34 closest to the right side of our field of view to erupt in flames. Next, the centre T–34 was hit. Finally, the third T–34, the one farthest left in our field of view, was on fire. Possibly one man, for sure badly burned, managed to get out of the middle tank. I last saw him sitting at the edge of the crew commander's hatch, kicking downward, as though trying to free himself from a tackler. There was no sign of others leaving any of the three T–34s.

Across the white fields, the wicked wind blew and blew, and, from the silenced T–34s, the black smoke poured and poured.

Minutes later, our Jagdpanzer IV still stood, framed, left and right, by the corners of two outbuildings about six metres apart. The West Prussian quadrangle–a farmhouse, a barn, and two sheds, all bordering a farmyard–had been as good a place as any at which to wait for Ivan. Rather than confine ourselves to a single, camouflaged blind, we wanted to see where he was coming from, and then drive into position and fire at him.

Although ours was the only Jagdpanzer IV at that deserted farm, there was a squad of German infantry somewhere inside the four buildings. Their Sergeant had spoken briefly with our crew commander, Sergeant Starke, right after we had arrived there.

Starke, no luminary, was a quiet, honest man of about 30 who would, it was known, go along with his gunner's ideas. He had, for instance let me decide which T–34 of the three to do away with first; in doing so, he, like me, hadn't considered the direction of the stiff wind. He was far from being critical, though.

Blowing from our right, the wind had, for less than a minute, carried a screen of relatively thin initial smoke from the burning knocked-out T–34 over to the other two T–34s. That veil of smoke had made it rather hard for me to aim, quickly and surely, our main gun at those two intact Soviet tanks still facing us.

We had done very well with just a few shells. Our three kills, 300 m distant and much too close abreast for their own good, stood burning in the white field. No 24251E Jagdpanzer IV at Sedice would do better that day. For one thing, there were only four, including ours, in the area.

Being crammed between two buildings was like wearing huge blinkers. We could observe what was going on in the fields ahead of us, but we couldn't see what was happening elsewhere close by. We hadn't poked our nose out past the corners any farther than necessary to deal with the T–34s. We hadn't seen the white-camouflaged Soviet infantry approaching the farmyard–and us–from a field much farther to our left.

One of the infantry Sergeant's men had been sent to let us know what was developing. We pulled back, first getting our ass end into the yard, and then slowly following with the Jagdpanzer IV's mid section, where the crew commander's periscopes projected from the roof. Starke was going to size up the situation, especially to the left of us.

What Starke saw was Soviets dodging about the premises, with more of them ready to throng in from the field. That's where a 360-degree turret would have been much better than a traverse limited to 20 degrees. He decided to get the driver to pull back still farther, turn around, and, taking our infantrymen with us, leave the yard by driving past the farm-house.

The big trouble was that the far end of our L/70 hadn't yet cleared the corner of the building to our left when the driver, acting on Starke's order, ripped 'er 'round to the left. The collision caused by that mistake heaved our main gun entirely out of whack.

Our L/70s mount ruined; we had all the more reason to leave D.-Sedice immediately, but not without our footsloggers. Between them and us it was a matter of one hand washes the other or, simply, cooperation. They knew how to deal with the Soviet infantry, just as we knew how to deal with Soviet tanks.

The Sergeant and his squad had been dropped off at the farm about two hours before we showed up, and their half-track APC, or armoured personnel carrier, had driven off. We had noticed tracks which the APC had left in the ankle-deep snow. There was no transportation, other than our Jagdpanzer IV, to take the squad away from the developing mess.

Despite the urgency of the situation, the men all displayed the self-assurance of experienced fighters. Most of their weapons were of the latest kinds, such as an MG42 and half a dozen StG44s, or assault rifles. There were also a couple of 98k bolt-action rifles for work at longer ranges. Their automatic fire, mainly, assisted our MG42 in keeping the farmyard and buildings hosed down.

All of them used our Jagdpanzer IV as a shield until after we had left the place. Then, the Sergeant made sure that his men had clambered aboard before joining them in sitting on our fairly smooth painted steel roof measuring 3.94 m in length by 2.76 m in width, or 10.87 square metres.

Our only requests to our passengers were that, if possible, they stay clear of the periscopes, that none of them get their trousers sucked off their asses by cooling air rushing through the air intake louvers and that others not get their balls cooked by the hot air expelled through the exhaust louver.

Starke had our driver backtrack the APC on the advice of the infantry's Sergeant, who was correct in saying that it would be a sure way out, considering, for instance, the sturdy bridges he had seen while in the APC.

For the nine-man squad it was, I am certain, a case of better to experience a bad ride than a good walk. The boys who rode up there should have gotten Adolf to holler to the world about their having insufficient *Lebensraum* (space in which to live) atop a Jagdpanzer IV.

Thinking about January 23, 1945, I still wonder whether that squad helped us get away from that farm next to the frozen field with the three blistering-hot T–34s on it, or whether we were the ones who did the helping. It was good for us, at any rate that the infantrymen were there. Equally good, for them, was that our Jagdpanzer IV was mobile–despite the loss of its damned good 7.5-cm *KwK* 42 L/70.

That gun on something more like a Panzerkampfwagen IV would have been the ticket.

In the afternoon of January 23, we, and the other three Jagdpanzer IVs, which had destroyed a total of five T–34s not far from Sedice, rendezvoused with two officers and several men from our Regimental HQ. Travelling in the company of our largely intact Panzer repair unit, they had managed to stay ahead of Ivan.

The HQ fellows and the workshop personnel were in touch with our Regiment and our Division by radio.

We didn't have to blow up our Jagdpanzer IV. The following day, when the tank workshop unit assumed responsibility for it, I learned that, because they couldn't get its main gun back into working order, they regarded that entire Jagdpanzer IV as spare parts. Actually, the workshop guys let on that they preferred to use it as a bulletproof means of transportation–at least for a while.

That same day, the Iron Cross 1st Class was, without benefit of a full awards ceremony, awarded to several of us Jagdpanzer IV crewmen who were holders of the Iron Cross 2nd Class. Whoever was not far enough advanced for the Iron Cross 1st Class got the Iron Cross 2nd. Paraded briefly in front of three Jagdpanzer IVs for the occasion, we stood in the snow, just above us the L/70 barrels of our trusted *KwK* 42s at maximum elevation.

Often, during a lull in the fighting, days or even weeks before a complete awards ceremony could be conducted in the presence of one's entire unit, a decoration was awarded, and documented quickly by means of a provisional certificate of award, usually in the form of a handwritten entry in one's paybook, with the entry signed by a senior officer, such as the C.O. of the Regiment and stamped. The formal certificate of award–typed, signed, and stamped–would be presented after things had quieted down. The paybook entry for an award was mandatory, no matter whether the decoration was awarded in a shortened ceremony or later.

Each of us got his Iron Cross–surprisingly, the medals, perhaps some of the last ones awarded within Panzer Regiment 25, were available–and the corresponding entry into his paybook. However, for us things never did settle down long enough for someone at Panzer Regiment 25 HQ to use the beat-up portable typewriter to fill in the certificates of award and have them signed by the C.O., and stamped. We Sedice guys never did receive the formal certificates for our Iron Crosses. We had to be satisfied with the entries in our paybooks.

By the next morning, it had become clear to us that Sergeant Starke and we, his crew, would have to join our Regiment's Panzer repairmen, at least temporarily, or hitch a ride with one of our intact Jagdpanzer IVs because they had lost contact with their unit, our foot soldiers were ordered to proceed westward aboard a Jagdpanzer IV or two. Surviving a whole string of actions against the Soviets along the way, their Regiment had managed to come to the Sedice area from the part of East Prussia that adjoined Lithuania.

Visualizing the seemingly foot-loose, but by no means defeated, fighters belonging to our Panzer Regiment who hung around the work-shop trucks and the three Jagdpanzer IVs that morning leads me to give the reader the following sketches of Sergeant Starke's four fellows.

Our oldest crew member, Fritz (Fritze) Keller, 22, was known to his buddies as the man who solicited favours from Russian and Ukrainian women in exchange for small black packs of wonderfully shiny sewing needles from Solingen. That's where he was from. Fritze was with our Regiment even before it, on its way westward from a point about 200 km southwest of Stalingrad, arrived in the Ukraine, where I first saw him.

Then there was, from Munich, Josef (Seppel) Huber, 20, who couldn't tolerate Ukrainian moonshine liquor called *somohon*. On one occasion, in our quarters in the southern Ukraine, Seppel urinated onto the earthen floor next to his bed, later leaving the imprints of his bare feet there upon arising.

Karl (Karlchen) Krapf, 21, after helping to clean up the soot caused by a quickly extinguished small electrical fire inside a Panzer IV, looked as though he had rubbed burned cork onto his face in preparation for a minstrel show.

I, wanting to wash my underwear in a nice clear Lithuanian creek in the summer of 1944, had tied it to the shore to let it soak in the water. For some reason, we had to leave the locale in a hurry, which kept me from retrieving my briefs and my undershirt. For a couple of weeks thereafter, wearing my scratchy pants without the briefs under them made me feel very uncomfortable in the hot weather.

Fritze, by the way, was our driver; Seppel, our loader; and Karlchen, our wireless man.

The Iron Cross First Class entry in my paybook proved to be of only relatively brief value to me because I had to surrender the book at a British Discharge Centre about six months after the end of the war. Then, its many entries–for instance, the dates of promotions in rank that I had received; the makes and models of the 9-mm pistols, with their serial numbers, that I had been issued; the medical shots that I had been given; the delousing facilities that I had visited; the awards that I had won; and the military hospitals that I had been confined to–were at once all lost.

In 1945, no one could, in an effort to retain a copy of such a fine bit of memorabilia, simply have the covers and pages of his paybook photo-copied.

Among the illustration presented in this book are the photocopies of the obverse and reverse of my Certificate of Discharge from the Army, dated October 24, 1945, which I received from the British in exchange for my paybook.

Soviet Armour Ambushed at the Lake at Lessen in West Prussia

My subchapter 'Soviet Armour Ambushed at the Lake at Lessen in West Prussia' became a great deal more significant for me when I later read, in General Hasso von Manteuffel's out-of-print 1986 book *The 7th Panzer Division in World War II*, pp. 438–39, the following two passages:

On January 22, the transfer to Bischofswerder takes place, from where the Division begins its counterattack south of Deutsch-Eylau. The Panzer Regiment, now under the command of Major von Petersdorff-Kampen, in these days again has more than 20 Panzers in action. In the encounter with the enemy southwest of Deutsch-Eylau on January 23, a tank-versus-tank battle ensues. From this engagement, Major v. Petersdorff-Kampen, the CO of Panzer Regiment 25, along with a number of officers and Panzer crews, does not return. 13 Panzers were–it turns out later–surrounded because of lack of fuel, and were, after firing all of their ammunition, blown up, and the crews overpowered by the enemy. A small number of the crews was able to bail out of their Panzers without being injured, and turned up at their unit after a few days. Along with Major von Petersdorff, the Lieutenants Rosskotten and Jakob were, among others, also killed in action.

On January 24, the Division is engaged in heavy defensive and withdrawal battles east of Graudenz, and on January 25 in the area southeast of Marienwerder. On January 26, the wheeled vehicles cross the Vistula over an ice bridge at Marienwerder, whereas the tracked [armoured] vehicles have to detour via Graudenz.

From the first passage above, I learned that on January 23, 1945, Lt. Jakob was killed in action. My own tank battles log shows an entry for that very date for a place called Gut D.-Sedice, certainly not far from where Lt. Jakob died. I have dealt with this tank battle in the previous subchapter, 'At Gut D.-Sedice, Our L/70 7.5-cm Gun Gave Us Excellent Results–Luckily Before Its Mount Was Accidentally Ruined'.

The second passage revealed to me that I was part of the rearguard ordered to protect the Division's tracked armoured vehicles crossing the Vistula at Graudenz from Soviet armour fast approaching that city from the east.

With the above preamble in mind, the reader, too, should arrive at a much greater appreciation of the following account.

Having written about our last certified tank-versus-tanks engagement with the Soviets, which took place on January 23, 1945, at Gut D.-Sedice, I realize that there are two other Jagdpanzer IV-related stories from a few days later which I must tell you before I get to the story of how I was wounded.

On January 24, the day on which we had bestowed our crippled Jagdpanzer IV upon our mechanics, one of the officers of 24251E, Lieutenant Krippendorf, needed a replacement for his gunner–like me, a Lance Corporal–who had been wounded by small-arms fire while standing close to their Jagdpanzer IV. As mentioned, 24251E was the field postal code of our unit, the *8. Kompanie, Panzer Regiment 25, 7. Panzer-Division.*

Being ordered to report to the Lt. did not make me unhappy. It was strictly a gunner's reputation within the Company that could get him employment in a hurry in a case like that–and my reputation had, so very recently, grown by virtue of the three T–34/85s that we had killed in a jiffy at Gut D.-Sedice.

Einsteigen, literally *to step in*, means, for instance, to get into an automobile. It also means to enter, as a burglar would, a dwelling. Then, too, it means, with regard to a tank or a Jagdpanzer, joining its crew. *Bei einem Kommandanten einsteigen* meant that one was going aboard an armoured vehicle as part of a commander's crew *auf Gedeih und Verderb* (for better or for worse).

In addition to the fact that I knew all of Lt. Krippendorf's congenial crew well, I had enjoyed serving in the Panzerkampfwagen IV of another officer, 2/Lt. Jakob, half a year earlier. I quickly became–for better, I felt, rather than for worse–a member of a crew that already had–or, better, still had–a Jagdpanzer IV.

Our crew commander was an experienced Panzer man. Regarding armour, that of friend or foe, he possessed a wealth of knowledge. We, his crew, were all specialists, each with regard to his own skill within the Jagdpanzer IV and then some. For instance, I held a *Wehrmacht* driver's licence for armoured, full-track vehicles.

Next day, on January 25, we, along with two other Jagdpanzer IVs also under the command of Lt. Krippendorf, found ourselves some 17 km west of Bischofswerder, very close to the highway that led westward directly to the Vistula River at Graudenz, a city about 39 km west of Bischofswerder and about 100 km south of Danzig. That road carried, from the east, many columns of modern Soviet armour, some of which we should, we hoped, be able to knock out, in true Jagdpanzer IV style, from an ambush.

Unchecked, Soviet armour, by travelling southwest from Graudenz, could quickly cover the 285 km to Frankfurt on the Oder River and, thereafter, the 83 km westward from Frankfurt an der Oder to the heart of Berlin.

Basically, the Lt.'s thinking regarding the use of our Jagdpanzer IVs was reminiscent of a well-known line–an ambusher's line–from the great German poet Friedrich von Schiller (1759–1805): "*Durch diese hohle Gasse muß er kommen.*" ('Through this narrow pass he has to come'.) For us, the singular pronoun *he* referred not to some person, but to a prospective prize which, for a change, might be a most modern Soviet heavy, such as one of the Joseph Stalin series. Prizes–as many as possible–was what we of course visualized.

Undoubtedly, Lt. Krippendorf knew that the IS–2 heavy tank, which had been put into service in April of 1944, weighed 46 tons, and could travel at 37 km/h maximum. Maximum road range 240 km. Maximum terrain range 210 km. Diesel engine of 600 hp. Hull front armour 120 mm. Turret front armour 160 mm. Length 9.91 m. Width 3.09 m. Height 2.73 m. A 12.2-cm main gun. Storage for 28 rounds of two-part, slow-loading main-gun ammunition. Armour-piercing, or AP, shot weight 25 kg. AP muzzle velocity 800 m/sec. One coaxial 7.62-mm machine gun. One 12.7-mm machine gun. Crew of four.

We crewmen realized that the IS–2 constituted a formidable adversary for the Jagdpanzer IV. Like our Lt., however, every one of us preferred, at that stage of the war, to chalk up victories over armour a lot heftier than the T–34/85. Still, we knew that we would have to deal with whatever Soviet armour happened to want to negotiate that proverbial narrow pass at Lessen in West Prussia.

Just as numerous Germanophiles of all social classes had all along been doing in other parts of Europe where fighting occurred in the Second World War, many German and pro-German West Prussians were at the time–early in 1945–assisting the German soldier. The Lessen area, too, had its share of German-speaking locals who readily gave us pointers regarding, for instance, the terrain, with which they had such great familiarity.

To give you an example of how long and how thoroughly West Prussia had been home to German and German-friendly souls, let me tell you that records in my possession show that in the late 1700s, more than 150 years before 1945, many of my mother's forebears, all Mennonites, lived in the Vistula lowlands of West Prussia at places like Marienwerder, about 25 km north-northwest of Lessen, and at Marienburg, about 56 km north of Lessen. Of course I had no opportunity early in 1945 to look for distant relatives in extant Mennonite communities in the area in which we operated. Mennonites from various parts of Western Europe had, by the way, settled in those lowlands along the Vistula since about 1530.

Some of my ancestors emigrated, in the early 1800s, from West Prussia to help establish Mennonite colonies in the Ukraine, where they multiplied, and their descendants prospering until the beginning of the First World War. My parents, for instance, grew up in a German-language Mennonite community about 50 km north of the western part of the Sea of Azov. In 1924, they emigrated from the Ukraine to Canada, where I was born in 1925.

It may not have come from some remote West Prussian cousin of a Panzer man born in Canada, but we did receive invaluable information about the area near the main highway at Lessen. We also got free lime to make whitewash, with which we coated the exteriors of our three Jagdpanzer IVs. Our vehicles had to be in perfect condition, even in appearance, for the job ahead.

The snow lay round about while, day and night, the frost was, as an old English Christmas carol describes it, cruel. We hoped that, after inflicting vast damage to the Soviets at Lessen, we would be able to stay inside warm billets for more than just an hour at a time. As it was, tending our almost albino vehicles kept us out in the cold for inordinately long periods.

Immediately to the south of the highway at Lessen, our topographical map told us, stretched a lake about 4.6 km long and between 0.4 and 0.75 km wide. Our best bet was to take up positions with that lake between the road and us, and with our guns directed northward, more or less, ready to fire across the lake. We would, we were certain, best sight slowed-down Soviet armour travelling just east of the town, and broadside to the direction in which our guns would be pointing. We would then shoot each target of ours through its relatively thin flank.

Concealed, largely, by brick-walled, lake-front farm buildings, our three Jagdpanzer IVs, once again operating without benefit of infantry support, would be invisible from the stretches of highway northeast and northwest of us, and practically invisible from the stretch to the north of us. We would conduct a clean ambush, followed by a quick getaway from the southern shore of the lake, the frozen surface of which could hardly be trusted to carry heavy armoured vehicles, so that any Soviet battle tanks wanting to kill us after we had fired our 7.5-cm L/70s would be deterred from venturing onto the ice. Yes, we would hit a column of Soviet armour fast and hard, and then slip away.

In carrying out the promising plan of ours for the ambush at Lessen, we would of course display a good measure of the audaciousness charac-teristic of the Panzer man. For sure, we had many audacious fighters, exemplified by Lt. Krippendorf, a man no one could, however, accuse of being overly reckless in action. He was not altogether a daredevil. His men all approved of his intrepid, yet level-headed, style of fighting.

With regard to our daring, we Panzer soldiers, frequently forced to risk our lives, had a great liking for an encouraging idea that is expressed most eloquently in the following couplet by Friedrich von Schiller: *"Und setzet ihr nicht das Leben ein, / Nie wird euch das Leben gewonnen sein."* (And if your life you will not bet, / Never will you your life as winnings get.) Partly reminiscent of those lofty words of Schiller, the following two lines were deemed by the Panzer men to be extraordinarily quotable: *"Wer nicht wagt, der nicht gewinnt; / Wer nicht vögelt, kriegt kein Kind."* (Whoever nothing ventures, nothing gains; / Whoever never screws, childless remains.)

Certainly, from those friendly West Prussian civilians we had received priceless information about the topography of the area. We had, above all, learned much from them about their roads and bridges, and about the farm buildings that would, to a great extent, keep our Jagdpanzer IVs from being spotted by the enemy at the other side of the lake.

At dawn on January 26, Lt. Krippendorf, accompanied by his two crew commanders, walked 100 metres up a gentle slope to the preferred farm buildings for some quick reconnaissance. Viewed from there through their binoculars, everything across the lake looked favourable for the accomplishment of our plan, they told us upon returning.

Just before both crew commanders left for their vehicles, Lt. Krippendorf ordered them to keep their radio receivers switched on, and to commence firing only after his Jagdpanzer IV had let fly.

Since the wind in our back was blowing in the direction of Lessen, approximately, we hoped that the noises prevailing there, mainly the engine roar of the Soviet vehicles moving on the highway would drown out the inevitable low-gear howl created by our three engines moving the Jagdpanzer IVs into positions.

Continuing to observe radio silence, we, as planned, jockeyed the Jagdpanzer IVs into hiding alongside several appropriate buildings in the light of early day, so that our guns would cover the highway at the eastern outskirts of Lessen. Very soon, I had my telescopic gunsight trained, at about 0 degrees traverse, on the imaginary narrow pass. I was preparing to get to work.

Cold and clear, the weather that morning was ideal for pinpoint shooting. Using my main gun's telescopic sight–it had 5x magnification, which gave me a 259 m field of view at 1,000 m, making it about 194 m at 750 m–to check the 750 m mandatory, I first observed that the six-metre length of a broken-down Opel Blitz truck standing at the near side of the highway subtended two full point intervals of the reticule. Thereupon, I, by means of the standard range-finding formula drilled indelibly into the mind of the Panzer gunner, mentally calculated the range as follows:

2 point intervals, each of 4 mils = 8 mils
8 mils = 6 m
1 mil = 6 ÷ 8 = 0.75 m
.75 x 1000 = 750 m

Finally, I set the sight's AP or armour-piercing, shell range scale at *750*. With that, I was–as far as range was concerned–ready for action. Calculating lead would have to wait until the Soviet armour showed up.

The English poet John Milton (1608–74), alluding to a spell of professional inactivity which he experienced as a young university graduate, wrote, "He also serves who stands and waits." This line applied to us 15 men as we endured the cold, silently waiting for our preferred targets to appear at the other side of the lake. Had Soviet aircraft been active in the area, we would have had reason to consider ourselves extremely vulnerable while standing, or lying, in wait. However, no enemy planes bothered us.

At about 9:20 a.m., the wished-for word quickened our intercom system. Crew Commander: "Attention! Lurking here is finally paying off. From the right, a proper convoy, consisting of two T–34/85s, then two Stalin 2s, and finally two further T–34/85s. Their point vehicle is now about 400 m from the edge of town. Speed fairly slow–about 15 km/h. Intervals approximately 25 m."

The death-dealing dialogue between the crew commander and his gunner had begun.

Gunner: "Understood! Let the blokes drive ahead, so that I get several of them into my gunsight."

At that point, because I already had their range, a verified 750 m, I quickly calculated the required lead, or aim-off, for AP for a target travelling at 90 degrees, or broadside, to our guns at 15 km/h. Performed mentally, the brief calculation, using *3*, a constant, as the first divisor–for the high-explosive shell the divisor would have been *2*–ran as follows:

15 km ÷ 3 = 5 mils
5 mils ÷ 4 mils = 1¼ point intervals

As long as the column maintained its speed at 15 km/h, every one of those six Soviet tanks required 1¼ point intervals of lead, with the main point of the reticule held that far ahead of the half of the target's length, and with zero set for navel height. Allowing a moving enemy tank's length of track in contact with the ground to skim any, or all, of the reticule points—it was called a six-o'clock hold—automatically put the main gun's zero a little more than halfway up the total height of that tank, namely 1.6 m above the reticule points, at the level of the imaginary navel of that tank.

Crew Commander: "Good! When the time comes, give the lead vehicle a solid punch. Simply fire at will."

Gunner: "Yes, sir! I already have the first T–34 in my reticule. Lead correct. Six-o'clock hold. Fire!"
Crew Commander: "Direct hit low in the turret! Next, knock out the first Stalin. You'd best drive one into his superstructure, directly below his turret. Take steady aim."

With their entire column suddenly stopped—the Soviets may even have thought they were up against remotely detonated concentrations of anti-tank mines—there was no further need to apply aim-off.

Gunner: "Hold six o'clock. Fire!"

Crew Commander: "Direct hit in the superstructure! There's smoke rising out of his paunch! He can never be patched up! The second Stalin, too, is already afire!"

Gunner: "What other damage can we inflict?"

Crew Commander: "The second-last T–34, right behind the second Stalin, apparently hasn't had enough yet."

Gunner: "Fire!"

Crew Commander: "Good hit! Right in the turret! Man, the Devil has fetched the entire column! No survivors to be seen! Cease firing!"

Gunner: "I'll continue to observe. Maybe something will still move."

Crew Commander: "Good. Switch on the transmitter!"

Wireless operator: "Transmitter and receiver ready for use!"
Lt. Krippendorf's next order, purposely terse and directed at the two crews with whom we had no visual contact because of their Jagdpanzer IVs' separate hidings, forced him to break radio silence for a moment.
Crew Commander: "*Feierabend! Feierabend!*"

Primarily, the word *Feierabend* means the tranquility and leisure of eventide. However, we Jagdpanzer IV crews instantly recognized *Feierabend* as part of a colloquial phrase, namely *Feierabend machen*, meaning, for instance, to call it quits instantly, to knock off work at once, or to cease a tank engagement right away. Heeding the *Wehrmacht*-wide warning that the enemy is listening in, Panzer crews using their radios generally resorted to colloquialisms, which the enemy would find much harder to understand than formal German.

Lt. Krippendorf's *"Feierabend! Feierabend!"* was, according to instructions he had issued earlier that morning, the code for "We're scramming fast now. Start engines. First, back up a hundred m, then turn around, and follow me."

We all rode away from those buildings immediately without, as far as we could tell, being pursued. We had not been shot at much, if at all. A clean ambush it was and a clean getaway.

Before we had turned them about, as well as after that, all three of our Jagdpanzer IVs were, I would say, driven with greater relish than any other vehicles of that type had ever been driven in West Prussia or, for that matter, anywhere on the German Eastern Front.

We were downright elated. The two IS–2s and the four T–34/85s killed on the highway just east of Lessen had reconfirmed the deadliness of the 7.5-cm L/70s of our Jagdpanzer IVs. Besides, the roads were, we knew, there for us south and west of the lake at Lessen, as were the bridges.

What troubled us more than just a little, though, as we covered km after km, was the columns of whirling snow whipped up by the six 40-cm-wide tracks of our three vehicles. Worse, still, was the fact that, wherever we drove, those same three pairs of all-steel tracks–each Jagdpanzer IV's pair was 2.05 m apart–left uninterrupted parallel ruts in the snow. Those furrows could easily help Soviet ground-attack aircraft pilots pinpoint our whereabouts and attack us, something their vengeful commanders might well order them to do.

Ivan certainly had to be utterly incensed about our having reduced a column of his armour to giant smoke pots–just before it got to Graudenz on its way westward.

Soldatenklau, and Anti-tank Mines at Graudenz

We knew that most of Graudenz lay on the eastern side of the Vistula River, and that its eastern outskirts were about 30 km west-southwest of where we had accomplished our ambush at Lessen. From Lessen, the main highway entered the northeastern part of Graudenz, and swung south not far from the Vistula, thereafter turning west, directly towards the big bridge which funneled the highway traffic across the river. Just to the south of that bottleneck lay the bridge for the main railway line.

After driving westward, largely, all the while staying south of the highway between Lessen and Graudenz, we, knowing that we would have to use the northernmost bridge to get across the water, entered Graudenz from the south on January 26. We saw a few German light anti-aircraft guns positioned at the southern part of the city's perimetre, and the closer we got to the eastern end of the bridge, the more anti-aircraft defences we passed. We were inside the ring of flak. For a spell, we would no longer have reason to fear being attacked by Soviet ground-attack aircraft.

I should explain that the pilots of the Soviet Ilyushin IL–2, or Shturmovik, ground-attack aircraft usually made use of either of their two favourite tactics when operating against a column of Panzers in the open. One tactic was to attack the column from astern, flying very low in a roughly circular path, firing anti-tank rockets and, if necessary, repeating the circular sweep before leaving the scene in the direction opposite to the one from which they had approached the Panzers. This tactic was known as the circle of death. The other tactic, termed the scissors, consisted of having several aircraft approach the Panzer column from astern at a low height, then widely weave–or zigzag, if you like–from one side of the column to the other, each aircraft firing its two 37-mm cannon. These tactics took advantage of the fact that a Panzer was much less heavily armoured at its sides than at its front, and that, broadside, each Panzer provided a larger target than did its front or its rear. What is more, the scissors tactic confused the few Panzer crew members who, outside of the Panzers, attempted to use hand-held machine guns as anti-aircraft weapons.

The *Army Service Manual No. 462: Anti-aircraft Use of the Machine Gun and the Rifle*, dated January 18, 1935, and in force throughout the Second World War, states, on page 92, that, when firing at an aircraft approximately 10 m in overall length, one should allow one aircraft length of lead for an aircraft flying at 250 km per hour, and five aircraft lengths of lead for one flying at 350 km per hour. Maximum speed of the Shturmovik, which had an overall length of 11.65 m., was 372 km per hour; therefore, the lead for it at that speed had to be, say, slightly more than five aircraft lengths. The above leads–the manual does not give the method of calculating lead, nor does it state the distance at which each lead applies–had to pertain to aircraft passing at 90 degrees to the direction of the machine gun or rifle fire.

Inside Graudenz, the buildings prevented the Soviet pilots from using either of the tactics referred to above. For sure, we didn't have to worry about Soviet ground-attack aircraft. Not in the city.

Close to the bridge at Graudenz, thousands of German soldiers, many with their vehicles and equipment, thronged. Untold numbers of refugees, old and young, most of them clutching their few possessions, crowded there. In all, a vast crowd, its members wanting to cross the bridge so as to put the ice-covered Vistula between themselves and the Soviets who were hounding them.

Some venturesome civilians, mostly those with relatively little to carry, walked, with unnaturally short steps, the ties of the railway bridge, undoubtedly hoping that no belated German train would make them abort their shortcut before they had gotten to the west bank of the Vistula–and to Pomerania.

We also saw the battered remnants of mechanized units, none of which belonged to the 7th Panzer Division, the one with the bold white capital Y painted onto its armour. Our Division hadn't yet arrived at the bridge.

It seemed as though we Panzer men would mentally forever be doing, out in the cold and a couple of blocks away from the bridge, what was called marking time. That is how we felt throughout the following night.

Well, shortly after sunrise on January 27, we three Jagdpanzer IV crews and our vehicles were grabbed by a Schörner-style *Soldatenklau* gang commanded by a Major of Military Engineers. Those rustlers of honest soldiers had a few military policemen clear the way for us–not towards the bridge, but in the opposite direction–to a warehouse on a side street, where they doled out coffee and something to eat, and, for our Jagdpanzer IVs, some fuel, but no armour-piercing and high-explosive shells. In Graudenz, *Soldatenklau* was much larger than the usual roadside operation.

Soldatenklau had no choice but to leave Lt. Krippendorf in command of his three Jagdpanzer IVs. Thus, we weren't integrated too thoroughly into *Soldatenklau* in the full Nazi sense, although at the warehouse *Soldatenklau* assigned to Lt. Krippendorf ten Panzer support infantry, who had all been treated to coffee and a bite to eat long before we got there.

Technically, *Soldatenklau* had made our Lt. one of its leaders because of his acceptance of the ten infantrymen, who all looked efficient enough. The fact that we and our Jagdpanzer IVs had been brought into the warehouse after the infantrymen had had to wait there reminded one of a steal-to-order enterprise. Maybe that's what the *Soldatenklau* scoundrels continued with in civilian life after the war–if they lived that long.

Armour was what *Soldatenklau* was looking for at Graudenz. Consequently our days in West Prussia appeared to be not quite over.

Soon *Soldatenklau* took us still farther away from the vicinity of the bridge, and to the eastern edge of the city, an area which our Division–as far as we knew, it still hadn't arrived anywhere close to the bridge in Graudenz–was unlikely to pass through on its way to the bridge.

The small sector assigned to us by *Soldatenklau* lay just north of the railway line which cut through the city from west to east.

From our infantry we quickly learned a bit more about the efforts of *Soldatenklau* to make Graudenz impregnable to the Soviets. We heard, for example, that *Soldatenklau* at Graudenz had a reputation for clandestinely pressing personnel from various branches of the Army, especially, into somewhat prolonged periods of local military service. That had been going on for some time, not just recently. Another oddity regarding Graudenz was that at the warehouse, *Soldatenklau*'s headquarters, a few men wore the Nazi Party's brown uniform featuring the wide swastika armband. Such cooperation of some officers with political leaders may have been even more conspicuous closer to Berlin.

Every Jagdpanzer IV would fight its best from an ambush, which meant that its crew had to have a suitable place at which to hide it. However, because we didn't want the ultralong barrels of our Jagdpanzer IVs close to the destructive walls of any of the buildings at that godforsaken extremity of the city, Lt. Krippendorf decided that we best check out some thickets, about 200m eastward, regarding going into position there. He, with his crew commanders and the Sergeant in charge of the infantry, walked the snow-covered 200m, soon summoning the rest of us to get our Jagdpanzer IVs and the infantry over there. Of course, we were giving up the warmth of the sheltering buildings.

I hadn't had our driver go ahead more than about 150 metres when I felt, and heard, the damndest blast under the front of the hull of our Jagdpanzer IV. An acrid stink enveloped us. Our driver, stunned, mumbled about our having run onto an antitank mine.

We had blundered onto an unmarked field of such mines, probably laid in staggered rows. Then, our last Jagdpanzer IV, about 100 metres behind us, experienced a similar blast. Our middle Jagdpanzer IV was following in our tracks; it, too, within minutes had the misfortune to set off an antitank mine. The whole damned district was loaded with mines.

Each of our Jagdpanzer IVs had suffered severe mine damage to its tracks and its road wheels, and couldn't be driven, but our radios and intercom systems still functioned.

As the Lt.'s gunner, I was the senior deputy crew commander, and my first message, by radio, was that, in bailing out, no one should jump from his Jagdpanzer IV's roof to the ground. Generated by jumping, kinetic energy would increase the force with which the men hit the earth and, possibly, antitank mines. Rather, everyone should climb down.

I recalled that as an apprentice electrician I had often jumped from scaffolds at least as high as the Jagdpanzer IV's roof, 1.85 metres above the ground. Each time, but especially in cold places, I had felt the jolt.

I also thought of the stories that I had heard about late-model submachine guns which, with their safeties off, could be made to fire simply by holding them vertically, butt down, while jumping from a relatively high vehicle. That would not have occurred with the one MP40 belonging to Lt. Krippendorf's Jagdpanzer IV; he had taken it with him to the copses. There were, however, the infantrymen, some of them with such weapons.

Moving gingerly, the guys, a few of them supported by others, all alighted safely, after which they followed the footprints left in the snow by the four men who had traversed the fields shortly before.

We recalled that, in part, the *Battle-Line Avowal of the Soldiers of the 7th Panzer Division* reads as follows:

> Never will I yield my tank, my vehicle, or other war material. If an order requires that weapons or other materials of war have to be left behind, I will ensure that nothing falls into enemy hands without having been destroyed.

There was no question about what we, with the latter part of that passage in mind, would have to do next. Lt. Krippendorf signalled that all three Jagdpanzer IVs had to be blown up. Retrieving and repairing them was impossible under the circumstances. The Soviets, some of whom we had encountered the day before at Lessen, must have been just down the road from Graudenz.

Each gunner waited till his buddies and the nine infantrymen were close to the thickets; then he pulled the igniter of his one-kilogram demolition charge. Walking, most warily, we three gunners, too, got to the congregation at the first thicket.

Sure enough, the Jagdpanzer IVs blew up, but not quite simultaneously, because the charge in the last one was touched off first.

Lt. Krippendorf had enough! To hell with scheming *Soldatenklau*! Just get across the Vistula on foot and away from Graudenz!

If a few of us hadn't known a bit about German anti-tank mines, all of us might have been trapped out in the bare fields for God knows how long. Some of Germany's most common anti-tank mines, the plate-shaped anti-tank mines, were designed to explode only under heavy loads. For instance the mine 42 required a firing load of 110 to 180 kg; the mine 43, 200 to 270 kg. The No. 42 had a 5.4-kg filling of TNT. In each of these mines, the spring-loaded striker was retained by a shear pin. The weight of one person was unlikely to cause either of these mines to explode. One German type of anti-personnel mine required an operating load of approximately 34 kg, and contained 1.50 kg of TNT.

Probably months earlier, before the snow had started to fall, *Soldatenklau* had the mines laid without posting mine warning signs. Perhaps the local coziness of *Soldatenklau* with the often meddlesome Nazi Party, the former relying on the latter to put the finishing touches on their minefield, led to the bungled mining. In the end, maybe *Soldatenklau*, seeing what had happened to the three Jagdpanzer IVs that it had requisitioned for itself; speedily saw to it that mine warning signs were placed at the fields, provided they had detailed records of where the mines were laid, and provided that the Soviets weren't already at those fields.

Konstantin Rokossovsky, Marshal of the Soviet Union, in his *A Soldier's Duty*, p. 290, terms Graudenz *a fortress*. On p. 297, Rokossovsky writes that towards the end of February, 1945, Graudenz, according to POW statements, contained up to 15,000 officers and men. Furthermore, on p. 304 Rokossovsky states,

The Nazi [*sic*] command was merciless towards its soldiers, forcing them to fight even when the hopelessness of resistance was obvious. The Graudenz garrison, cut off from friendly troops, fought to the end, and only on March 6, after days of street fighting, was the town finally taken ...

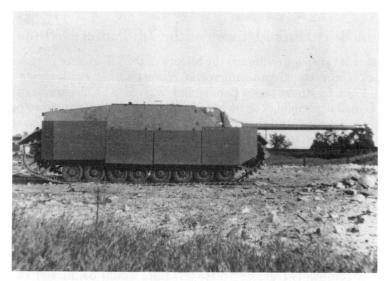

Prototype of Jagdpanzer IV/70 (V), featuring early-type gun mantlet. (The Tank Museum)

Early production Jagdpanzer IV/70 (V). The vehicle has been covered in Zimmerit paste, used to prevent magnetic mines being attached to the vehicle. (The Tank Museum)

CHAPTER 16

Some Historical Details about the 7th Panzer Division and Wounded

A Brief Partial History of the 7th Panzer Division

In part, a two-page outline of the history of the 7th Panzer Division, the book *Uniforms, Organization and History of the Panzertruppe*, San Jose, 1980, by Roger James Bender and Warren W. Odegard, states that the Division participated, in March of 1944, in the retreat across the northern Ukraine, and that, in July of 1944, it was engaged in the central sector of the Eastern Front during the Soviet summer offensive.

The Division was, we are told, transferred to the Baltic States in August of 1944 as part of the 3rd Panzer Army. It fought in Raseiniai in Lithuania and later in Kurland and Memel until November of that year. It was heavily engaged in January of 1945 during the Soviet winter offensive west of the Vistula.

Finally, we learn that the Division gradually withdrew to the west, fighting defensively until it surrendered to the British at Schwerin on May 3, 1945.

My comments regarding these few lines would be, first of all, that, since Kiev lies in the northern Ukraine, the Chernovtsy area, where at least part of Panzer Regiment 25 was to be found at the end of March, and early in April, of 1944, it must have been at what was considered to be the extreme southern flank of the 7th Panzer Division.

Also, regarding the statement that the 7th Panzer Division was transferred to the Baltic States in August of 1944, I can point out that my log of tank engagements shows some dates between July 7, 1944, and July 20, 1944, attesting to our pre-August presence in Lithuania, one of the Baltic States. Incidentally, Raseiniai lays 150 km north-northwest of Leipalingis, named in my log, which could indicate that there; too, Panzer Regiment 25 may have had something like a flanking role.

Furthermore, I can state that Panzer Regiment 25 was, according to my log, east of the Vistula during the latter part of January, 1945. Let me add, with regard to my second-next paragraph, that any 7th Panzer-Division troops east of the Vistula must have, by February 2, 1945, been virtually cut off from the west by the Soviet front line, which then ran along the Vistula to a point about 50 km south of Danzig.

By February 24, 1945, the Soviet front line extended to the Baltic Sea just east of Danzig. Farther west, the Soviet February 24 front line lay about 100 km south of the Baltic coast. It is comprehensible that troops west of the Vistula, especially those that were there earlier than about

February 2, moved westward in the 100-km wide tract before Pomerania, too, was overrun by the Soviets. The battle for the part of Pomerania north of the February 24 front line continued until about the middle of March.

Finally, regarding the 7th Panzer Division's surrender to the British at Schwerin, 90 km east of Hamburg–and, by the way, 490 km west-southwest of Danzig–I was very surprised, despite the fact that its difficult way west had apparently led through Pomerania, to find out that even part of the Division had escaped from the Soviets.

There is no reason to doubt that the authors of the brief history which I have just commented upon did their best to get at, and publish, the truth, for, as General a.D. [Ret.] Hasso-Eckard Frhr. von Manteuffel wrote in his foreword to Roger James Bender and Warren W. Odegard's *Uniforms, Organisation and History of the Panzertruppe*: "The authors have provided a vivid description of the development, organization, and fate of the German tank units on the basis of a detailed and conscientious study of the source material."

Contrary to the impression one gets from reading *Uniforms, Organisation and History of the Panzertruppe*, the 7th Panzer Division did not go through Pomerania on its way to Schwerin. Page 154 of Hasso von Manteuffel's book *The 7th Panzer Division: An Illustrated History of Rommel's "Ghost Division" 1938–1945*, published in 2000, states the following:

> From March 12th to 24th, 1945[,] the Division was engaged in heavy fighting round the Danzig-Gotenhafen bridgehead. When the Gotenhafen bridgehead had to be given up on March 25th, the Division was moved to the Oxhöf[t]er Kämpe area where the fighting continued until April 4th, 1945. The Division was moved then [*sic*] to the Hela peninsula and was transferred via sea to Swinemünde harbour on April 15th.

Wounded

It seems that, in the turmoil of war, a small group of low-echelon soldiers can lose track of their Division about as quickly as their Division can lose track of the whereabouts of that small group of soldiers.

That's exactly what we were–a small group of eight Panzer soldiers who had arrived at Rahmel, a northern suburb of Gdynia, then called Gotenhafen, ten km north of Danzig. Earlier we had outrun the Soviets after what might collectively be called Bischofswerder, east of the Vistula, had crossed the Vistula, and had then entered the eastern reaches of Pomerania, intending to travel westward. We had, however, been prevented from doing so by the Soviets' thrusts from the southern part of Pomerania towards the Baltic. Bereft of higher leadership in the final throes of the war, we felt like orphans.

We band of brothers–these four words are part of the king's soldierly, stirring Saint Crispin's Day speech in Shakespeare's *Henry V*, IV, iii, 60, fine reading for any military man–stood in a yard in Rahmel. Corporal Fehler, our ranking man, had found a box of cigars and was playing the big shot. Half of the boys were occupied with the cigars Fehler had handed out. Mostly, though, we were wondering about finding something to feed on. A clear day it was, that March 12, 1945.

Right after Fehler had asked something like "How are the shares doing?" or "How's the stock market?" one–just one–unexpected, violent explosion in our midst changed all our jollity into stark tragedy. Fehler suddenly lay face down, his cigar crumpled. Fehler looked dead. He was.

Another guy, his back leaning against a brick wall, sat on the ground, staring at one of his feet. Something had made it awfully pigeon-toed; he couldn't move it.

Flung by the blast, I found myself flat on the ground, a couple of steps from where I had stood while watching the cigar puffers. I could see. I could hear. I could speak. I could feel that I was wounded. I could smell the explosion–and, soon, my own blood.

Later that day, the diagnosis would be multiple shell fragment wounds. My right shoulder, right arm above the elbow, right buttock, and left shin had been hit. I kept the shell fragments that were removed from my shoulder a year later, and I wish they were able to tell me exactly what kind of weapon they were part of. My guess has always been that a mortar shell got us in that yard.

Three of our group were dead, the rest wounded, some very badly, far worse than I. We survivors had to get to where medical help was available. That meant heading into Gdynia.

No more than half a block away from that fateful yard ran the main thoroughfare of Rahmel, on it an unbroken line of refugees on their way to Gdynia. Many of them drove compact, narrow-bottomed, more or less slant-sided, rubber-tired, two-horse agricultural wagons, loaded with possessions of all sorts. Taking one of our wounded with me, I limped up to such a wagon, got us aboard, and with my left hand redistributed the upper part of the load to make it comfortable for us to lie on. That was the very best I could do for the two of us.

Whereas the rig's hunched driver remained impassive towards his load, a German Red Cross nurse, walking towards Gdynia, accompanied us for a while. A good-looking, compassionate person she was, although she could actually do no more than advise us to seek medical attention forthwith. In the city.

Hours later, our churl's horses tugged us into town, where, it seemed, the *Kriegsmarine* was running things. We got off the wagon near the main gate of the Gdynia dockyards, and walked into solid *Kriegsmarine* territory to have our wounds looked after for the first time.

Certificate for my *Verwundetenabzeichen in Schwarz*

No screwing around in that place. To get at the holes in my right arm and shoulder, the prep gents simply cut open the sleeve and shoulder of my uniform jacket, ruining it, but leaving it with me. I still have the black-cloth-backed national emblem and rank chevrons, which I removed from the jacket later on in a military hospital, where I was given a field-grey uniform. I also have my *Panzerkampfabzeichen in Silber*, my *Verwundetenabzeichen in Schwarz*, my *EK II*, and my *EKI*.

Each of us was triaged with regard to what mode of transportation would be required to further move him—standing, seated, or lying. They gave me lying, and placed me on the floor of a huge warehouse. I'll bet a hundred guys lay there in rows. Each of us had a blanket, compliments of the *Kriegsmarine*. At that stage, I had lost track of the black-uniformed fellow who had made it, in my company, from Rahmel into Gdynia and the dockyards. I was in with guys from here, there, and everywhere. All half dead or worse.

The following day—triage officers had, in the meantime, been around to make sure that the wounds or injuries of the many men warranted lying—we were loaded aboard a hospital ship at Gdynia. I heard no more shooting, but I heard many cries of pain coming from somewhere farther below in the vessel. Amputations were being performed there, I heard.

We hadn't known where we were to land, but it turned out to be Denmark. There, somewhere, a hospital train was ready for us. Again, a diverse bunch together for a long ride. One man, I recall, lamented the loss of his penis, intermittently consoling himself by recalling that he was the father of two children. The Soviets had hit his fly with a small caliber fragmentation bullet. Tales galore of that sort.

In Altenburg in Thuringia, a city destined to lie, shortly thereafter, in East Germany, the hospital train was unloaded. Thuringia, in those days, was a province to stay away from. After all, we had, not long before, eluded the Soviets at Gdynia, and who, wounded or not, would want to fall into their hands?

The staff of the military hospital in Altenburg didn't want their place to become lousy—infested with lice that was. No matter how poor his condition, every man entering that hospital as a patient had to strip by himself and use soap and water in the back yard before being allowed to enter the building. Either the place had before that time not received many wounded from the Eastern Front, or it had received too many.

Not all of my wounds were healing nicely in Altenburg. A shin wound, for instance, heals very slowly. On a different floor of the hospital there worked a homely nurse with a reputation for great skill in ˙bandaging wounds. Bandages applied by that lady wouldn' sag, and the guys flocked to her station to have her do the daily job—until they were shooed back to their proper stations.

Official medical papers, addressed to the medical officer at Panzer Regiment 25 in Bamberg and entrusted to me for personal delivery, show that I was discharged from the Altenburg hospital on April 10, 1945, with two weeks' leave.

Dated April 10, 1945, one of the full-page documents bears the following sentence: "*F. wird heute als k.v. [kriegsverwendungsfähig] zu seiner Ersatzeinheit entlassen.*" ([Lance Corporal] F[riesen] is today being discharged to his replacement unit as fit for wartime service.) Also, there are the words "*Verwundetenabzeichen in Schwarz wurde verliehen.*" (Wounded badge in black has been awarded).

I departed on foot from the hospital, went to the railroad station, and stood for hours and days while travelling in the trains, heading west. Gone were the days of lying. Still, life would be much better in the British Zone of Occupation of Germany than anywhere close to the Soviets.

Our train had travelled no longer than one hour after leaving Altenburg before it was stopped outside a village because of some sort of trouble there. Never will I forget what I, looking through one of the train's windows, saw at that small place. In front of the still-smouldering ruins of a house, no doubt the aftermath of a bombing raid, stood a lone bareheaded woman, perhaps 40 years of age. Her hands clasped above her head in despair, she typified the wife and mother whose family was either buried in the ruins behind her, or was far off, elsewhere in the war.

Mostly, I recall that her eyes pathetically expressed the horror of war. Their look exemplified that of hundreds of others in the parts of Germany through which I travelled slowly by train less than a month before the end of the war.

There was, not much later, no need for me to report in Bamberg, which by then lay in the American zone.

CHAPTER 17

Making Do in Postwar Germany

By the time the war ended, I lived in the British Zone–in Wilhelmshaven, to be exact–looking for suitable employment. I never did surrender anywhere. I never was a P.O.W. I never was interrogated. I never attended de-nazification lectures.

The first job–working shifts as a translator and interpreter–that I had immediately after the Second World War can be regarded as a kind of extension of my military service, for I was then still in uniform–mind you, with the national insignia removed from my jacket and cap.

Let me tell you a bit about the place at which I worked at that time, and about some of the personnel there.

Operating by authority of the Royal Navy, the Senior German Naval Officer (Wilhelmshaven), or SGNO (W), had his headquarters aboard the *Tanganjika*, a bombed former Africa steamship with her keel resting on the floor of the harbour, but with her upper decks not submerged and listing only slightly to starboard alongside the Wiesbaden Quay.

The large rooms on those intact decks served as offices for the SGNO (W)'s staff, which consisted of about three dozen competent men, most of whom had served in the *Kriegsmarine* until their country's surrender.

Many of the blue-clad young fellows aboard the *Tanganjika* were wireless operators who, by way of the then still fully functional naval radio station at Sengwarden, eight kilometres northwest of the centre of Wilhelmshaven, and the lofty antennas on the North Sea coast at Norddeich, 59 kilometres west of Sengwarden, kept the SGNO (W) in touch with, for instance, German submarines still out on some of the Seven Seas.

For that kind of work, those wireless operators often employed Royal Navy-sanctioned, genuine *Kriegsmarine*-style shortcuts, such as their *Quatsch* groups. *Quatsch* means *nonsense*, but the Q-groups constituted short signals designed to thwart direction finding. Each such group consisted of a Q followed by a couple of other letters of the German alphabet.

All shortwave enthusiasts, those men delighted in demonstrating to visitors to their large radio shack the brief delay which a radio signal of theirs showed after being transmitted clear around the world. As well, each of them could quickly identify the personal style of anyone, German or not, communicating with him at SGNO (W) via Morse code.

The *Tanganjika*'s cabins were home for the staff. In some of those quarters, the wireless boys, a fun-loving bunch, occasionally amused themselves with such things as studying, very closely, the colour of the

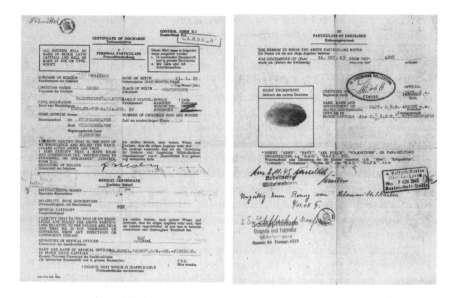

Certificate of discharge, front and back, from the German Army

flame resulting from the ignition of methane gas contained in the farts of some of their off-duty chums.

One day, I, in uniform, arrived at the family's apartment in Fedderwardergroden to find my father there. Never before, and never since, did I see him smile as much as he did that day.

Towards the end of the war, the Soviets had captured him along with many others in the province of Mecklenburg, close to what had been part of the German Eastern Front. They had, however, let their older POWs, as well as their very young ones, go. A gesture unheard of, actually, in dealing with the Soviets. One lucky young POW, whom my father knew, hailed from Bremen; his last name was Schaumlöffel.

When he was about to be captured my father was shepherding some Russian POWs. He had a tough decision to make: allow himself to be captured or pretend to be one of the Russian POWs. Some of the Russian POWs had, he told me, simply said to him the equivalent of "Come along; you're one of us." Had he gone with his Russians, he might have been off badly in the end. The Soviets did not always treat their repatriates kindly.

Of course my father had been interrogated by the Soviets. An ignition key that he had picked up somewhere and put into his pant pocket had been the subject of many of their questions. What high-ranking officer had he driven? He hadn't let on that he understood his interrogators' asides in Russian. Anyway, he got away from his captors and headed for Wilhelmshaven. God, was he happy to see me.

Oscar had been killed in action by a low-flying Allied aircraft near Houffalize in Belgium the previous winter.

The British operated discharge centres in their zone of Germany, and, to me, getting out of a uniform that was looked upon with disdain practically everywhere seemed a good idea. Therefore, I resigned from the staff of the SGNO (W) and got free room and board at the extensive naval barracks at Ebkeriege, near Mariensiel in the south of the city, where the naval ordnance depot covered a huge area. I was discharged by the British on October 24, 1945, at Wittmundhafen.

Next, I worked as an interpreter-translator for the American Graves Registration Command concerned with disinterring and then positively identifying, in a requisitioned small German meat packing plant which they used as a morgue, the bodies of many Americans, most of whom had been killed over the Wilhelmshaven area or over the adjoining parts of the North Sea.

I still visualize the putrid corpses, and I still readily recall the stories about some of them that we heard from various German civilians. For instance, a farmer showed us a water-filled, manhole-size depression in one of his marshy fields. That hole, the farmer said, had been made by an American airman who, feet first, hit the ground with his parachute unopened. His temporary grave was in the closest churchyard. Ultimately, all of the American dead were conveyed to a military cemetrey in Belgium.

The H.Q. of the Graves Registration Command was located in the centre of Jever. Because the Command operated throughout a large district, I had no trouble getting a jeepful of U.S. soldiers to tour the country north of Jever, and to drop in at Carlseck. It was, of course, the era of post-war de-nazification, and that normally overbearing lady, Frau Iben, who, half a dozen years earlier, had thought so very little of my German, looked as though she would suffer a heart attack when she saw real Americans in my company at her door. At that place, there was no more cockiness at all towards the boy who had been the Ibens' *Amerikaner*.

After the Command had finished its work, I easily landed a job that combined the work of a mail courier with that of an interpreter and translator at the *Kreis* (District) H.Q. of the British Element of the Control Commission for Germany at Varel, pronounced *Far-ell*, a small city 20 kilometres south of Wilhelmshaven, and on the same large bay in the North Sea coast.

As a mail courier, I got around a lot. To the British Army Post Office in Oldenburg early in the day, then back to Varel, and on to places like Jever and Wilhelmshaven. By that time, the British had established a boarding school, called Prince Rupert School, in the barracks of the former submarine base at the other side of the high brick wall opposite the one end of Kasernenstrasse in Wilhelmshaven.

Despite my foremost post-war plight at the time–being kept, by the Canadian government, from returning to Canada–Varel turned out to be an extraordinarily good place for me. In the evening of March 27, 1947, at the C.C.G. *Kreis* H.Q.'s own telephone exchange, two of the fellows who worked that switchboard, as well as I, met three young female telephone operators from the Varel telephone exchange of the German federal postal service, which operated the country's telephone system. The three girls had come to see the place that dealt with so many of the calls that passed through their switchboards. It was during the girls' visit that I, for the first time, admired lovely, blue-eyed Helga Christine Marianne Meyer, a 19-year-old native of Varel.

In 1947 all of West Germany was still a vast black market in which I became involved to a modest extent mainly because the itinerant nature of my work at the C.C.G. was conducive to trading.

I did not have to look far for expert tutelage because all of the drivers at the Varel C.C.G., or Military Government, *Kreis* H.Q. were discharged German soldiers with experience as black marketeers.

Two such good men, Arthur B. and Willi R., spent much time at the H.Q.'s motor pool in a requisitioned garage in the Nebbsallee in Varel. Like their fellow drivers, the two had no trouble appropriating a few jerry cans full of gasoline now and then. Next, they sounded me out regarding where to trade with that liquid gold. Inasmuch as I was something like a tank crew commander to this pair of gents, who took turns being the driver of the day for the entire mail route, I always told them that all of our deals had to be made on the mail run, outside of Varel.

Our favourite trading partner lived in Diekmannshausen, east of Varel, on the highway to Rodenkirchen on the Weser River. There, Arthur and I, or Willi and I, traded gasoline for baked goods. The old master baker even threw in 500-gram packages of premium-quality butter to make sure that his activity on the black market suffered no slump.

Those were ultra-lean times in Germany, especially for the people in the cities and towns.

Shortly after the end of the Second World War, practically, I began to try to get permission from the Canadian government to return to Canada. In this regard, I had to deal initially with the Canadian Military Mission in Berlin and, subsequently, with the Canadian Consulate in Frankfurt am Main.

The sixth of the nine letters I received from the Canadian Military Mission confirms that I was born in Canada, and that, despite the fact that my father was naturalized in Germany in 1940, I am deemed to be a Canadian citizen. The letter also states that, in view of the fact that I served in the German armed forces during the war, it is not proposed that I be given any assistance by the Canadian government to enable me to return to Canada at the present time.

Of my eight letters from the Canadian Consulate, the penultimate, dated March 16, 1950, and the last, dated March 28, 1950, show that I was issued a Canadian travel document. My long wait was over.

Preceding, by approximately four months, the arrival of my last two letters from the Canadian Consulate, my greatest coup on the black market involved two pounds of ordinary Canadian tea sent to me by one of my second cousins in St. Catharines, Ontario.

To comprehend how my remarkable tea deal could come about, one has to know that a great many of the people living along the North Sea coast of Germany are, just as their forebears were for centuries, inveterate tea drinkers. It has been stated that, long ago, many of the wells in that low-lying area of Europe provided bog-tinged drinking water, commonly made potable in the form of strong tea.

At about the time I received my parcel containing the two pounds of tea, the aging uncle of one of Helga's neighbourhood girl friends had come from Los Angeles to visit Varel. Uncle Hermann had left Germany many years before the Second World War.

Uncle Hermann went about doing his old home town a lot of good. Among other things, he had the two crumbling stone pillars with the large wooden gate at the Windallee entrance to the Varel forest replaced anonymously. He had good use his for large sums of German currency.

The transaction might not have made the *Guinness Book of World Records*, but my two pounds of Trumpet-brand tea, sold on the black market, brought in enough money for me to hand to Uncle Hermann, in an at-par exchange, for the U.S. dollars I needed to pay at a travel agency in Bremen for an open passage in my name from Hamburg to New York.

Yes, the black market in Germany was still active towards the end of 1949, a good 4½ years after the termination of the Second World War in Europe, and 1½ years after the country's currency reform.

I departed from Hamburg aboard the United States Lines' steamship *Washington* on April 29, 1950, and, after entering the U.S.A., stayed briefly with Mennonite friends in Doylestown, Pennsylvania. En route by car from Doylestown to St. Catharines for a short sojourn there with relatives from my mother's side of the family, I crossed the Canadian border at Niagara Falls, Ontario, on June 10, 1950. On that day, I was asked at Canadian Customs how long I had remained abroad continuously. "Since March of 1939," I answered.

From St. Catharines I travelled straight to Kitchener.

Canadian Military Mission
Berlin

22 September 1947.

Dear Sir,

Further to my letter of 12 August 1947, concerning your case, I have now received further instructions from the competent authorities in Canada that your birth in Canada on 25 May 1925 at Westbourne, Manitoba, has been confirmed.

The fact that your father was naturalised in Germany in 1940 has no effect upon your Canadian status and you are deemed to be at present a Canadian citizen.

However, in view of the fact that you served in the German armed forces during the war, it is not proposed that you be given any assistance by the Canadian Government to enable you to return to Canada at the present time.

Yours truly,

(J.J.Hurley).

Mr. Bruno Friesen,
(23) Meneke St. W.
Varel i. O.,
Germany.

145, Fuerstenberger Str.
FRANKFURT/MAIN, Germany

January 26th, 1950.

Dear Sir,

Since I last wrote to you on the 26th of July, 1949, there has been a change in the regulations pertaining to those Canadian citizens who served in the German Armed Forces during the late war. It is now possible for such people to enter Canada and as soon as I receive proof from you that your passage to Canada is paid I shall consider the issuance to you of a Canadian Passport.

Your friend Rudolph Friesen, to whom you refer in your letter has made arrangements to return to Canada as have the other members of his family and that is why passports have been issued to them.

Yours truly,

(A.J. Hicks)
Consul

Bruno Friesen
Salzastrasse 92
Wilhelmshaven N
British Zone

AJH/hc

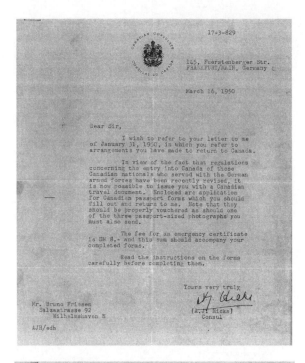

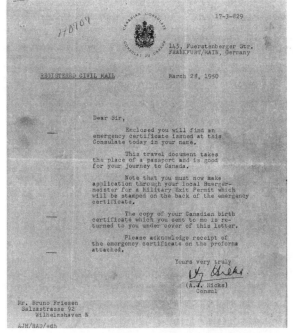

Four letters from Canadian authorities concerning my effort to return to Canada

CHAPTER 18

Back in Canada

A Year of Bachelorhood

In the summer of 1950, after returning to the Twin Cities–to Kitchener and Waterloo, that is–I first reacquainted myself with much of the length of King Street from North to South in Waterloo, and from West to East in Kitchener. For one thing, the old dark-green, cast-iron, five-globed street lights in Waterloo's business district had been replaced. For another, the old streetcars had, not long before, given way to buses.

In Kitchener, I purposely walked the stretch of King Street from Frederick Street out to the corner of King East and Kent Avenue, where our last home in Canada had stood. Actually, the old frame house on its spacious, sandy lot had belonged to the Kitchener Lumber Company which, adjacent to the house, sprawled along the eastern side of the King Street end of Kent Avenue, just as it had in 1939.

Mr. Hauck was still the manager at Kitchener Lumber. His chat with me proceeded civilly despite his telling me emphatically that my parents had not bothered to dispose of their chickens before leaving for Germany. He told me that the Kitchener *Daily Record* had written about it as a case of pet abandonment. The story was on file in the *Record's* morgue.

My parents' pets? It had to be the two Bantam hens that I had left at home in March, 1939. The hens' hubby, as beautiful a "Bantie" rooster as ever crowed, was killed by a car on Kent Avenue during my time in Kitchener. I doubt that the two widowed hens were confined to a coop. Probably free-ranging, they understandably looked uncared-for in the vicinity of a house suddenly deserted. In Waterloo and Kitchener, I had at different times kept pigeons, guinea pigs, rabbits, a cat, and bantam chickens, but not a dog. The other kids in our family never had pets of their own, at least not in those days.

At any rate, after mentally placing that fair, but embarrassing, disclosure by Mr. Hauck under *noted well*, I got around some more, looking up people and places closely connected with my childhood in Canada.

Although most of them had not been sent overseas, some of my old Sunday and German school buddies had served in the Canadian forces in the Second World War, and had entered university soon after being discharged. By 1950 they were well prepared for employment.

Generally, the ex-servicemen of Mennonite extraction, who in 1950 were still warmly referred to by their folks as "our boys" in lasting recognition of their service to their country, had come home from the war none the worse for their experience.

However, one Mennonite fellow, a former N.C.O. in a Canadian Intelligence unit, had picked up some highly questionable interrogation techniques during his wartime military service, which included a spell overseas. According to him, the least offensive item in his whole assortment of "Intel" interrogation tricks–he liked to dwell on all of those various procedures at his home for the benefit of his guests–consisted of being "real nice" to persons, military or civilian, who were to be questioned by his unit, with him acting as the interpreter whenever the English and German languages were involved.

The gist of his most lenient, but time-consuming, method of getting at the truth: Provide the persons slated for interrogation with all the beer– yes, beer!–they can drink, and then watch them squirm when they get around to having to relieve themselves. Do not allow them to leave the waiting rooms. Sooner or later, they will confess in exchange for being permitted to urinate properly in private. After all, cultured persons do not want to wet their clothes in the presence of others.

I still believe that that boastful ex-N.C.O., a celibate, had the makings of a sadist.

In 1950, the General Service War Service Badge worn by many Canadians my age–I was then 25 years old, but had no right to wear that badge–marked, for one thing, its wearers as having priority for employment in Canada.

While looking for work in Kitchener and Waterloo, I became aware that, mainly because I displayed no General Service War Service Badge, employment interviewers probed especially hard for details of my past, whereupon some of them went so far as to suggest impolitely that I should, even at such a late date, be penalized because of where I had spent the war years. It was then that Ted Nettleton gave me his preventive dictum: "Don't tell people your troubles … " What is more, he gave me a job.

To those who earned their living there, the B. F. Goodrich plant was simply a "rubber shop." An entire floor of the building was devoted to manufacturing tyres, namely to stock preparation, tyre building, and tyre vulcanizing. The company's non-salaried employees had been on strike in 1949; in 1950 they were interested in making up lost pay. The plant operated three shifts daily, namely 7–3, 3–11, and 11–7, with the employees' schedules moving back one shift at the beginning of each week.

For my first three years at B. F. Goodrich, my work consisted of servicing a quadrangle of tyre building machines, meaning that I had to keep four tyre builders, all on piece work, happy by giving their stock supply prompt attention. The heavy rolls of sticky fabric which, depending on the strength rating of the tyres being built, could run up to six different-width rolls per machine, made better body builders than any expensive gym equipment. It was the kind of job at which I worked off the extra calories that derived from the Canadian-, German-, and Russian-style cooking of a number of kind, old Mennonite ladies.

The foul air coming into the tyre building room from the press room and elsewhere in the building had a deleterious effect on the workers, especially if they stayed with the company for the better part of a lifetime or longer. Really, a "rubber shop" was not the ideal place in which to accumulate a lot of seniority. Still, I worked there for almost 16 years, quitting in 1966 to be able to attend university.

After three years in the tyre building room, I had transferred to the small department whose members calculated the specifications for tyre production.

Let me get back, for a bit, to 1950, the year by which the majority of my friends had entered, or were about to enter, matrimony. Helga was still in Germany, preparing for her immigration to Canada. Her neat letters–we never did speak with each other by telephone during the year that we were apart–brightened my room-and-board existence. She and I had to wait until the following year for our wedding in Canada.

The Waterloo-Kitchener United Mennonite church building had been extended to twice its original length by 1950, and the old organ, one of its silver-coloured pipes badly dented in the process, had been relocated accordingly. The church basement, in contrast to the upstairs, had retained its original size and appearance. Down there, the dark-brown, glossy paint on the wooden chairs that belonged to the Sunday and German schools felt the least bit sticky–as it always had.

During a Sunday school session some time before 1937, I pulled back one of those chairs just as a chum of mine was about to seat himself on it, causing him to plunk onto the floor. Former pupils who witnessed that misdeed still talk about how ill-behaved I was that day, as well as at other times in the early 1930s.

At the 1950 Christmas service in the old church, the Sunday school superintendent surprised many a man and woman in the congregation by gravely announcing, during the Sunday school kids' part of the program, that a young man, Bruno Friesen, who was proof that Sunday school could lastingly elevate a person, would, next, say a few words. I believe that the super felt that what was then about to transpire would serve to illustrate to his fellow Mennonites that a boy's Sunday school attendance overshadows even the effects of exposure to radical militarism. He must have been certain that most, if not all, of the adults present knew, just as he did, that I had spent much time among men generally regarded as the worst of the Occident's bad boys.

Temporarily given the role of a Sunday school pupil, I had to recite my short German Christmas poem, which ended "*Tante Janzen half gut nach, / Und es ward mit Weh und Ach.*" (Auntie Janzen nicely prompted me, / and I made it with dif-fi-cul-ty). As a boy, years before 1950, I got stuck while presenting my Christmas poem, but I finished it with help from one of the Sunday school teachers, Mrs. Janzen, who was the wife of Bishop Janzen, the church's minister.

I didn't falter at Christmas in 1950 and, along with the participating genuine Sunday school kids; I was rewarded with a paper bag full of sweets, nuts, and cookies at the distribution of gifts later that evening.

On July 1, 1951, at Union Station in Toronto, I picked up my radiant Helga, then 23. She looked as splendid as she had the day I first met her in Varel a good four years earlier. She had come to Canada to stay. She had left her home and had travelled to a far-off country all on account of me. Now, more than 50 years later, I appreciate, more than ever, that such a fundamental move on her part was a sign of her immense faith in her prospective partner and in a country new to her.

The Canadian Consulate in Hannover, Germany, had issued a non-quota immigrant visa to Helga with the stipulation that she and I get married within 21 days after her arrival in Canada. A shotgun wedding, we jokingly called it.

Before the wedding, Helga stayed in Waterloo with elderly relatives from my mother's side. Aunt Lina, one of the best Mennonite cooks in the Twin Cities, and Uncle Cornelius showed Helga off at every opportunity. Besides, a group of girls I knew from Sunday and German schools made Helga a member of their club. For that, I remain very grateful to them.

At the 1951 church picnic, Mrs. Dyck, the wife of the farmer on whose property the picnic was held annually, said to me in correct, but overly formal German, "*Sie haben guten Geschmack!*" (You have good taste!). She meant not only that Helga was easy to look at, but also that Helga had the approval of the community.

In the Mennonite colonies in the Ukraine, every woman from a Lutheran German colony in the Ukraine, who became the bride of a Mennonite, was traditionally subject to an extra measure of scrutiny by the ladies. Traces of that old custom shone through at the church picnic.

CHAPTER 19

Married in the Absence of Close Relatives

Recalling the circumstances in which I found myself after returning to Canada, but before Helga and I were married, I chuckle at the carefree view of marriage expressed in the following four lines:

In der Heimat angekommen,
Fängt ein neues Leben an.
Eine Frau wird sich genommen,
Kinder bringt der Weihnachtsmann.

(Returned to his homeland,
A guy starts life anew.
He gets himself a wife and,
Brought by Santa, kids ensue.)

Although none of Helga's relatives and friends were able to attend our marriage at the Waterloo-Kitchener United Mennonite Church on July 21, 1951, and no one from my immediate family was there, many well-wishers joined the two of us—Helga and me—in the sight of God, as the Minister put it.

The Reverend Henry Epp, whose wife Mary is a none-too-distant cousin of mine, conducted the ceremony. Mary Toews was Helga's bridesmaid, and Wally Reimer my best man. Mennonites galore.

That day, Joe and Katie Nyce of Doylestown, Pennsylvania, jokingly presented Helga with a short-handled, wooden paddle, made at the Nyce's planing mill. Traditionally, such a Pennsylvania-Dutch Mennonite utensil served a wife to control her husband, although I have never felt its effect.

Our wedding rings we had bought with money a couple of my co-workers had collected on my behalf at B.F. Goodrich. During a lunch break in the shedhouse, they presented me with 24 dollars in paper currency.

Helga in her wedding dress sewn by her Aunt Henny of Delmenhorst, not far from Bremen, looked splendid. I believe that my grey suit, bought at George Fine's men's clothing store on King Street West in Kitchener a few days before the wedding, didn't detract from the picture. Old George was known to many Goodrich guys because his shop was only four blocks away from the Goodrich plant.

George had watched his senior man, Jerry Leyes, help me choose a suit. After I, having tried our ultimate selection on for fit, remarked, "Not a bad suit," George quickly asked, "Vell, vy don' you buy it?" So I did.

STORE: 0089   REG: 04/53   TRAN#: 2188
SALE   10/14/2010   EMP: 00274

Returns

Returns of merchandise purchased from a Borders, Borders Express or Waldenbooks retail store will be permitted only if presented in saleable condition accompanied by the original sales receipt or Borders gift receipt within the time periods specified below. Returns accompanied by the original sales receipt must be made within 30 days of purchase and the purchase price will be refunded in the same form as the original purchase. Returns accompanied by the original Borders gift receipt must be made within 60 days of purchase and the purchase price will be refunded in the form of a return gift card.

Exchanges of opened audio books, music, videos, video games, software and electronics will be permitted subject to the same time periods and receipt requirements as above and can be made for the same item only.

Periodicals, newspapers, comic books, food and drink, eBooks and other digital downloads, gift cards, return gift cards, items marked "non-returnable," "final sale" or the like and out-of-print, collectible or pre-owned items cannot be returned or exchanged.

Returns and exchanges to a Borders, Borders Express or

CHAPTER 20

Acquiring a Formal Education and Teaching English at a College

For me to get a formal education took a lot longer than it did for me to become married. From 1956 to 1967, mostly while I was an employee of B.F. Goodrich Canada Limited, I took the Advanced Technical Evening Classes, modeled on the British Higher National Certificate curriculum and run by the Ontario Ministry of Education. Most of my fellow A.T.E.C. students didn't pursue all three of the Certificates. After we had our Certificates I and II, the course was discontinued in Kitchener, and I had to travel, a couple of times weekly, to Guelph, about 25 kilometres north of Kitchener. I often referred, in fun, to the whole thing as Advanced Evening Technical Classes. A copy of my third A.T.E.C. Certificate–the three certificates made me a Certified Engineering Technologist, but not a Professional Engineer–is shown in this chapter, as is a copy of the congratulatory letter that accompanied my Certificate III. Also shown is a copy of my C.E.T. Certificate.

Working in industry can show a person the good aspects of society and the bad. I experienced an instance of the bad after I had asked the

Third Advanced Technical Evening Classes certificate

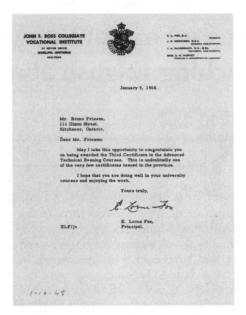

A letter related to the award of my third ATEC certificate

sycophantic manager of the Tyre Development Department, in which I worked, if he'd like to see my A.T.E.C. Certificates. That bicycle rider, meaning a person who displays an obsequious posture towards those above him while trampling on those below him replied, "Not particularly."

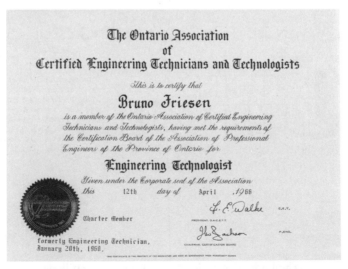

Diploma for Certified Engineering Technologist (CET)

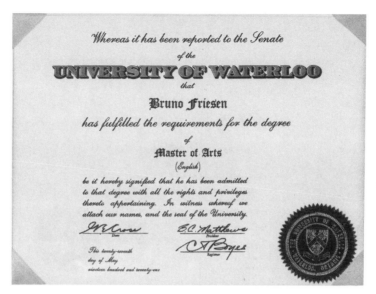

Whereas it has been reported to the Senate

of the

UNIVERSITY OF WATERLOO

that

Bruno Friesen

has fulfilled the requirements for the degree

of

Master of Arts

(English)

be it hereby signified that he has been admitted
to that degree with all the rights and privileges
thereto appertaining. In witness whereof we
attach our names, and the seal of the University.

This twenty-seventh
day of May
nineteen hundred and seventy-one

Diploma for Master of Arts (English) degree

The tyre industry in Kitchener has long had an overabundance of self-styled engineers; all of them impostors shy of academic qualifications. When one looked about at a picnic, a backyard party, or pub sessions, the lickspittles, were there, toadying shamelessly.

At the age of 41, I was glad to leave "engineers"-infested B.F. Goodrich in the summer of 1966, even though I knew that I had years of hard work ahead of me at university. By the time of the fall convocation at the University of Waterloo in September of 1971, I had a B.A., an M.A.(English) and an M.Phil. (English) to my name. The M.Phil. stands for Master of philosophy, a degree between an M.A. and a Ph.D.

The foreign language requirement for the graduate degrees presented no problem for me. After one visit to the Department of Germanic and Slavic Languages and Literatures, I was certified as having a thorough knowledge of German. Neither faculty nor students in the English Department ever knew of the nature of my connection with Germany.

Throughout my five years at university, Helga, in addition to working full-time, spent many hours with me at the university library. She fetched books for me from the stacks, allowing me more time for research. She also typed my essays and, starting in 1969, my thesis.

Helga could not have received a more sincere and meaningful accolade for all her hard work in supporting my studies than the one expressed in the presence of the members of the committee convened to hear me defend my thesis. Addressing me, George Hibbard, a Professor of English opened the proceedings by saying, "I must congratulate you. I have read your thesis, and I haven't found any [typographical] errors." Those words set the tone for the

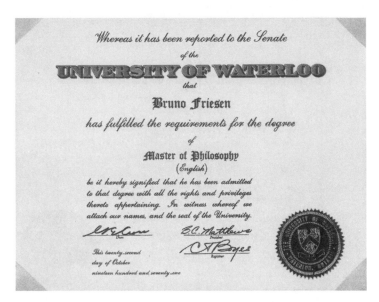

Whereas it has been reported to the Senate

of the

UNIVERSITY OF WATERLOO

that

Bruno Friesen

has fulfilled the requirements for the degree

of

Master of Philosophy
(English)

be it hereby signified that he has been admitted
to that degree with all the rights and privileges
thereto appertaining. In witness whereof we
attach our names, and the seal of the University.

This twenty-second
day of October
nineteen hundred and seventy-one

Diploma for Master of Philosophy (English) degree

entire meeting, which resulted in the English Department's acceptance of my thesis. The excellent work done by Helga on her Smith-Corona electric typewriter gave me a tremendous advantage on that crucial occasion.

Entitled "Meteorological Imagery in the Poetry of Henry Vaughan," my Masters' thesis deals essentially with the use, by the Welsh poet Henry Vaughan (1621–95), of geocentrism's heavenly phenomena to inspire his contemporaries to lift their eyes contemplatively towards God, who dwelt beyond the *primum mobile*, the prime mover of the universe. Vaughan availed himself of the Ptolemaic geocentric rather than the Copernican heliocentric universe at a time when the controversy regarding the two systems was at its height.

Although I knew all too well in 1971 that, had I acquired my last two university degrees when I was 26 and not 46, my income would have been far greater for two decades, I had the satisfaction of knowing that I had caught up, academically, with the tens of thousands of government-assisted Canadian veterans who had achieved their degrees a few years after the Second World War.

Working, as of 1971, for 19 years at the painstaking job of Professor of English–lecturing effectively was a full-time job, and grading students' papers was another–has given me the satisfaction of dealing professionally with what I would have taken up years earlier, had I been given the opportunity. Teaching English at the post-secondary level has made me feel that I have contributed to the betterment of some of the youth of the country of my birth, which I had to leave as a lad.

CHAPTER 21

My Retirement and Volunteer Work at the Canadian War Museum

After I retired on June 30, 1990, at the age of 65, relatives and friends in Southern Ontario urged Helga and me to relocate to Waterloo or to Kitchener, where we had lived until 1971 following our marriage in 1951. However, we elected to stay in Ottawa. Retired, I had time to mull over what I had achieved since I was a kid.

On May 27, 1995, I gave a lecture on the Jagdpanzer IV on display at Vimy House, the Canadian War Museum's annex. Don Holmes had asked his friend and neighbour, Dan Glenney of the Canadian War Museum, to make arrangements for the talk. My audience included Jim Whitham, Chief of Mechanized Warfare at the Museum.

I stayed in touch with Jim after that lecture and, in February of 1997, he, while walking ahead of me past some of the armoured vehicles on display close to his office at Vimy House, asked me, "How would you like to be a volunteer for me?" I referred to the fact that I was a shade over 70 years of age, and that I wouldn't be doing any bull work at the Museum. Jim's innate salesmanship immediately made him take me to the Museum's library at Vimy House, now called the Hartland Molson Library, where he headed straight to what can be called the *UG* section because the call numbers of the books on tanks and other armour begin with UG. I could, he said, work at answering queries involving research and writing. That was how I got into answering letters on behalf of the Museum.

At that time, I, as I was writing some of my memoirs, couldn't help comparing the lot of the German World War II veteran with that of his Canadian counterpart. To this day—well over 60 years after the end of the Second World War—the stories of that war that a German veteran of the *Wehrmacht* might want to tell are unwelcome in Germany. The man has no Legion branch or armoury at which to reminisce in the company of his wartime associates. He might have the opportunity to attend, biannually, a Regimental or Divisional gathering, provided the organization has not, like the unit that spawned it, passed into oblivion.

If his Regimental or Divisional veterans' organization still does exist, it is compelled, by law, to masquerade as a benevolent society. Since 1953–Germany was then arming its *Bundeswehr*, the successor to the *Wehrmacht*–German veterans' organizations have had to conform with the decree regarding the common good, of December 24, 1953. The Registered Traditional Association for the Assistance of Former Comrades of the 7th Panzer Division, whose activities, including get-togethers, I was unaware of before 1995–I was a member of that Division–was founded in Cologne in 1953. According to p. 466 of *The 7th Panzer Division in World War II*, the lawful purpose of the association is as follows:

> ... to promote assistance to comrades, [and] to issue printed material dealing with the purposes of the association. Moreover, to advise continually all authorities somehow having to do with assistance to comrades, to advise all organizations and individuals somehow connected with the work of assisting comrades, as well as to support the dependents of those missing in action and of the needy.

The 1953 German regulations governing veterans' associations were followed, on July 26, 1957, by the law governing Third-Reich military awards. Accordingly, the swastika in all classes of the Iron Cross was replaced by the 1813-style three oak leaves. The swastika was excised from all other awards, leaving a void in most of them. Although they may be worn openly in Germany, de-nazified military awards have not much been in evidence among Second World War veterans–unless their wearers served in the *Bundeswehr*.

Austria prohibits the wearing of any Third-Reich awards by members of its armed forces or its civil service. However, Austrian costume clubs and similar groups may wear them, even in their original form. Imagine having to wear *Lederhosen* (leather shorts) for the sake of displaying one's original *Panzerkampfabzeichen in Silber* (tank battle badge in silver).

The removal of the offensive symbols is calculated to mean that the awards were for service to the nation, and not to the regime. There is, we are told in *Symbole und Zeremoniell in deutschen Streitkräften vom 18. bis zum 20. Jahrhundert* (*Symbols and Ceremonial in the German Armed Forces from the 18th to the 20th Centuries*), p. 62, a precedent for such a change. The appearance of the French Legion of Honour was altered after the demise of Napoleon. The likeness of his head was replaced by that of another person, and the emperor's eagle on the reverse of the medal was replaced by three lilies.

No possibility exists for the post-war award of most Third-Reich medals. The exception is any one of the three classes of the *Verwundetenabzeichen* (wound badge–black, silver or gold–which may be worn, de-nazified of course, without its having been awarded before the unconditional surrender of Germany in 1945.

Regardless of where he resides, the German veteran of the Second World War has long been familiar with the frame of mind that gave rise to the following lines–note well that they are in English–which, according to *Bartlett's Familiar Quotations*, 12th ed., p. 698, were found on an old stone sentry box in Gibraltar:

God and the soldier
All men adore
In time of trouble
And no more;
For when war is over
And all things righted,
God is neglected–
The old soldier slighted.

I see the Canadian War Museum partly as a kind of meeting place for the not-so-reticent veterans and the reticent ones. Often, after I have listened at length to war stories told by Canadian World War II veterans, I am asked what branch of the service I belonged to during the war. "Hold onto your hat," I'll say, following which I'll disclose that I was a gunner in a Panzer Regiment. "On the German Eastern Front," I'll quickly add. That admission seems to perk the gentlemen up and, comparing notes, we'll talk some more.

Among the large numbers of visitors to the Museum are the veterans of Canada's NATO forces, many of whom were for years stationed in Germany after 1949, ready to face the Soviet Union, a former wartime ally of Canada. These ex-soldiers–some of them appear old enough to be taken for veterans of the Second World War–do not wear the medals that mark off those who took part in war, but they are, by and large, as amicable as their older comrades. Some have German-born wives. None speaks badly of his experiences in Germany.

The visiting Canadian vets who fought in Korea are also a friendly lot. I equate the Asian enemy they encountered with that which my comrades and I many times were up against on the German Eastern Front. Some veterans from each of the above categories are, as I have been for years, members of the Friends of the Canadian War Museum. One of our functions is to conduct regular guided tours of the Canadian War Museum.

I am delighted that my being a volunteer at the Museum has led to my getting to know many older Canadian veterans, a dozen of whom I join for lunch every Wednesday at the Army Officers' Mess in Ottawa, of which I have become an associate member.

A few days before November 11, 2000, one of the twelve fellows who had served with a Canadian armour unit during the war asked me if Germany observes the equivalent of Canada's Remembrance Day. I answered that Germany does not, at least not on as grand a scale as Canada does.

From 1920 to 1934, Germany annually observed *Volkstrauertag* (Day of National Mourning). Subsequently, until 1945, the day was called *Heldengedenktag* (Heroes Remembrance Day). Since 1945, it has again been termed *Volkstrauertag*, a day that should not be confused with *Totensonntag* or *Totenfest* (Commemoration Ceremony) of the Evangelical Church, or with *Allerseelen* (All Soul's Day) of the Roman Catholic Church.

The 1959 edition of *Knaurs Lexikon* gives the following definition of *Volkstrauertag*: "Day of National Mourning for the dead of both World Wars; the second Sunday before the first day of Advent." Since Advent begins four Sundays before Christmas, *Volkstrauertag* occurs on the sixth Sunday before Christmas, just about coinciding with November 11.

It is important to note that the government of the Federal Republic of Germany has declared, by law that *Volkstrauertag* must serve to commemorate all victims of despotism, as well as all other victims of war.

Volkstrauertag is generally void of funereal martial music, medals, marching, speeches and public wreath-laying. It is, instead, the day on which each family recalls, at home, the loss of its dead due to war or despotism.

However, throughout Germany there are countless powerful mnemonic devices—the artistic old cenotaphs—pertaining, in particular, to the country's heroes. For instance, on the warriors' memorial just outside of the main entrance of the large twelfth-century church in Varel, a small city between Oldenburg and Wilhelmshaven in North-west Germany, the inscription above the long columns of the names of the community's heroes—those who did not return from the wars—reads as follows: "*Rausche ewig, du Eichenwald, und verkünde ihren Ruhm*" (Rustle eternally, you forest of oaks, and spread their [our heroes'] fame).

The above ten words in English can be understood to mean that, whereas mortal man's remembrance of heroes can fade and die, eternal Nature can vigorously commemorate heroes everlastingly. In other words, by means of the above inscription Nature is called upon to help pass the proverbial torch in commemoration of heroes.

Maintained exemplarily, German military cemeteries, including those inside Germany, also honour the military dead. The Heroes Cemetery in Wilhelmshaven, where many of those who died in the Battle of the Skagerrak, or Battle of Jutland in 1916 lie, is one such monumental repository.

At the Canadian War Museum's Vimy House, there is the congenial full-time staff, whose every member has years of experience in his or her field, and who is, therefore, adept at giving guidance to the Museum's volunteers.

Of the small number of managers at Vimy House, most—and here I think primarily of Dan Glenney—have excellent rapport with the volunteers.

My experience at Vimy House leads me to believe that, by working diligently and with a minimum of supervision, the volunteer carves out for himself more than one niche of expertise; he has the opportunity to practice versatility, which makes his museum work even more interesting to him. However, a volunteer will not attain anything like versatility by constantly asking one supervisor or another, what it is that has to be done next. Certainly, every volunteer has his preferred sphere of interest. Mine is–you guessed it!–armour of all kinds. Still, because many of the Museum's artifacts are of German origin, I am just about guaranteed diversity as a researcher without being confined to deal with things German.

Typical of the length of the body of each of many letters that I write at Vimy House is the following one that I wrote on August 21, 1998:

> Thank you for your letter of enquiry dated July 22, 1998, which was passed to me with the request that I respond to it on behalf of the Museum. The photograph accompanying your letter certainly facilitated identification of the weapon it depicts.
>
> In addition to photocopies of the title page and the reverse of the title page of *Japanese Combat Weapons*, I enclose a photocopy of the book's one-page description of the 20-mm A.A./A.T. Automatic Cannon Model 98 (1938)–the weapon you enquire about.
>
> Please note, incidentally, that the enclosed photocopy of the front cover of the book shows *Second World War Combat Weapons: Japanese* as its title and subtitle.
>
> Records here at the museum show the following dimensions for the Museum's Japanese 20-mm Automatic Cannon Model 98: height 127 cm, length 275 cm, and width 120 cm. These figures apply to the gun as it stands on display.
>
> The same records also reveal that the gun was manufactured in 1936 [*sic*] at the Nagoya State Arsenal in Japan, that it bears serial number 836, and that it was transferred from National Defence to the Canadian War Museum on November 16, 1945.

Below is the recipient's unsolicited reply that caused a minor sensation at the Canadian War Museum. It expresses the sort of acknowledgment that each volunteer there dreams of getting, but seldom, or never, does.

August 20, 1999

Passing The Torch Campaign
Canadian War Museum
General Motors Court
300 Sussex Drive
Ottawa, Ontario K1A 0M8

Re: Donation

Attached below is my donation cheque in the amount of $1,000.

This donation is made, in part, in appreciation of the effort made by Bruno Friesen in responding to my inquiry regarding one of the items seen by me at the Museum's Vimy location (see attached photocopy of August 21, 1998 letter from Bruno to me).

(Signature)

cc: (w attachment) Bruno Friesen

Another sensation at Vimy House was triggered not by a thank-you letter, but by the realization that some equipment dating from the Second World War still proves to be of surprisingly good quality.

Starting to let a German inflation flotation vest, life jacket, or Mae West, manufactured in December of 1940, tell me its story, I turned, ever so gradually, the broken bakelite valve handle at the end of the compressed-air cylinder, inflating the jacket's air bag, which retained the air, holding its inflated shape. The small metal seal clamped to a severed black cord at the valve handle was, I had noticed, ready to be lost.

The photographer at Vimy House, hearing of this marvel, impulsively grabbed the old Mae West, took it to his studio, planted it on a plastic mannequin, and proceeded to show it off, even e-mailing invitations to higher-ups at the Museum to come to him to see it.

There is, in Appendix E, the memorandum which I wrote in response to the request, by one of the managers at the Canadian War Museum, for an answer to the question of how many Canadians encountered, or saw, German Panther tanks in Italy and North-west Europe in the Second World War. The memo should be of interest to military historians.

Sometimes, on my way through the military technology gallery at Vimy House, I ascend the half dozen steps to the wooden viewing platform that Jim Whitham has wisely placed along the right side of the superstructure of the Jagdpanzer IV, from which he had removed the 20-mm-thick roof armour. Then I look down into the fighting compartment of the unrestored Jagdpanzer IV V–note the addition of the *V*, which stands for *Vomag*, or *Vogtländische Maschinenfabrik A.-G.*, of Plauen in Saxony–and I see the massive breech mechanism of the once-powerful 7.5-cm main gun, into which, I know, the production code *bcd* is impressed. That code belonged to the Gustloff Works, Weimar plant.

Weimar, in turn, brings to mind Germany's greatest poet, Johann Wolfgang von Goethe (1749–1832), who spent most of his productive years there. The following four lines, written by Goethe and entitled "Soldier's Consolation," reflect a life differing vastly from that in the fighting compartment:

Nein, hier hat es keine Not:
Schwarze Mädchen, weisses Brot!

Morgen in ein ander Städtchen:
Schwarzes Brot und weisse Mädchen!

(No, here there is no need:
White the maidens, brown the bread!
Tomorrow to a different town:
White the bread, the maidens brown!)

By adhering more closely to the artistic sequence of the ideas in Goethe's original, I arrive at my second translation of "Soldier's Consolation":
(Here our life is good and sweet:
The maidens black, the bread of wheat!
Tomorrow to a different site:
The bread of rye, the maidens white!)

Before long, my thoughts turn to the four lines of the fifth, and last, stanza of the *Panzerlied* (Panzer Song), lines which are about the possibility–even the probability–of death occurring in the fighting compartment:

Und lässt uns im Stich einst das treulose Glück,
Und kehren wir nicht mehr zur Heimat zurück,
Trifft uns die Todeskugel, ruft uns das Schicksal ab,
Dann ist unser Panzer ein ehernes Grab.

(And if faithless luck lets down our small band,
And if never again we see our homeland,
If we are shot dead, and if fate bids us go,
Then our Panzer is our coffin of steel, all aglow.)

Finally, as I descend the steps from the viewing platform, I am glad that the old Jagdpanzer IV, at whose side I have just meditated briefly, did not end up being a shot-pierced, remains-splattered and sooty dumpster.

I am glad, moreover, that the Canadian War Museum evokes, not only in us veterans, but also in many of its other visitors, a decidedly contemplative mood.

Three newspaper articles reflecting pre–World War II Nazi activity in Canada

Kitchener Daily Record

KITCHENER, ONTARIO, THURSDAY, MARCH 16, 1939

Kitchener Lads Induced to Go to Germany

Given Attractive Offers to Labor in Reich, Is Claim

Love of the Nazi doctrine of Chancellor Adolf Hitler or the monetary inducement offered them to go to Germany to take an active part in affairs there has led several Kitchener young men to sign up.

According to information supplied The Record by a person, whose identity, for obvious reasons, must remain unknown, several members of one family of former Russian Mennonites and one or two others are sailing for Germany shortly.

Not Former Residents

None of those concerned have ever lived in Germany. They lived in a section of Russia that was peopled by persons of German extraction and came to Canada as immigrants. However, a desire to become part of Hitler's movement for a Greater Germany has led them to decide to become citizens of a land they have never seen.

According to *The Record's* informant inducements have been offered these youths to go to Germany by a Nazi agent in this country. Their fare to that country is being provided on the understanding that they pay it back when they can do so.

Attractive Offers

As an inducement to join up with Germany the youths receive attractive offers, it is understood. One of them is going to work on a farm where he will be paid a considerable amount for such work and the other expects to join the air force in Germany.

One of the youths who is returning, when questioned about it, denied that he is going to Germany other than voluntarily or even because he expects any special concessions will be given him. He is at present a Canadian citizen and has a position in Kitchener.

"I thought that the inducement to go to Germany was being offered to any Nazi sympathizer but now I believe that these boys are the only ones that are getting it," *The Record's* informant said.

Prior to their departure for Naziland it is understood the youths are being given a send-off party by a German club here.

Kitchener Daily Record

KITCHENER, ONTARIO, MONDAY, MARCH 20, 1939

To Continue Investigation

Father of Four Going to Germany Received $4,300 in Relief Aid

Hon. Gordon Conant, attorney-general of Ontario, said today in Toronto he could not undersand what "all the excitement is about" in connection with the reported departure of five young Kitchener Canadians, of German descent, to take up residence in Germany.

Even if reports that Germany was subsidizing the immigrants were correct, there was nothing wrong about it, said Mr. Conant. Canada had subsidized immigrants from other lands and Germany was free to subsidize those who desired to leave Canada for Germany.

Sail from New York

The minister's remarks were voiced in connection with the departure from Kitchener early today of Helena Esau, 16, her three brothers, Jacob, George and Henry, and another unidentified man. The five were given a farewell party by the Deutscher Bund Club in Kitchener Saturday night and are believed to be sailing tomorrow from New York.

The attorney-general is communicating with federal authorities today regarding the departure.

Provincial police at Kitchener, Mr. Conant said, are investigating the circumstance of their leaving. Meanwhile he intends to learn what Ottawa knows of the matter.

The attorney-general expressed doubt as to what action Ontario authorities can tak. Rumors the four young men and one

young woman are having their passage paid by pro-Nazi sources
are being looked into, he stated.

A Federal Matter

"I presume these young people would require a passport," Mr.
Conant said. "That is a matter entirely within Ottawa jurisdic-
tion. As far as I can see at the moment, unless the Foreign Enlistment Act has been violated, there is no action Ontario can take."

Mr. Conant said he believed it possible that Ottawa may have
had information on the departure of the five for Germany.

He made it clear, however, he intends to find out if there is
any organized effort to entice young people of German extraction
to return to Hitler's domain.

As the attorney-general continued his investigation into the
circumstances regarding the departure of the five, the Kitchener
relief department delved into its files for information on George
P. Esau, father of four of them.

On Relief 10 Years

Department officials learned that Esau had been on relief ten of
his 11 years in this country. During that period he received
approximately $4,200 in assistance from the welfare division.

Chairman C. C. Hahn was indignant at the report four
members of the family are going to the old country. They had
good jobs here, he pointed out, and there was no purpose in their
leaving because of unemployment.

"Just at the time when they should be working and helping
support the family, which includes 12 children, they pull out and
go to some other country.

"It amounts to this. We have supported them here and helped
bring them up and now they go to Germany without assisting us
in any way. In the event of war involving Germany and Britain it
is quite possible they might be drafted to fight against our boys.
We have taken care of them here so that they might aid in
destroying our own youth," he said.

Kitchener Daily Record

KITCHENER, ONTARIO, TUESDAY, MARCH 21, 1939

Ottawa Won't Detain Five
Government Cannot Do Anything to Stop Group from Sailing

By Charles Lynch, Kitchener Record Correspondent

OTTAWA. March 21.–The Dominion government will take no action to prevent five Kitchener young people from leaving Canada for Germany.

The government can do nothing to prevent their departure. It can control immigration into Canada but cannot prevent any Canadians from going where they please.

It was stated today that during the Great War the War Measures Act was invoked to prevent men of military age leaving Canada without a permit. This was the only time in Canada's history when a prohibition against people leaving Canada was put into force. It began when enlistment pressure was brought to bear.

Act Ineffective

The War Measures Act has long since been ineffective. Canada's door does not swing both ways. It opens inward for those willing to settle in the Dominion and complying with immigration regulations.

(The five people concerned, Jacob, George, Helen and Henry Esau, and another unnamed man, left Kitchener yesterday and sail today from New York on the Europa.)

(The rumored investigation by Attorney-General Gordon Conant did not produce any evidence of violation of provincial laws, it was reported from Toronto, and the matter was referred to the federal government.

(It is understood the Royal Canadian Mounted Police have been keeping an eye on the activities of the Nazi party here, of which there are 17 known members.

(Many Germans in Kitchener have consistently maintained that they are as opposed to dissemination of Nazi propaganda here as are Canadians. Suggestions that they are not good Canadian citizens have roused many of them to protest.

("We are just as annoyed as other citizens when evidence of Nazi propaganda comes to light but what can we do? The authorities will not take any action and we are helpless to do anything on our own. Canada may regret some day that it treated this matter so lightly," one German Canadian resident in Kitchener for several years said today. "This unobtrusive working from within is the manner of the Nazis to gain strength for future use.")

7th Panzer Division Historical Summary, 1944–45

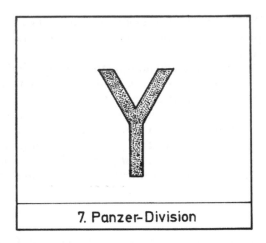

7. Panzer-Division

Organisation

Panzer Grenadier Regiment 6
Panzer Grenadier Regiment 7
Panzer Regiment 25
Panzer Aufklärungs Abteilung 7
Panzerartillerie Regiment 78
Panzerjäger Abteilung 42
Panzer Pioneer Battalion 58
Heeres Flak Abteilung 296
Panzer Nachrichten Abteilung 83
Kdr Panzer Division Nachschub Truppen 58
Feldersatz Battalion 78

Combat service 1944–45

Resting and refitting middle April-end June 1944, at the disposal of 4th Panzer Army, west of Brody. Entrained beginning of July, moving from Brody-Stanislau to Army Group Centre, near Lida.

July-September 1944 counter-attacks at Lida, defensive operations northwest of Vilnius, in the area of Merkine (4th Army). Transferred to 3rd Panzer Army, collecting areas west of Riga, north-west of Autz/Doblen. Middle of August, counter-attack (as part of XL Panzerkorps) in the area Schaulen-Doblen, Lithuania/Latvia. September, defensive actions northwest of Doblen (as part of XXXIX Panzerkorps). October/November in defences north of Doblen/west of Libau, withdrawal to the Baltic. Defence of the bridgeheads around the town and harbour of Memel (XXVIII Corps). At end of November evacuation by sea to Pillau, rest and refitting. December 1944-January 1945 in reserve, 2nd Army, Army Group North, behind Narev Bridgehead.

Middle January 1945 counter-attacks and defensive actions in southern East Prussia (VII Corps, Second Army). Withdrawal into West Prussia via Graudenz, in the direction Marienburg-Danzig. Counter-attacks southeastward of Kolberg, between 3rd Panzer Army and 2nd Army. Defensive actions in the area Rummelsburg and Konitz (still with VII Corps). Withdrawal into defensive positions around Gotenhafen-Danzig, defence of Danzig, evacuated via Hela to Swinemünde. Shattered remnants used as reserve units with 3rd Panzer Army. The majority of the division went into American and British captivity in the Mecklenburg area, 5 May 1945.

Bibliography

Brehm, W. *Mein Kriegstagebuch 1939–1945. Mit der 7. Panzer-Division 5 Jahre in West und Ost* (Kassel, privately published, 1953)

Huber, J. *So war es wirklich. Das letzte Kriegsjahr an der Ostfront (21.8.1944-August 1945). Ein Panzermann berichtet* (Berg am See, Vowinckel, 1989)

Manteuffel, H. von *Die 7. Panzer-Division im Zweiten Weltkrieg. Einsatz und Kampf der "Gespenster-Division" 1939–1945* (Köln, Traditionsverband ehem. 7. Pz. Div., 1965)

Manteuffel, H. von *Die 7. Panzer-Division 1935–1945. Die "Gespenster-Division"* (Friedberg, Podzun Pallas, 1978)

APPENDIX C

Circus Mirandola

Technical Data

Panzerkampfwagen IV Ausf H (Sd Kfz 161/2)

Type: Medium tank
Manufacturer: Krupp-Gruson, Vomag, Nibelungenwerke
Chassis Nos.: 84401–91500
3,774 produced from April 1943 to July 1944

Crew: 5	Engine: Maybach HL120TRM
Weight (tons): 25	Gearbox: 6 forward, 1 reverse
Length (metres): 7.02	Speed (km/hr): 38
Width (metres): 2.88	Range (km): 210
Height (metres): 2.68	Radio: FuG5

Armament: One 7.5cm KWK40 L/48	One 7.92mm MG34	One 7.92mm MG34
Traverse: 360° (electric)	=	hand
Elevation: –8° +20°	=	
Sight: TZF5f/1	=	KgZF2
Ammunition: 87 Pzgr, Sprgr+Nebel	3,150 Patr SmK	

Armour (mm/angle):	Front	Side	Rear	Top/ Bottom
Turret:	50/10°	30/26°	30/15°	15/84°–90°
Superstructure:	80/10°	30/0°	20/11°	12/85°–90°
Hull:	80/14°	30/0°	20/8°	10/90°
Gun mantlet:	50/0°–300°			

Panzerkampfwagen IV Ausf J (Sd Kfz 161/2)

Type: Medium tank
Manufacturer: Nibelungenwerke
Chassis Nos.: 91501-
1,758 produced from June 1944 to March 1945

Crew: 5	Engine: Maybach HL120TRM112

Weight (tons): 25   Gearbox: 6 forward, 1 reverse
Length (metres): 7.02   Speed (km/hr): 38
Width (metres): 2.88   Range (km): 320
Height (metres): 2.68   Radio: FuG5

Armament: One 7.5cm KwK40L/48	One 7.92mm MG34	One 7.92mm MG34
Traverse: 360°(hand)	=	hand
Elevation: —8° + 20°	=	
Sight: TZF5f/2	=	KgZF2
Ammunition: 87 Pzgr, Spgr+Nebel	3,150 Patr SmK	

Armour (mm/ angle):	Front	Side	Rear	Top/Bottom
Turret:	50/10°	30/25°	30/ 15°	18/86° & 26/ 90°
Superstructure:	80/8°	30/0°	20/ 10°	12/85°–90°
Hull:	80/15°	30/0°	20/ 10°	10/90°
Gun mantlet:	50/0°–30°			

Jagdpanzer IV/70(V) (Sd Kfz 162/1)

Type: Tank destroyer
Manufacturer: Vomag
Chassis Nos.: 320001–321725
930 produced from August 1944 to March 1945

Crew: 4   Engine: Maybach HL120TRM
Weight (tons): 25.8   Gearbox: 6 forward, 1 reverse
Length (metres): 8.5   Speed (km/hr): 35
Width (metres): 3.17   Range (km): 210
Height (metres): 1.85   Radio: FuGSprf

Armament: One 7.5cm PaK42 L/70   One 7.92mm MG42
Traverse: 10° left 10° right (hand)   hand
Elevation: –5° +15°
Sight: SflZF

Ammunition: 55		600		

Armour (mm/angle):	Front	Side	Rear	Top/Bottom
Superstructure:	80/50°	40/30°	20/35°	20/90°
Hull (upper):	80/45°	30/0°	20/11°	10/90°
Hull (lower):	50/55°	30/0°	20/9°	12+10–10/90°
Gun mantlet:	80/Saukopfblende			

The information in this appendix is taken from Peter Chamberlain and Hilary Doyle, *Encyclopedia of German Tanks of World War II (Revised Edition)*, London, Arms and Armour Press, 1993. Due acknowledgement is hereby given to the copyright holders.

Copy of a memorandum regarding the number of Canadians who saw the Panther tank in Italy in World War II

MEMORANDUM

Date: May 3, 2002
To: Jim Whitham
From: Bruno Friesen
Subject: The number of Canadians who encountered, or saw, German Panther tanks in Italy and NW Europe in World War II

One method of determining the approximate number of Canadians who in World War II necessarily got to know the German Panther tank in Italy and NW Europe is to make use of certain data tabulated in *The Gunners of Canada*, by G.W.L. Nicholson. This book's index list the Canadian armour, anti-tank, and infantry Regiments that served in those two theatres of World War II.

Multiplying Nicholson's enumerations of the Canadian tank-fighting Regiments in Italy and NW Europe by their wartime personnel strengths results, approximately, in the number of Canadians who perforce recognized the Panther tank.

The Gunners of Canada, pp. 740–41, 743, 752, shows the following figures, to which the personnel complements, recalled by World War II veterans who are members of The Friends of the Canadian War Museum, are applied.

Armour
16 Regiments, each with 600 men, equals 9,600 men

Anti-tank
8 Regiments each with 550 men, equals 4,400 men
Infantry each with 800 men, equals 32,000 men

The 46,000 Canadians who served in those 64 Regiments were bound to know their adversary's Panther tank. Undoubtedly, too, many Canadians serving outside of those units saw abandoned or destroyed Panther tanks, for instance at roadsides in Italy and NW Europe.

The Crucible of War, 1939–1945: The Official History of the Royal Canadian Air Force, Vol. III, p. 308, states, "The Luftwaffe in Italy was so weak that there could be no justification for keeping fighter squadrons employed exclusively on air superiority duties." Consequently, Italy was not a country in which Canadian aircraft fought Panther tanks.

Although this book seldom states that Panther tanks were involved, it tells again and again of the destruction, mostly by Hawker Typhoon fighter-bombers of the R.C.A.F., of German tanks in Normandy.

The Canadian Army 1939–1945: An Official Historical Summary, by C.P. Stacey, pp. 353–54, lists, under the heading "Enemy Forces," the 14 Panzer Divisions that faced the Canadians in Italy and NW Europe.

Werner Haupt's *A History of the Panzer Troops 1916–1945,* p. 191, states that in 1944 a Panzer Regiment—each Panzer Division had, as its core, one such Regiment—was equipped, at the most, with 73 Panther tanks.

Those 73 Panthers belonged to the four Companies of a Panzer Regiment's 1st Battalion. By the way, in 1944 a Panzer Regiment's 2nd Battalion, also consisting of four Companies, had a maximum of 86 Panzer IVs and/or Jagdpanzer IVs.

Theoretically, 14 Panzer Regiments, each with 73 Panthers, meant 1,022 Panther tanks in the field.

Published production figures for the Panther tank vary. Bruce Culver and Don Geer, in *Panther in Action,* p. 4, state, "The Germans built 4,814 Panther tanks ... " Ian V. Hogg's *The Greenhill Armoured Fighting Vehicles Data Book,* p. 80, states that about 5,500 Panther tanks were built. *Tanks and Armoured Vehicles of WW II,* by Jim Winchester, p. 38, gives the total production as 5,976 Panthers. *The Encyclopedia of Tanks and Armoured Fighting Vehicles,* Gen. Ed. Christopher F. Foss, p. 242, reads, "Total Panther production by February 1945 had reached only 6131 ... "

Regardless of the differences between the above production figures, Panther tanks must have been encountered, or seen otherwise, by tens of thousands of Canadians serving in Italy and NW European World War II.

The following interesting short pieces of information pertain to Canadians who served in Italy in World War II.

The Canadian Army 1939–1945: An Official Historical Summary repeatedly refers to the deadly German anti-tank positions consisting of Panther tank turrets in concrete emplacement, which Canadian troops encountered in Italy. This book shows two paintings by Canadian war artists, depicting Panther-turret pillboxes.

Roman J. Jarymowycz, in *Tank Tactics from Normany to Lorraine,* p. 273, states the following: "The first Panther knocked out by the Allies in Europe was in Italy, during the attack on the Hitler Line on 24 May 1944 (two weeks before D-Day) by a Canadian crew of the British Columbia Dragoons." Actually, the Soviets had destroyed numerous Panther tanks in the European part of Russia, namely at the battle of Kursk, in July of 1943.

The Canadian Army 1939–1945, p.p. 154–55, relates a most note-
worthy incident involving Panther tanks:

> During the Seaforth defence of their hard-won bridgehead, there
> occurred a very notable act of individual heroism. As the right
> forward company was consolidating its objective, it was suddenly
> counter-attacked by a group of three Panther tanks, supported by
> two self-propelled guns and a platoon of infantry. With extraordi-
> nary coolness, Pte. Ernest Alvia Smith, a member of the Seaforth
> tank hunting platoon, let one of the Panthers approach to a range
> of 30 feet before he fired his PIAT and put it out of action.

Bibliography

Army Service Manual No. 462: Anti-aircraft Use of the Machine Gun and the Rifle. High Command of the *Wehrmacht*, January 18, 1935.

Army Service Manual No. 86: *Field Cookbook.* High Command of the *Wehrmacht*, August 16, 1941.

Bartlett, John. *Bartlett's Familiar Quotations*, 12th ed. Boston: Little, Brown and Company, 1951.

Bender, Roger James, and Warren W. Odegard. *Uniforms, Organization and History of the Panzertruppe.* San Jose: R. James Bender Publishing, 1980.

Chamberlain, Peter, and Hilary Doyle. Technical Editor Thomas L. Jentz. *Encyclopedia of German Tanks of World War Two.* London: Arms and Armour, 1999.

Dean, I. C. B., General Editor. *The Oxford Companion to World War II.* Oxford: Oxford University Press, 1995.

Encyclopedia Americana. Canadian Edition. Montreal: Americana Corporation of Canada Limited, 1962.

Jentz, Tom, Hilary Doyle, and Peter Sarson. *Kingtiger Heavy Tank 1942–1945.* London: Osprey, 1995.

Knaurs Lexikon A-Z. München: Droemersche Verlagsanstalt Th. Knaur Nachf., 1959.

Macksey, Kenneth, and John H. Batchelor. *Tank: A History of the Armoured Fighting Vehicle.* New York: Ballatine, 1971.

Manteuffel, Hasso E. von. *Die 7. Panzer-Division im Zweiten Weltkrieg: Einsatz und Kampf der "Gespenster-Division."* Friedberg 3: Podzun-Pallas-Verlag GmbH, 1986.

Manteuffel, Hasso von. *The 7th Panzer Division: An Illustrated History of Rommel's "Ghost Division" 1938–1945.* Atglen, Pa.: Schiffer Publishing, 2000.

Nafziger, George F. *The German Order of Battle: Panzers and Artillery in World War II.* Mechanicsburg, Pennsylvania: Stackpole Books, 1999.

Perrett, Bryan. *The Panzerkampfwagen IV.* London: Osprey, 1991.

Perrett, Bryan. *The PzKpfw V: Panther.* London: Osprey, 1991.

Rokossovsky, K[onstantin]. *A Soldier's Duty.* Trans. Vladimir Talmy. Moscow: Progress Publishers, 1970.

Scheibert, Horst. *Jagdpanzer: Jagdpanzer IV–Jagdpanther.* West Chester, Pennsylvania, 1991.

Scheibert, Horst. *Tiger I.* Trans. Dr. Edward Force. West Chester,
    Pennsylvania: Schiffer, 1991.
Scheibert, Horst, und Ulrich Elfrath. *Panzer in Russland: Die deutschen
    gepanzerten Verbände im Russland-Feldzug 1941–1944.* Dorheim:
    Podzun-Verlag, 1971.
Schroeder, William, and Helmut T. Huebert. *Mennonite Historical
    Atlas*, 2nd ed. Winnipeg: Springfield Publishers, 1996.
Spielberger, Walter J. *Panther & Its Variants.* Trans. Don Cox. Atglen,
    Pennsylvania: Schiffer, 1993.
Stein, Hans-Peter. *Symbole und Zeremoniell in deutschen Streitkräften
    vom 18. bis zum 20. Jahrhundert.* Herford: Verlag E. S. Mittler &
    Sohn,1991.
The Random House College Dictionary, Rev. ed. New York: Random
    House, Inc., 1975.

Stackpole Military History Series

Real battles. Real soldiers. Real stories.

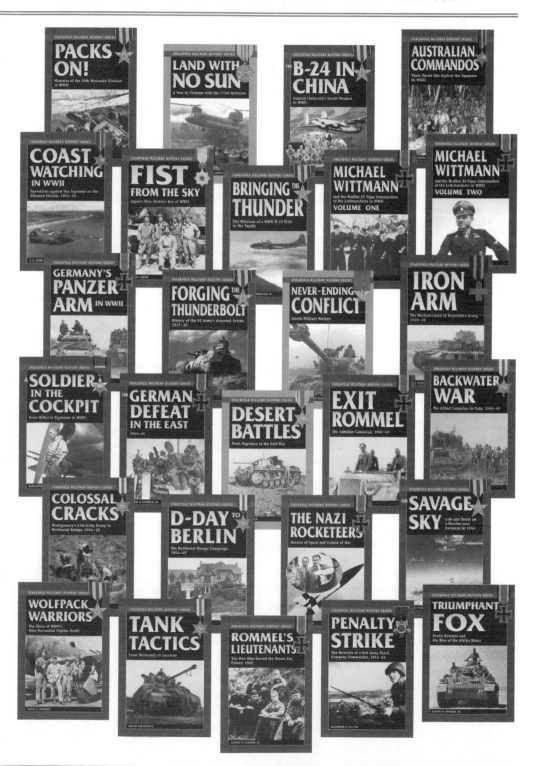

Stackpole Military History Series

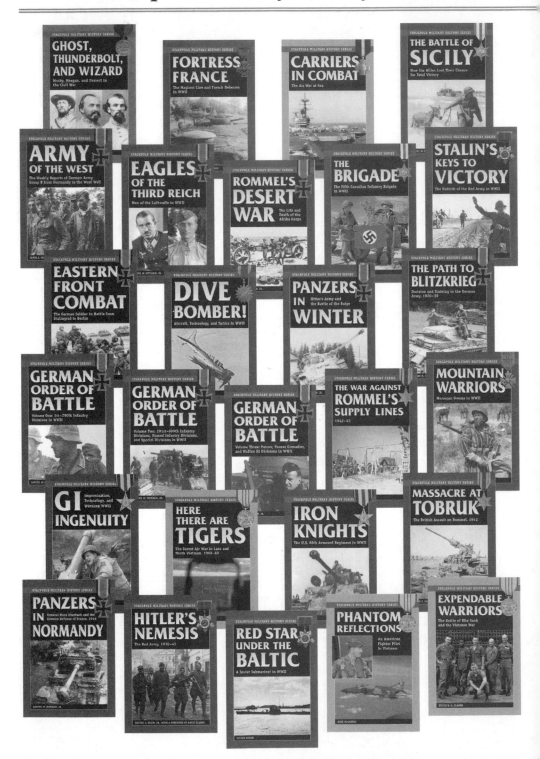

Real battles. Real soldiers. Real stories.

Stackpole Military History Series

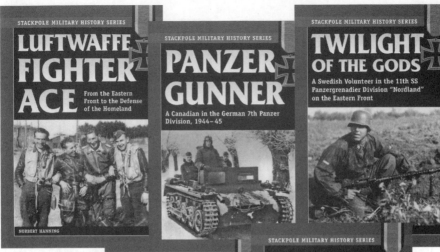

STACKPOLE MILITARY HISTORY SERIES

LUFTWAFFE FIGHTER ACE
From the Eastern Front to the Defense of the Homeland

NORBERT HANNING

STACKPOLE MILITARY HISTORY SERIES

PANZER GUNNER
A Canadian in the German 7th Panzer Division, 1944–45

STACKPOLE MILITARY HISTORY SERIES

TWILIGHT OF THE GODS
A Swedish Volunteer in the 11th SS Panzergrenadier Division "Nordland" on the Eastern Front

STACKPOLE MILITARY HISTORY SERIES

THE SIEGFRIED LINE
The German Defense of the West Wall, September–December 1944

STACKPOLE MILITARY HISTORY SERIES

BEYOND STALINGRAD
Manstein and the Operations of Army Group Don

DANA V. SADA

NEW for Fall 2009

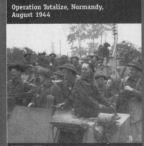

STACKPOLE MILITARY HISTORY SERIES

NO HOLDING BACK
Operation Totalize, Normandy, August 1944

BRIAN A. REID

STACKPOLE MILITARY HISTORY SERIES

THE CANADIAN ARMY AND THE NORMANDY CAMPAIGN

JOHN A. ENGLISH

STACKPOLE MILITARY HISTORY SERIES

BATTLE OF THE BULGE
Volume One: The Losheim Gap / Holding the Line

HANS WIJERS

Real battles. Real soldiers. Real stories.

STACKPOLE MILITARY HISTORY SERIES

THE KEY TO THE BULGE
The Battle for Losheimergraben
STEPHEN M.

STACKPOLE MILITARY HISTORY SERIES

ZHUKOV AT THE ODER
The Decisive Battle for Berlin

STACKPOLE MILITARY HISTORY SERIES

RANGER DAWN
The American Ranger from the Colonial Era to the Mexican War
COL. ROBERT W. BLACK

STACKPOLE MILITARY HISTORY SERIES

SIEGES
From the Siege of Jerusalem to the Gulf War
BRUCE ALLEN WATSON

STACKPOLE MILITARY HISTORY SERIES

CAVALRY FROM HOOF TO TRACK
ROMAN JARYMOWYCZ

NEW for Fall 2009

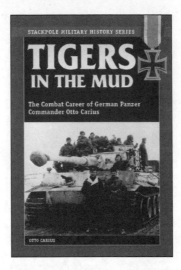

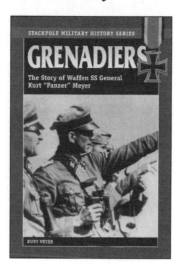

Stackpole Military History Series

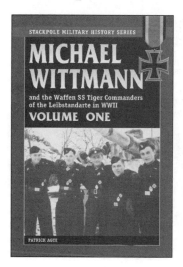
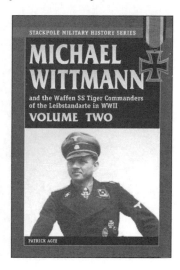

MICHAEL WITTMANN AND THE WAFFEN SS TIGER COMMANDERS OF THE LEIBSTANDARTE IN WORLD WAR II

Patrick Agte

By far the most famous tank commander on any side in World War II, German Tiger ace Michael Wittmann destroyed 138 enemy tanks and 132 anti-tank guns in a career that embodies the panzer legend: meticulous in planning, lethal in execution, and always cool under fire. Volume One covers Wittmann's armored battles against the Soviets in 1943–44 at places like Kharkov, Kursk, and the Cherkassy Pocket. Volume Two picks up with the epic campaign in Normandy, where Wittmann achieved his greatest successes before being killed in action. The Leibstandarte went on to fight at the Battle of the Bulge and in Austria and Hungary before surrendering in May 1945.

Volume One: $19.95 • Paperback • 6 x 9 • 432 pages
383 photos • 19 maps • 10 charts
Volume Two: $19.95 • Paperback • 6 x 9 • 400 pages
287 photos • 15 maps • 7 charts

WWW.STACKPOLEBOOKS.COM
1-800-732-3669

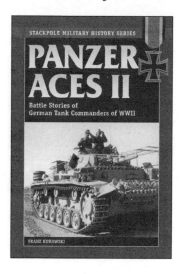

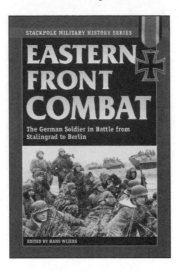

BORDERS.

BORDERS
Books * Music * Cafe
6151 Columbia Cross Circle
Columbia MD 21045
410.290.0062

STORE: 0089   REG: 04/53 TRAN#: 2188
SALE   10/14/2010 EMP: 00274

PANZER DESTROYER
        3189548   CL T   26.77
 39.95 33% BR PROMO
COUPON 159047760000000000
PANZER ACES
        7638518   QP T   19.95
PANZER GUNNER CANADIAN IN GER
        9875650   QP T   18.95
BR   :8385028942 S

            Subtotal   65.67
            MARYLAND 6%   3.95
 3 Items   Total   69.62
            VISA   69.62
ACCT # /S XXXXXXXXXXXXX5772
            AUTH: 02548D
NAME: LONGFORD/ROBERT

        CUSTOMER COPY

You Saved $13.18

    10/14/2010 11:53AM
TRANS BARCODE: 00890421880027410140

        Shop online
        24 hours a day
        at Borders.com

BORDERS.

Returns

BORDERS.

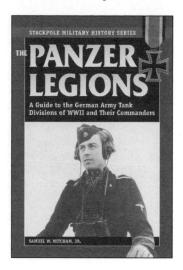

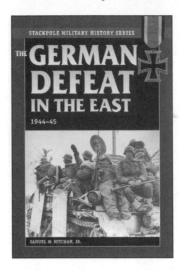

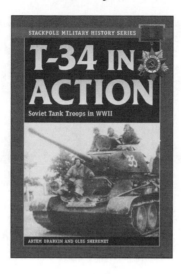

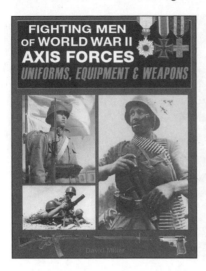
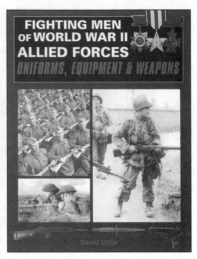